MM 1841 **315028** 8005

Leabharlanna Atha Cliath
CHARLEVILLE MALL LIBRARY
Invoice : 00/3823 Price IR£9.99
Title: Hurling heroes   fourt
Class: 796. 351

Hurling Heroes

Eddie Keher

BLACKWATER PRESS

D1078697

Editor
Aidan Culhane

Design/Layout
Paula Byrne

Cover
Liz Murphy

ISBN
1 84131 502 8

© Eddie Keher 2000

Produced in Ireland by
Blackwater Press
c/o Folens Publishers
Hibernian Industrial Estate,
Greenhills Road,
Tallaght, Dublin 24.

All rights reserved. No part of this publication may be reproduced or transmitted in
any form or by any means electronic, mechanical, photocopying, recording, or
otherwise without prior written permission from the Publisher.

This book is sold subject to the conditions that it shall not, by way of trade or
otherwise, be lent, re-sold, hired out or otherwise circulated without the
Publishers' prior consent in any form or cover other than that in which
published and without similar conditions including this condition being
on the subsequent purchaser.

While considerable effort has been made to locate all holders of co
material used in this text, we have failed to contact some of these. Shoul
wish to contact Blackwater Press, we will be glad to come to some arrange

Acknowledgements

I would like to thank everyone most sincerely who helped me in so many ways to produce this book.

First of all, my wife Kay, my son Colm and his wife Sinead who encouraged me all the way and helped me to improve my computer skills in the process. They painstakingly read each chapter and offered constructive criticism and advice which was invaluable.

To John O'Connor and his staff at Blackwater Press, and particularly editor, Aidan Culhane, who played a 'full-back's' role by ensuring that nothing untoward went to print.

There were many books, publications and newspapers I had to refer to for facts and figures. I want to especially acknowledge the late Raymond Smyth's *Complete Handbook of Gaelic Games*, Tom Ryall's *Comhairle Laighean Record Book* and the Kilkenny GAA Yearbook committee's *The Kilkenny GAA Bible*, all of which provided excellent references for my research. Thanks also to Ray McManus and Sportsfile for the photographs provided.

I am deeply grateful to AIB for their sponsorship support.

Finally, a very special thanks to all my hurling friends and families and former hurling colleagues who agreed so willingly to participate in the book, and to their wives who made me so welcome when I visited them.

Muhammad Ali gets a lesson from Eddie Keher, 1972.

Eddie, marked closely by Cork's Sean Lucey.

Contents

Legends are made of this. vii

Introduction. viii

1 – Tom Cheasty 1

2 – Joe Cooney 11

3 – Ray Cummins 22

4 – Tony Doran. 33

5 – Jimmy Doyle 43

6 – Pat Fox 54

7 – Len Gaynor 64

8 – Pat Hartigan 75

9 – Fan Larkin 87

10 – Ger Loughnane. 98

11 – Paddy Molloy. 114

12 – Michael O'Grady 124

13 – Noel Skehan. 135

14 – Tom Walsh 148

Index of Names 163

Legends are made of this

I had the good fortune of having watched Eddie Keher, hurling master craftsman supreme, in action regularly over his long and distinguished career. It was a truly wonderful experience, one of the most rewarding I have had in Gaelic games.

The Kilkenny stylist's senior inter-country championship career began in his teens at the highest possible level – the 1959 All-Ireland final replay against Waterford. He went into that game as a substitute after having some weeks earlier played in the All-Ireland minor final.

Then followed an amazing 22 years in the top flight, years during which Keher laced a razor-sharp finishing technique with co-ordination, balance, intelligence and the ability to effortlessly produce flashes of genius under the most intense pressures.

Razor-sharp finishing technique? He was the nation's top scorer in hurling ten years outright between 1965 and 1976 for all competitions. Indeed, between 1963 and 1976, he was out of the top two scorers nationally only once – in 1964 when he finished in third place.

Not only that, his amazing standard of a staggering 20–134 (194 points) in only 21 games in 1972 is still standing as the record for a yearly programme. The prospects of that marker being passed out in the years ahead look remote in the extreme.

Keher, who won two All-Ireland Colleges' medals with St Kieran's, was a consistent match-winner with Kilkenny. He helped the country to capture six All-Ireland senior titles between 1963 and 1975 and he also had the distinction of leading the Noresiders to their 1969 Liam McCarthy Cup triumph.

The Kilkenny ace, who hurled with the Rower-Inistioge club, was included in the first All Stars team in 1971 and he went on to win five such awards in succession.

Add in three National League medals and nine interprovincial souvenirs and those achievements further underline the tremendous contribution that Keher made to Kilkenny, Leinster and, indeed, hurling in general in close on 300 appearances – a record that says much for his dedication and the consistently high-standard hurling he produced over such a long period.

Legends are made from rare and successful careers like Eddie Keher's. Who, then, could have been in the least surprised at his inclusion at left full-forward in the An Post/GAA Hurling team of the Millennium during the year 2000?

Owen McCann

Introduction

During Christmas week in 1999, I got a telephone call from John O'Connor, Managing Director of Blackwater Press asking me if I would be interested in writing a GAA book for the following year's Christmas market. Having no experience whatsoever of writing a book, my immediate reaction was to say 'no'. I explained that, while I had retired from AIB Bank, I was happily working with *Ireland On Sunday* and that I had no desire to take on any additional projects. I was supposed to be winding down, for God's sake.

Sensing my reluctance, he told me not to make any decision until he had a chance to meet with me. I should have known that Offaly men don't give up easily and I was half way back to Kilkenny following our meeting in January before I realised that I had agreed to take on the task. Panic began to set in then as I really had no idea how to approach the job. The following day I sat down to draw up a plan and very quickly listed about 25 names of players I would like to feature. 'Too many', said John 'you'd never get that many done in the time available, and anyway the book would run into volumes. Send me the list and I will cut it for you by eliminating people who have already been featured recently in other books.' There was no escape so I had to commence the project.

It turned out to be a most interesting and rewarding experience. I enjoyed so much visiting all the players and their families and talking about the game we all love so much. The hard part was when I had accumulated all the information and had to sit at the computer to compose each chapter. My biggest fear was that I would not be competent enough to do each player justice.

The players featured in this book are a good cross-section of the many hurling heroes that have thrilled us over the years. By telling their stories I have tried to convey to the reader that every hurling star had to start at the beginning, had to practise long hours at the skills of the game and was coached and influenced by many people along the way. Some of them had the ability and the opportunity to give their time to passing on their knowledge by coaching teams themselves when their own playing days were over.

I hope that people will find it an interesting read, but I hope also that young hurlers will be inspired from reading about the exploits of these great heroes and that they will see how they developed their skills to become legends on the hurling fields of Ireland.

Hurling is the greatest game in the world and we need every generation to produce its own hurling heroes so that our unique game will continue to thrill and excite sports lovers for centuries to come.

Eddie Keher
October 2000

1 – Tom Cheasty

Christy Ring, Eddie Keher and Tom Cheasty

On Christmas Eve 1995, a huge crowd gathered around a graveside in St Kieran's cemetery in Kilkenny to pay their respects, and to offer their support to the family of one of Kilkenny's hurling heroes. Ted Carroll, an outstanding centre-back in the 1960s, and Texaco Hurler of the Year at right-full-back in 1969 had prematurely and suddenly passed away. When Ted's inter-county days were over, he had continued to play for Lisdowney before moving into administration and he eventually succeeded the popular Paddy Grace as county secretary of the GAA in Kilkenny. Ted proved to be very popular in that role, and as he was laid to rest within a puck of a ball from his beloved Nowlan Park, thousands of GAA administrators and past and present hurlers from every county in Ireland stood in shocked silence while former GAA president, Paddy Buggy delivered a graveside oration. Within a few yards of the grave, a stocky, big-shouldered, muscular figure with familiar wavy hair listened as the former president outlined Ted Carroll's outstanding career. Paddy highlighted Ted's performance in the 1963 when given the task of marking Waterford's Tom Cheasty, as his greatest hour on the field of play.

He was paying a great tribute to the Kilkennyman, but in doing so, he was indirectly paying tribute to an outstanding Waterford hurler who had been feared, loved and admired by Kilkenny hurling followers during their three great

All-Ireland clashes in 1957, 1959 and 1963. As the stunned crowd, slowly and reluctantly started to drift away from the graveside, people crowded around the Ballyduff man to shake his huge hand. Tom Cheasty was a legend in Kilkenny too.

The first time I saw Tom Cheasty in action was in the 1957 All-Ireland final. I had played in the minor final against Tipperary, and, in those days the minor teams were accommodated in seats to one side of the Railway Goal for the senior game. It was very hard to see what was going on at the Canal end of the field, but being almost on the pitch, we certainly got a worm's eye view of the action in front of the Railway goal.

I was in the same position for the 1959 drawn final, and while my memories of both games are somewhat clouded, the performances of two individuals remain clearly in my mind. Ollie Walsh performed heroics in the Kilkenny goal making unbelievable saves right in front of our eyes from a relentless Waterford attack who seemed to take delight in bringing out the best in him. The cavalier centre-forward who was leading most of those attacks was one Tom Cheasty. Tom had just one thing in mind when he ran on to that ball, make for goal, and it didn't matter who came to meet him.

Martin Óg Morrissey had obviously been instructed to send every ball down to Cheasty who, with the familiar 'genuflect' to pick up the ball on the run, was on his way. If he did find himself in a cul-de-sac, he knew there must be forwards loose, and he had perfected the accurate hand pass to Mick Flannery, Frankie Walsh or Larry Guinan who capitalised on the space created.

I am on record as saying that the Waterford team of the late 1950s and early 1960s was one of the finest hurling teams of the century. I qualified that statement by saying that their style of play was ahead of its time, and, had they been playing under the rule changes introduced in the early 1970s, they would have been unbeatable.

When I asked Tom if he would have liked to play under those 'new' rules, he told me that some aspects appealed to him, particularly the 70-minute game. He was a man that prided himself in his fitness, so he feels that his physical condition when he was at his peak would have served him well. He did hard physical work on the home farm in Ballyduff, and he also took part in cross-country running, which often gave him an advantage over less fit players.

When asked about other players in his own time and in the present day, he singled out players like Pat Hartigan, who was also a champion shot putter, and his brother Bernie Hartigan who were both superb athletes. 'Pat was a very skilful hurler too,' said Tom, 'and Bernie was the fittest man I ever hurled on,' he admitted.

Of the present-day hurlers, he liked Jamesie O'Connor because of his running, and his ability to cover so much ground as well as being able to finish scores. Having seen both of them play, I would say that the Clare man's style of play is very similar to that of a young Cheasty.

Cheasty admitted that he would miss the hard, fair shoulder tackle, which was part and parcel of the traditional game.

My view is that the make-up of the Waterford team was ideal for the modern game with a strong backbone of Flynn, Morrissey, Cheasty and John Kiely. They had two long-striking, stylish centre-fielders in Philly Grimes and Seamus Power, and speedy and accurate wing and corner forwards in Walsh, Flannery and Guinan. The wing and corner backs were stick men, and preferred to play the ball rather than play the role of 'stopper,' which they were expected to do under the 'old' rules. Tom Cheasty would be equally at home in any era. He loved the physical contact that was very much part of the old game, but his speed and love of scoring would have stood him in good stead had he been born a decade later.

The strong, firm handshake was the same when I arrived at the Cheasty home in Killure on the outskirts of Waterford city. As we sat before a welcoming fire, it wasn't long before the tea and cake arrived so I knew that we were in for a long session. The Cheastys are great company, and we had a lot to talk about.

Tom's wife Kathleen (née Kelly) came from Curraghballintea, near Carrigbeg in County Waterford. They had four children. The eldest, Siobhan, suffered a brain haemorrhage and passed away in the bloom of youth some five years ago, which was a devastating blow to the family. Siobhan had qualified as a doctor and was a gold medal winner in her class at UCD. Tom and Kathleen are blessed with two other girls and a boy. At the time I called, Margaret was waiting for a job, and was teaching part-time in a local school. Catherine is a Business Studies student at Trinity College, while Geoffrey was in transition year at De La Salle College and playing hurling with Ballygunner.

Tom's brother took over the home farm in Ballyduff when Tom purchased Killure in the 1970s. He is now retired from farming, and laughingly told me that he was a man of leisure. Tom's father was a typical hard-working farmer of his time, with a mild interest in hurling. His brother played in goal for Ballyduff. But the young Cheasty's love of hurling was fostered in Kilkenny where he used to spend his summer holidays. His mother, Kathleen Walsh, was from Grange, Mooncoin, and he remembers as a six or seven-year-old looking enviously over the gate of the hurling field at the young Mooncoin lads hurling. They appeared to him to be very handy hurlers, and although he did possess a hurl, he felt that he was good enough to join in.

The tenacity and competitiveness that was in later years to be his trademark was already in evidence, and he remembers going back to Ballyduff and practising for long hours with a sponge ball against a wall. When he returned to Grange for the Christmas holidays, he was confident that he was good enough to join in. The game normally played was 'backs and forwards' comprising of four backs, four forwards, goalie and centre-field to puck the ball in.

Mooncoin, of course was steeped in hurling lore, and the great team of the early 1900s and their battles with Tullaroan were still talked about. Tom remembers that his mother was very friendly with Mike Doyle who was the youngest of the famous Doyle brothers. He always got great encouragement from Mike and Martin Murphy, who were related by marriage.

Back in Ballyduff, the love he had developed for the game was nurtured by the Foran family, who were next-door neighbours and they spent many happy hours training together. In later years, Tom's training partner was Mick Power, who worked on the family farm. Mick was two years younger, and played centre-field on the Ballyduff team. When the day's work was done, they hurled every evening until nightfall. Tom credits Mick with the development of many of the skills that were to stand to him later in his career. He remembers that he was weak and had little confidence in shooting for scores on his right side. They spend hours working on that deficiency and it paid off in the 1959 All-Ireland replay when he soloed in to finish two first-half points on his right side.

His first competitive 15-a-side game was as a 16-year-old when he was asked to play with Ballyduff junior team. They had difficulty in fielding a team, and he played with his stockings pulled up over his trousers. It may seem funny now, but it was not that unusual at that time. He had a cousin playing that day who just pulled the jersey on over his shirt.

He came to the notice of the county minor selectors in 1950 in the same year. Tipperary were All-Ireland champions the previous year, and Waterford drew with them only to be beaten in the replay. In his second year as minor in 1951, they were beaten by Tipperary in the first round. Tom did not regard his minor days as very successful, either for himself or his county. There was a great upsurge of hurling in Waterford around that time following their great All-Ireland senior victory in 1948. Tom was honoured to have been selected to wear the county blue and white for the minor team, but he did feel that the interest of the people around his own area was not as passionate as he experienced in Mooncoin where they ate, drank and slept hurling.

Nevertheless, the interest grew and the Ballyduff team succeeded in winning the junior championship in 1961. Centre half-back on that team was John O'Donnell who was on the fringes of the Waterford senior team, and who died from an illness in the prime of his life. Willie Power played at full back, and his training partner, Mick Power at mid-field. Other prominent players were Noel Larkin, Hopper McGrath and John Kirwan. They played Four Mile Water in the final. Tom was marking Mick Connolly who later became a good friend.

Ballyduff later merged with Portlaw, and they won their first senior championship in 1970, by default perhaps, when the other semi-finalists, Ferrybank and Erin's Own were thrown out because they could not agree over the fixture. The parish split up the following year, and Tom threw in his lot with Portlaw. They won their second title, defeating Carrigbeg in the final.

He won three more county medals, the last in 1977 when he was 43 years of age. He kept fit all those years, and continued to play at centre-forward. He felt that he made a good contribution to their success right up to the end. The most enjoyable win was against the great Mount Sion Club, and he was marking Jim Greene who starred for the Waterford seniors at corner forward in later years.

The Phelan (Whelan) brothers were the backbone of the Portlaw team, which also boasted of John Galvan, who was the first Waterford man to win an All-Star

Award in 1974. Martin Hickey, Paul Kelly, Hugh Maher, Paddy Henebry, Ben Delaney and Big John Kirwan all made their own contributions to the club's successes over the years.

That was all more than 20 years after he had begun a most illustrious senior career in the famed white and blue jersey of Waterford. He earned a permanent place on the team in the 1956 Championship. They played Cork at Fermoy and he was marking Mick McCarthy who was very young. Tom's strength and fitness enabled him to get the better of the young Corkman, and the Cork mentors moved back Willie John Daly from corner forward to mark him. The experienced Willie John started to get the better of him in the last ten minutes, but he had done enough to get his place on the 'Rest of Ireland' team who played All-Ireland champions, Wexford later on in the year. He was marking Billy Rackard that day who was getting the better of him. He was very hurt to be then moved in to corner forward where he came up against Bobby Rackard, but that might have been the spur he needed, as he finished up whipping three goals past Art Foley!

In the mid–1950s, hurling in Waterford was at a low ebb, in that they were unable to field a team to play Kilkenny in a League game. Tom had played well in a junior match the previous week, and he was called down from the bank in Walsh Park to make up the team. He was given boots, stockings and togs and was positioned at centre forward. He was marking Mick Brophy that day, who later played centre-field for Kilkenny. Mick in fact was a relation of his mother.

But by 1956, John Keane, star of the 1948 side, and in 1984 selected at centre-back on the 'GAA Centenary Team,' and this year on the 'Team of the Millennium' had taken over the running of the team. Although, they were beaten that year, John felt that he had good prospects with this group of players. John worked on building up the confidence of the players and it started to pay dividends. They beat Limerick, Munster champions of 1955 in the first round of the 1957 Championship, and faced Cork in the Munster final. The Leesiders were without Christy Ring that day due to injury, and Waterford romped home by 1–11 to 1–6. Tom was playing on Vince Twomey who was an extremely skilful ball player. However, the Waterford man was able to get possession first and use his strength to get past Vince, who was unable to dispossess him. Tom won his first Munster senior medal in style.

They defeated Galway in the semi-final to set up a showdown with neighbours Kilkenny. Tom did not really experience the intense rivalry that built up on the borders of these counties for this game. In fact he thought that he probably had a sort of 'sympathy vote' from the Mooncoin area where he had spent much of his youth, and had even trained with the Mooncoin team. He had many good friends there including Mickey and John Fribbs and Pat 'Blondie' Murphy. There was no Mooncoin man on the Kilkenny team, so he felt that they regarded him as 'one of their own.'

John Keane put them through their paces at Walsh Park and Dungarvan, concentrating on skill and team play. But Tom worked hard himself on his own fitness and kept up the 'ball against the wall' practice and other skills with his training partner, Mick Power. The Ballyduff man had prepared well, and with the confidence gained by their defeat of Limerick and Cork inculcated in them by John Keane, Tom left the Grand Hotel Malahide on the first Sunday in September expecting to overcome a previously unimpressive Kilkenny.

He was so focused as the teams paraded around the pitch that he did not notice the strange looking 16th man togged out with Kilkenny as the players followed the Artane Boys Band around the field. He was not alerted either by the build- up of the 'buzz' in the stands, as the spectators from both sides wondered who the stranger was. Waterford fans wondered if Kilkenny had pulled a fast one by parachuting an 'unknown' potential match-winner at the last minute. The Kilkenny fans were equally perplexed, and were somewhat relieved to see the tall dark-haired stranger make for the dressing room and not the 'dug-out' after the parade. I was in the minor dressing-room that year which adjoined the senior one, and there was equal consternation there as we emerged to see this strange figure in the black and amber strip surrounded by a weird bunch who turned out to be film directors and crew. The stranger, of course was the movie star of the 1950s John Gregson, who was over doing a scene for the film 'Rooney.' Rumour has it that the directors of the film first asked the Waterford mentors if they would agree to allow him to walk in the Waterford strip, and they refused, as they feared that it might upset the team. The jovial Paddy Grace, Kilkenny county secretary saw it as a mild distraction that would calm the team's nerves before the big game.

Tom felt that his analysis of the possible outcome of the game was correct with ten minutes to go. They had beaten Kilkenny in most sectors of the field and were leading by six points and cruising. Then, as they had done so many times in the past, Kilkenny struck and crashed in two goals by Billy Dwyer and Mick Kenny. After Dwyer's goal, Phil Grimes steadied the Decies men with two points, but Mick Kenny replied with a point and his well-taken goal. Clohosey levelled with a point, before Mickey Kelly sent over the winning point, while on his knees on the ground for a sensational victory for Kilkenny, 4–10 to 3–12.

Tom was of the opinion that, but for the brilliance of Ollie Walsh, they would have built up an unassailable lead coming in to the last ten minutes that even Kilkenny could not recover from. 'Ollie was unbelievable that day in his first All-Ireland final,' he said. It was a big disappointment for the team to be beaten like that, though Tom said that it was not as devastating as it must have been for Limerick in 1994 when they went down to Offaly in even worse circumstances.

That team was too good to stay down for long. They got to the Munster final in 1958 only to go down heavily to Tipperary. But their spirit was not broken, and they came back in 1959 to beat what Tom called the 'big three' in winning their first All-Ireland medal.

They had a big win over Galway, who had opted to play in the Munster Championship that year, by 7–11 to 0–8 in the first round. Then they faced Tipperary, who had given them a hiding the year before, and were the reigning All-Ireland champions. This match was played in Cork and many Tipperary fans didn't travel, expecting another landslide for their team. Waterford played with a strong wind in the first half and built up an amazing lead. I remember listening to intermittent reports coming over the radio giving this unbelievable half-time score of something like 7–3 to 0–1. Everyone expected that there would be a big Tipperary comeback in the second half. We were playing a club match on that day and we could not believe our ears when we heard the final score as we came off the pitch – 9–3 to 3–4 in favour of the Decies men. Tom said that he really had very little to do, that most of the scores came from their full-forward line who were able to get a step ahead of the Tipperary backs to whip the ball to the net. Their backs held out well in the second half against the gale.

They now faced Cork in the Munster final. They had beaten them in 1957, but without Ring. There were doubts amongst the Waterford supporters that their could beat them again with the maestro on the field, but Christy was well marked for the 60 minutes by an uncompromising Joe Harney, and they overcame the Leesiders in a dour contest by 3–9 to 2–9.

Now there were two of the 'big three' beaten as they faced Kilkenny yet again in a final. Despite their defeat by the black and amber brigade in 1957, Waterford were established as 'favourites' to win this time.

That tag seemed to be justified when they led by 0–9 to 1–1 at half time. I remember Cheasty was devastating in that first half, causing havoc in the Kilkenny defence with his runs, and his passing for his colleagues to convert. Waterford had been warned by John Keane to take their points and he considered that it would be impossible to get goals against Ollie Walsh who seemed unbeatable. Nevertheless, from my perch behind the goal, I can remember many fantastic saves that Ollie had to pull off to keep his goal intact. The Ballyduff man continued where he left off in the second half and scored four great points from his searing runs.

Kilkenny came back in the second half and scored four goals, three from the stick of 20-year-old Tommy O'Connell. Waterford continued their policy of taking points and had accumulated 0–17 just on the call of time, but were still three points behind Kilkenny. I can still remember Seamus Power running through in the last minute and unleashing a shot from outside the 21, which Ollie moved to cover. Unfortunately for Kilkenny, the 'Link' Walsh tried to get a hurl to it and deflected it away from Ollie and over the line for a goal. Waterford had equalised and the match ended square. Ollie Walsh and Tom Cheasty shared the coveted 'Sports Stars of the Week' award in the following Friday's *Irish Independent*.

For me, the draw was a mixed blessing. I had to get over the disappointment of losing another minor final, and seeing the seniors hauled back to a draw, but I was surprised to get a call-up to the senior panel for the replay on 4 October. Johnny McGovern was a doubtful starter for the replay having injured his shoulder in the drawn game. However, the Kilkenny selectors took a chance on his fitness, but the lion-hearted Johnny had to be called ashore after 15 minutes of the first half, and I was called in to a re-shuffled Kilkenny line-up for my first senior final. Tom Cheasty and myself were now standing on the same field for the first time, but Tom was playing one of his best games ever in the white and blue and had a personal tally of 2–2 chalked up before half time.

Tom recalled both goals. 'I slipped my marker, Timmy Kelly, and went on a solo run and sent in a shot which Ollie saved. However, I met the rebound just before Ollie reached me and the ball hit the net.' The second goal was from a "70" by Mick Lacey. As the ball dropped in the square, I got my hurl to it and deflected it past Ollie,' he recalled. Tom thought that Ollie was caught between two stools as he came out to challenge the dropping ball. 'If he stayed back, he might have been able to stop it,' he said. Tom had paved the way for this great Waterford victory, and they ran out easy winners by 3–12 to 1–10.

Cheasty felt that this win compensated for the disappointment of 1957, and that it was well that they did win their All-Ireland medal in that year, because the great Tipperary team of the 1960s had now arrived and were to dominate the Munster Championship for the next decade. However, the now ageing Decies men did make a final burst in 1963, and made an all-out effort to oust the Premier County in that year.

They met in the League final that was described by the late John D. Hickey in the *Irish Independent* as one of the best matches he had ever witnessed. Tom told me that he regarded that League final as his best ever performance, and the records show that he was again named 'Sports Star of the Week,' having played on the great Tony Wall. Waterford came out on top to win the League title, and they also won the Oireachtas competition that year. They now set their sights on the All-Ireland, and they reached the Munster final for another encounter with Tipperary. On the way to the final they defeated Limerick, but Tom missed that game having been suspended following a minor incident in a junior club football match.

After the fantastic League final, everyone expected another classic, but it turned out to be a poor game, and Waterford scraped through by 0–11 to 0–8. Tony Wall tightened up considerably, and Tom felt that he just about 'held his own' on the day.

Waterford were the form team that year and came to the All-Ireland as favourites against an untried Kilkenny team that contained a few of the 1957–1959 team and a number of newcomers including 19-year-old Tom Walsh, Tom Murphy and Ted Carroll. Although I was only 21, the late Padraig Purcell listed me as one of the 'veterans' of the side. The team was described in the match previews as a blend of youth and experience.

It turned out to be a sensational game and finished up with the scoreline of 4–17 to 6–8, a record score for a 60-minute game. Tom was marked by the late Ted Carroll, who I had played with and marked on occasions in training for the county at minor and senior level and in St Kieran's College. Ted was unspectacular, but extremely tight and would never give space to his opponent. Tom confirmed this, and added that he was extremely fair and never pulled a dirty stroke, 'we just about cancelled each other out on the day.' Of course, the Kilkenny mentors felt that if they could get anyone to do that with Cheasty, they would be half way there. Tom was the hub of the team, and all scores came through him. The other, lighter forwards needed the supply of ball from him to score. By breaking even with Tom, Ted had his job done.

The team and supporters were very disappointed that they did not get a second medal, and felt that they had a better team. Despite the huge score, they were only three points behind at the end. However, Tom said that they took consolation in the fact that this team had won three Munster medals, beating Cork and Tipperary in the process.

Tom won five Railway Cup medals with Munster and generally got on well with colleagues from the other Munster counties. Nevertheless, he always bore in mind that these players would be the opposition in a few months time, and he tended to 'pal' with Phil Grimes on the day of these matches. He felt it a great honour to share a dresssing room with the legendary Christy Ring, and watched closely every move he made to see what made him so great. He felt that his greatest asset, other than his skill of course, was his ability to come from nowhere after a quiet 50 minutes to win a game. In contrast, Tom admitted that if he himself did not get a good start, he would never make an impact on the game.

As an anecdote on the maestro, Tom told the one about a frustrated Limerick man coming out of the Munster final in 1956 after Ring scoring three goals in the second half to steal the match. 'Ring, we'll have to shoot you,' he sighed. 'You might as well,' retorted Ring, 'you've tried everything else.'

John Keane was his own early hero, and he saw him perform at club level with Mount Sion towards the end of his career. Mick Hickey and Mick Hayes were other heroes of his from that 1948 team. He spoke highly of all his colleagues from his own era and picked Austin Flynn on his provincial team for his consistency over a long career at full-back. Jimmy Doyle, he described as a beautiful stick man with superb control and a great finisher of scores. He was also an unselfish player and a supreme sportsman.

He enjoyed the limited success of the 1998 Waterford team, and thought that they were unlucky to go down to Kilkenny in the semi-final that year. He felt that they deserved a draw and that a replay would benefit whatever team that emerged victorious in their preparation for the final. He considered Fergal Hartley, Tony Browne, Tom Feeney, Sean Cullinane and Paul Flynn to be players of high quality, but they were short a few to make a really good team.

He believes that the back-door system had some merit, but it still only benefited Kilkenny and Offaly. Waterford still had to beat Tipperary and Clare to get to a Munster final to get a second chance. His preference was for a complete 'open draw' which would give Waterford a chance to get out of the shadow of Tipperary and Cork. He was not sure how it would affect the provincial championships, but it was worth a try. Tom would love to see Dublin make a breakthrough in hurling. 'The capital city should be strong in hurling,' he said.

Tom Cheasty has wonderful memories of an outstanding hurling career from his first game as a junior hurler with Ballyduff to his last game with the club when he was well into his 40s. In the period between, he reached the top of the hurling ladder and gave outstanding service to his county. He will always be spoken about when men sit down to talk of great hurlers.

Tom Cheasty's Team of the Century

Ollie Walsh
(Kilkenny)

John Doyle	Pat Hartigan	Bobby Rackard
(Tipperary)	*(Limerick)*	*(Wexford)*
Jimmy Finn	Billy Rackard	John Keane
(Tipperary)	*(Wexford)*	*(Waterford)*

Phil Grimes   Frank Cummins
(Waterford)   *(Kilkenny)*

Eddie Keher	Mick Mackey	Jimmy Doyle
(Kilkenny)	*(Limerick)*	*(Tipperary)*
Christy Ring	Nicky Rackard	Paddy Kenny
(Cork)	*(Wexford)*	*(Tipperary)*

Munster Team Of The Century

Tony Reddin
(Tipperary)

John Doyle	Austin Flynn	Brian Lohan
(Tipperary)	*(Waterford)*	*(Clare)*
Jimmy Finn	John Keane	Mick Hayes
(Tipperary)	*(Waterford)*	*(Clare)*

Phil Shanahan   Phil Grimes
(Tipperary)   *(Waterford)*

Jamesie O'Connor	Mick Mackey	Jimmy Doyle
(Clare)	*(Limerick)*	*(Tipperary)*
Christy Ring	Jimmy	Paddy Kenny
(Cork)	Barry Murphy	*(Tipperary)*
	(Cork)	

Tom looked for the qualities of speed, strength and skill when making his choice.

2 – Joe Cooney

Joe Cooney in action.

Joe Cooney had already a very distinguished career behind him as a minor and under-21 star in the maroon and white jersey before I really saw him at close quarters. In fact, he had played with the senior Galway team in the All-Ireland semi-final of 1985 when they overcame champions, Cork in atrocious conditions by the unusual score of 4–12 to 5–5. Joe made his first appearance in an All-Ireland senior final that year when they were favourites to beat an ageing Offaly team.

But, at the tender age of 20 years, he was to learn that Offaly is a hard team to beat. Galway could not break free of them that day, and the beautiful, flowing, attacking movements that they displayed against Cork in the semi-final were never repeated in the final. The endless supply of attacking ball that was delivered by that superb half-back line of Pete Finnerty, Tony Keady and Gerry McInerney against Cork, was stifled by that hard-working, strong-running Offaly trio of the Corrigan brothers and Brendan Bermingham. The dogged Offaly men held out to win by 2–11 to 1–12. Joe remembers hitting one ball that appeared to be dropping over the cross-bar, but it dipped under the bar and landed behind goalkeeper Jim Troy's line on to his spare hurley and bounced out. The quick-thinking Troy caught the ball and cleared it away. The loss of that 'goal' was obviously crucial to the result. 'The Sunday Game' cameras caught the incident, and showed the ball as being over the line. But Joe, in a typical sporting manner accepted the decision made on the day, and gives full credit to the Offaly team for their victory. He has often joked with Jim Troy about the score, but the Lusmagh man was always non-committal.

Joe Cooney was one of a team of stars in those two first years as a senior, but he really burst magnificently on the scene in the All-Ireland semi-final against Kilkenny in 1986. I was unfortunately on the sideline in Thurles that day as a selector with the Kilkenny team as we frantically tried to contain a rampant Galway side who gave us a lesson in all aspects of the game. That was the day when Galway manager, Cyril Farrell introduced the famous/infamous three-man centre-field tactic that worked so well. The Galway mentors had decided on the tactic in order to leave room in front of goal for the speedy Joe Cooney and the crafty Noel Lane. After the throw-in, the 'named' full-forward, Pierce Piggot roamed out-field to play as a third mid-fielder which took our backs unawares and broke up our defence pattern. We (the selectors) made the mistake (in hindsight!) of re-arranging the defence, and sending out Joe Hennessey to track Piggot. This move played into Galway's hands, and the youthful Joe Cooney went to town!

Joe's two goals in the second half of that game ensured that Kilkenny had no hope of mounting a late comeback. For his first, Cooney was on hand to whip in the ball to the net after Kevin Fennelly had parried Noel Lane's hand-passed effort. His second goal was a gem and was named by Joe himself as his favourite goal of his career. 'I ran on to a ball,' he recalled, 'and it fell slightly behind me. I kicked it on and it rose lovely into my hand as I rounded Frank Holohan, which left me with only Kevin Fennelly to beat. Kevin had no chance from that distance.' Joe finished the game with a tally of 2–6 and established a reputation as one of the most lethal finishers in the game during a long and distinguished career.

The Cork mentors had plenty of time to study the new Galway tactic before the All-Ireland final, and Cyril Farrell and his colleagues made the cardinal error of merely repeating the dose for the final which totally backfired on them. Piggot continued to send in balls from centre-field to his grateful 'marker' Johnny Crowley who took up a position slightly in front of his colleagues in the full-back line. The experienced Crowley had plenty of time to make intelligent clearances over the heads of the centre-field players to the Cork forwards who capitalised on those quality deliveries. The Galway mentors took too long to revert back to the traditional three-man full-forward line, and with no plan B to call upon, the players were somewhat demoralised for a time. Nevertheless, they did rally in the second half. But the damage was done, and Cork held on to win 4–13 to 2–15. Johnny Crowley won the 'man of the match' award. As a young player, playing in his first All-Ireland senior final, Joe never got going after the three-man centre-field tactic had misfired, and he had to merely put it all down to experience.

A trip to Galway is always a pleasant experience (except perhaps when you have to take them on in a League game in winter conditions!). I went to Portumna on the May bank holiday weekend for the final of the No Name Club

Cabaret Competition, and the Annual Youth Awards, and I decided to use the opportunity to meet with Joe in connection with this chapter of the book. It was glorious weather, and my trip out to Joe's house in Carramore was very pleasant. It was uplifting to experience the friendliness of the Galway people as I sought directions, and to enjoy the countryside with the sun gleaming on the stone walls on that beautiful summer's day.

I was greeted by Joe's broad smile as I drove into the driveway of his lovely dormer bungalow. His wife Catherine was in Galway City completing the final exam for her degree, and Joe was looking after their four young children, ages nine to two, Joseph, Maria, Aoife and Kevin. I noticed the fine style of young Joseph as he pucked a ball around the front lawn. Unlike his father, he is right-handed, and holds the hurley with his right hand on top. When I discovered that Catherine's brother was Tomás Mannion who was one of the stars of the Galway All-Ireland-winning football team of 1998 and a panellist for a time on the hurling team, I concluded that the pedigree was good! I was probably looking at a future Galway star.

Joe Cooney was born only a short distance from his present home into a farming family. His father, Michael played hurling with the local club, Sarsfields. His mother's brother, Pat Fahy played minor and senior hurling and football with the county before emigrating to England in the 1950s.

There were fourteen children in Joe's family, six boys and eight girls. The eldest, Jimmy, played at corner back on the famous 1980 team who made history by bringing the McCarthy Cup to Galway for the first time since 1923. Pakie, Michael, Brendan and Peter all played for the local club, Sarsfields.

Joe was an excited 15-year-old spectator in the Cusack Stand as his brother won his All-Ireland medal. He was equally inspired by Joe Connolly's famous speech, and Joe McDonagh's rendering of 'The West's Awake' as the excited Galway supporters acclaimed their heroes. He hoped that one day he would emulate his brother's achievements.

The Cooney brothers spent most of their youth hurling in the field at the back of the house. They were all reasonably close in age, so the games were highly competitive. Jimmy, the eldest, moved to his uncle's house a few miles away at the age of 13, but the lads continued their matches. On Sundays, some neighbouring boys joined in for more serious games. They also developed some skill games against an outhouse wall. They competed with one another to see who could hit the ball through some air holes in the wall! Hours were spent there at that exercise which helped to develop strong wrists as well as accuracy.

The school bus collected Joe outside his door each morning to take him three miles to the parish school in Bullaun. His hurl was essential equipment for each school day, but they could only play after school, as hurling was banned during school hours. After some of the boys were injured during lunchtime games, some parents complained, and the teacher had to impose the rule. Frank Corcoran from the local club trained the boys after school. They had a school team, but had little success due to small numbers. The parish consisted of Bullaun and New Inn, which was sparsely populated. They played under the name of Sarsfields, a name that was to become nationally known in later years. The club field was in New Inn, but the community field in Bullaun was much better for hurling.

Joe played his first game with the school team at wing-forward and continued to be recognised as an attacker during his career, although he has played successfully at midfield, and even played in goal as a young hurler.

With no success at under-14, the team matured and had a great run in the under-16 Championship in 1980 and defeated Castlegar in the county final. The team was made up from seven or eight families and included Michael 'Hopper' McGrath who was later to play with Joe on the county senior team. Joe had already established himself as the free-taker and scored six points from frees and play that day.

The team continued to get stronger and play better as a unit, and the same group went on to take the under-21 county title in 1984. While other clubs had success at under-age level, they tended to fade away as they reached adulthood. Sarsfields, on the other hand became a very respected force as the years went by.

The under-21 final was played in November on an Indian summer's day. It is still regarded as one of the best games seen in the county at any level. Joe contributed five points to his side's total as they held on to win against a fancied Tulloughmore team. The game is also remembered for the final effort of Tulloughmore's Martin Naughton, who collected a ball around his own half-back line and soloed the length of the field to score a great goal. While the goal came too late to break down the Sarsfields men, it brought the then unknown Naughton to the notice of the county selectors, and a place on the county senior team. He was to perform that same feat with the Galway seniors in a number of big games before retiring prematurely due to an injury.

At the age of 18, Joe was called up to play with Sarsfields' senior team in the quarter-final of the championship against Gort in 1983. Josie Harte was a Gort stalwart at corner back and coming to the end of his career. The Sarsfields selectors decided to play Joe on him with instructions to come out to every ball and 'take him on.' Josie, now a sports reporter with Galway Bay FM, was also a great Kilkenny hurling fan, and frequently travelled to Kilkenny to watch them train. He was a very experienced hurler, having played for a short time with the county team. Joe and 'Hopper' McGrath did everything to try to get the ball, but Josie was always there to get in the hurley and tap it away. Joe eventually did get through for a goal, but the Sylvie-Linnane-powered Gort side went on to victory. Gort won the county final that year, only to go down to the Shamrocks of Kilkenny in the All-Ireland club final after a replay.

Sarsfields had won their first senior championship in 1980 with some of Joe's brothers on the team but they had no success for the following eight years. In 1989, they reached the county final and came up against Athenry who had many stars including inter-county man, PJ Molloy. Sarsfields had a young team who had been close to success during the 1980s, but never actually won through. They began to think that their chance was gone but they 'came of age' that day and won with a determined performance. The Sarsfields' goalie brought off some great saves to inspire them and keep them in the game. Joe scored some great points at centre-field. In the second half, against the wind, they were under severe pressure but held out to win a great game. Joe Cooney was awarded the 'man of the match' for his performance. They were looking forward to success in the All-Ireland club championship, but were beaten by the Shamrocks from Kilkenny in the semi-final at Ballinasloe by 2–8 to 0–12 on 11 February 1990.

Joe has a very good reason to remember that match. He was going out with Catherine at that time and arranged to pick her up to bring her to the game in what he described as a 'bad car.' It was a very wet February, and the roads were flooded. Now the car might have managed in normal conditions, but asking it to go through flooded roads was asking a bit much and it finally ground to a halt at Athenry. With time now a factor, Joe frantically called into a filling station and the proprietor told him that if Cooney could wait a few minutes while he got someone to look after the station, he would drive him to Ballinasloe. Every minute was now vital as they set out. Joe was sitting in the front seat willing the car through each flooded part of the road. The driver carefully tested the brakes as he came out of the water and this exercise added to Joe's frustration. It was coming near 'throw-in' time. Joe togged out in the car and was ready to run out on the field as soon as they arrived. The match was on about five minutes as he ran through the gates and down to the selectors to collect his jersey. Sarsfields were going well in the early stages, and the mentors couldn't decide who to take off to accommodate Joe. He was introduced as the game entered the second quarter. Despite that setback, they gave the Shamrocks a run for their money, and were only two points behind at the finish. The Kilkenny side went on to win the All-Ireland, beating Ballybrown by 1–16 to 0–16.

In 1992 Sarsfields were back again when they defeated Carnmore in the county final. They went on to have an easy victory, 4–13 to 1–10, over Buffer's Alley of Wexford in the All-Ireland semi-final. In typical fashion, Joe told me how he felt sorry for the Buffer's Alley goalkeeper on that day. Their regular goalie was injured and the Wexford team had to recall Henry Butler who had been retired for some time to fill the gap. Henry had a long and distinguished career between the posts for his club, but this game was one too many, and unfortunately for him and his team he dropped a few balls into the net.

After that comfortable win they went on to meet Kilmallock in the All-Ireland final, and the small club from Bullaun came home with their first AIB All-Ireland title. They defeated the Limerick side by 1–17 to 2–7. Joe was marking Mike Houlihan and they had some great tussles in the centre of the field. Crucial to their success was the fact that the backs succeeded in containing Paddy Kelly who was Kilmallock's chief scorer up to that.

It was a marvellous achievement for the club, and there was great excitement in the parish when they arrived home with the trophy. It was a very special day for the Cooney family when five All-Ireland medals went to the same household on the same day. It was a proud day for Pakie, Michael, Brendan, Peter and Joe. All the days spent hurling that ball against the wall had brought their just rewards!

Sarsfields, however, did not sit on their laurels. They were back again the following year, 1993, to win the county final and make an attempt to retain the All-Ireland title. They contested the All-Ireland semi-final with St Rynaghs of Offaly and beat them 1–11 to 1–7. Joe was not happy with his performance. 'I struggled against Hubert Rigney that day.' Nevertheless Sarsfields went on to meet Toomevara in the final. The Tipperary champions were favourites and their supporters were reported to have had a lot of money on their side. Toomevara was gambling country, but that was unheard of around Bullaun!

In the early stages, Toomevara justified their rating and went ahead and led by six points at half time. Sarsfields had an fantastic start to the second half with forwards scoring from unbelievable angles. The six-point lead was wiped out in as many minutes. The Tipperary boys rallied again and were three points up with five minutes remaining. Sarsfields were awarded a sideline cut, and Joe decided to go forward from his mid-field position to make one last effort to snatch the game. The ball landed in the square and Joe succeeded in catching it, but was surrounded by Toomevara backs. He gave a quick hand pass to Michael Kenny who blasted to the net to draw level. That score rocked the Tipperary men, and Sarsfields added a further two points to claim their second All-Ireland club title.

Cooney rated that match as his most enjoyable with the club, and he paid tribute to their various trainers Michael Conneely, former Galway goalkeeper, Michael Murray and Michael Mulkerins who coached them at various stages over the years.

In the 1997–1998 All-Ireland club series, Joe suffered a groin strain and had to have an operation. He watched his club draw with Dunloy in the semi-final and was still injured for the replay. Cooney remembers sitting on the bench and noticing how fast the game was. He had been told that he could not play for six weeks after the operation, and only three weeks had passed at this time. Sarsfields were under fierce pressure and the game was going away from them with 12 minutes to go. The selectors pleaded with Joe to go in and he answered the call. Shortly after taking the field, they won a line ball and Joe took it and sent it over the bar. Joe describes this point as one of his favourite scores. It rallied the Galway team and they went on to win by 1–15 to 1–11. The team, however, was a little 'over the hill' at this stage with most of them on the wrong side of 30. They went down to Birr in the final by 1–13 to 0–9.

Having watched his brother win an All-Ireland medal in 1980, Joe's ambition was to wear the county colours and go on to emulate Jimmy's feat. After attending county minor trials, he did not feel that he had a chance of making the team. However, before the All-Ireland semi-final that year, he was approached by one of the selectors and told that they would like him to join the panel. Joe was thrilled to pull on the jersey, but had to remain on the substitute's bench while the team went down heavily to Tipperary by 2–7 to 0–4 in the final. That team included Pete Finnerty, Gerry McInerney and Anthony Cunningham.

The following year, Cooney earned a permanent place at left half-forward on the team and they reached the All-Ireland final to meet Leinster champions, Dublin. The Dubs had come through Leinster mainly due to the phenomenal scoring achievements of their right full-forward who was identified at that time as Billy Quinn's son. Billy had played for his native Tipperary as well as Dublin and had starred for Faughs Club for many years. The tall, lanky Niall Quinn was most unlike his father in build, but had the same lethal finishing power. He came into the final with a huge reputation and Sean Treacy was detailed to mark him. Sean almost matched Niall for height and stuck to him like glue for the game until the Dublin selectors brought Quinn out the field in an effort to give their star forward a bit of space. Due to the superiority of Galway throughout the field, very few balls were being delivered to the full-forward line in any case. Joe remembers Niall scoring one great point when he doubled on a ball from a Dublin puck-out and sent it straight over the bar. Galway won by 0–10 to 0–7 and Joe Cooney collected his first All-Ireland medal with great pride. Niall Quinn turned his attentions to soccer and became one of the stars of Ireland's international soccer team.

In 1986, Joe collected his second All-Ireland medal with the Galway under-21 team who defeated Wexford by 1–14 to 2–5. Wexford had Tom Dempsey playing in the unusual position of centre half-back and Larry O'Gorman on his right. Joe played at full forward and made his usual contribution to the scoring. 'It was not a great game,' said Joe, 'but I was delighted to win my second All-Ireland medal.'

Cooney had been establishing his claim to a senior jersey with Galway from 1984, and was now an automatic choice on that star-studded Galway team of the 1980s.

Having lost two All-Ireland finals in a row in 1985 and 1986, Galway were determined to make the breakthrough in 1987. They defeated Clare by 3–12 to 3–10 in the League final, which was a great boost to their confidence. Also, the League gave them a good number of competitive games right up to May, and it was not that long to wait and prepare for the Championship. Tipperary had won the Munster title after a lapse of 16 years. They too were determined to go all the way and the All-Ireland semi-final between these two sides was very competitive with both badly needing a win. After a tremendous game, Galway's experience told and they surged forward to win by 3–20 to 2–17.

They faced Kilkenny in the final, and it turned out to be a dour contest. Joe was playing at centre forward against Ger Henderson, and he could not believe the strength and the determination of the Kilkenny man. Joe pulled on a high ball during the game and accidentally caught Ger on the hand between the fingers. It was bleeding profusely but the Kilkenny man continued to play a dominant role, and reminding his younger opponent at every opportunity that he 'owed him one!' But Henderson was always tough but fair, and even when his old adversary, Brendan Lynskey came out to mark him in a switch with the Sarsfields man, the challenges between these two players were tough but never dirty.

The match was close all the way through, and Joe felt that were it not for John Commins' great reflex save from Liam Fennelly's hand-passed effort, the result could have been different. He also recalled that Ger Fennelly was unusually 'off-form' with his frees that day which could also have been a factor. However, Galway was the best team on the day and finished worthy winners, 1–12 to 0–9.

In 1988 the men from the West well and truly made up for the disappointments of previous years by winning a second title in as many years. They disposed of Offaly in the semi-final by 3–18 to 3–11 for another showdown with Tipperary. Tipperary had won a second Munster final and their supporters were crying out for an All-Ireland title but they could not match the Galway men for speed, strength and skill. The Galway half-back line of Finnerty, Keady and McInerney were at their peak and could not be broken down. Joe considered that he had a quiet game that day. He also felt that Commins again made some vital saves that kept them in control. Nevertheless, he now had two All-Ireland medals, one more than his big brother, Jimmy!

By the time Tipperary and Galway met again in the All-Ireland semi-final of 1989, an unhealthy rivalry had developed. There was high tension in the air when the players took the field and it was obvious that there was going to be trouble. The Tipperary players and mentors were under severe pressure from their supporters to deliver. The Galway camp had become embroiled in what was later known as 'the Keady Affair' and felt that they had been victimised by the GAA authorities. Despite the suspension of Tony Keady, they wanted to win badly to prove their point.

Joe, in his usual fair-minded manner, does not want to take away from the Tipperary victory but he did feel that Tony Keady had been unfairly treated and was singled out even though people were well aware of many other players who had played abroad illegally with impunity. He felt that Galway could still have won the match but lost their focus with all the hype surrounding the issue. In hindsight, Galway would have been better off to ignore the whole thing, make no protest and get down to the business of winning the match. In fairness to Tipperary, they distanced themselves from the affair despite the media's best efforts to embroil them.

Despite all the setbacks, Galway were in with a chance until Michael McGrath was sent off for a careless challenge when tempers had become frayed. This was followed by the sending-off of Sylvie Linnane. 'I have seen Sylvie making some questionable challenges that could have merited the red card but this was not one of them. His reputation had preceded him and he was the scapegoat when tensions were high,' noted Cooney. Galway had now only 13 men and were narrowly beaten by 1–17 to 2–11. Tipperary went on to win the final well against Antrim who surprised everyone by beating Leinster champions, Offaly in the other semi-final.

Following Sarsfields' win in the county final in 1989, Joe Cooney was appointed captain of the county team for the 1990 campaign – and what an inspirational captain he proved to be. Galway beat Offaly in the All-Ireland semi-final by 1–16 to 2–7. This great Galway team had beaten two of the 'big three' in All-Ireland finals, Tipperary and Kilkenny. While they had beaten Cork in semi-finals, they had never done so in a final. 1990 was the year that they could have achieved that unique distinction, but they lost out on a scoreline of 5–15 to

2–21. This was one of the great finals of the decade, and possibly the greatest. It had an abundance of scores, marvellous individual performances and a fantastic comeback by the Leesiders.

It was the greatest display I saw from Joe Cooney during his outstanding career. As captain, he led from the start of the game and bamboozled the Cork defence with his surging runs. Every ball that landed in the area he caught, and either scored himself or laid off to a colleague. With those other speed merchants, Martin Naughton and Anthony Cunningham flanking him in the half-forward line, they completely overwhelmed the Cork defence in the first half. I remember seeing the usually dominant Jim Cashman looking to the sideline expecting a replacement who might be able to cope with the rampant Cooney.

I remember Joe catching one great ball under intense pressure and racing through before shooting for a goal. Ger Cunningham managed to get his hurl to the ball, but Joe's momentum carried him forward and he was there to gather the rebound and kick it to the net. He created another goal for Eanna Ryan. Having burst through again, he delivered a precision pass to the Killimordaly man, but the referee called back the play to give a free to Galway which Joe sent over the bar. Cooney finished the first half by sending over a beautiful point while running down the left wing at full speed. Joe scored 1–6 of Galway's first-half total of 1–13 to Cork's 1–8.

Although they were to face the wind in the second half, I thought at the break that they were so superior to Cork all over the field, they would win comfortably. A number of factors contrived to deny them victory. Ger Cunningham's lengthy puck–outs in the second half took Galway's outstanding half-back line out of the game, and the Galway forwards no longer received the well placed deliveries they enjoyed in the first half. Cunningham also made a number of vital saves: a great reflex save from Noel Lane and a brave effort as he flung himself in front of a 'rasper' from Martin Naughton, catching it on the face. The ball went over the end line, but was signalled 'wide' by the umpire. Ger gratefully took another long puck out which ended in a goal for Cork. 'If you are going to win.' said Joe, 'you get those sort of breaks. We also made the mistake of dropping balls short into Ger's hand which put further pressure on our backs.' It must have been an especially disappointing day for Joe having come so close to being captain of an All-Ireland winning side, particularly when he had such an outstanding game himself.

That Galway team began to disintegrate over the following years and they suffered defeats in finals and semi-finals by Tipperary and Kilkenny. Joe was omitted from the panel in 1996 and 1997, but following his return to form with Sarsfields, Mattie Murphy asked him to rejoin the panel in 1998. I saw him back to his best when he played at centre-field against Clare in the 1999 quarter-final, but they allowed Clare to whittle away a big lead to snatch a draw in the final minutes. 'You don't allow the Bannermen a chance of a replay,' Joe observed regretfully. Clare went on to qualify for the semi-finals.

Joe's boyhood hero was Galway's John Connolly. He saw him mostly in videos of 1970s games and admired him for his skill. 'He was a lovely free-taker and was deadly from the penalty spot. He kept the team going when times were bad, and I was delighted to see him win his All-Ireland medal at the end of his career in 1980.' Joe met him for the first time when Connolly was appointed a selector of the Galway team. He never really spoke to him that much, because, as with many boyhood heroes, he was somewhat in awe of the great man.

He was also a great admirer of Joe Hennessey from Kilkenny. 'Joe was a great reader of the game, and a lovely, clean, stylish player. He had a great range of skills and could hit the ball equally well on either side. On top of that,' he continued, 'he is a lovely fellow to meet.'

Joe thought Cork's John Fenton was a lovely striker of the ball. 'He got some lovely scores in all his games, and we will never forget that famous goal against Limerick,'.

Of the present players, Cooney admires DJ Carey. 'He's a lovely player, with an abundance of skill,' Joe enthused. 'He has a great turn of pace, and if he gets on a run, there is no stopping him. He is a great finisher of the ball.'

Joe has four Railway Cup medals that mean a lot to him. He is disappointed that the Railway Cup competition has lost its appeal to the fans. All the players love to take part. To revive interest, he suggested that the final could be played the Sunday after the All-Ireland on the home pitch of the All-Ireland champions. Speculation on the picking of the team should arouse media interest, and the winning county would be anxious to see their own lads in action again. It is a suggestion worth considering.

While he concedes that the back-door system has given the public more good games and that the image of hurling has benefited from the television coverage, he feels that it has not done much for Galway. 'However, if we could get past the quarter-finals, the extra match would help in the semi-final or a final.' he agreed. 'I don't think an open draw would improve matters.'

Joe is happy with the high standard of skill in the present game. 'It's a lot faster now though', he said 'but maybe that's because I'm getting slower. I see young fellows flying past me in training, but you can get over a lack of pace with the use of experience.'

Joe cannot see the day when players would get paid. He feels that you would lose a lot of players from the game, particularly if the 'elite' were the ones getting money. He felt that the clubs would lose out in a big way. 'Most counties look after their players very well with expenses, and that is all anyone should want. If you went into hurling for money you wouldn't enjoy it. For my part, I'd play hurling for my county even if it cost me money!' He did not see the need for a players' association, as he thought that player's interests were being adequately looked after by the Player's Advisory Group set up by Joe McDonagh, and under the chairmanship of Noel Lane, a former player. He feared that the players' association could have the effect of setting some players against those with differing views, and that would not be a good thing.

Joe Cooney has won every honour in the game. He has five All-Star awards and a Texaco Award for his performances in 1987. He loved meeting all the players from other counties at the All-Star banquets. He was also fortunate to get an All-Star trip abroad where he struck up a great friendship with Jim Cashman of Cork and Liam Walsh of Kilkenny. Cooney was also delighted to meet sportsmen from other sports at the Texaco Awards. He remembers that Alex Higgins of snooker fame and Pat Eddery were there in 1987.

For a man who is so honour-laden, Joe is extremely modest. He was very slow to give details of his performances, or his scoring feats. In recalling victories, he always played down his own team and picked out instances where the other team was in hard luck not to win on the day.

Joe Cooney is a sportsman who is a credit to his club and county.

Joe Cooney's Team of the Century

Joe picked his teams from his own era, and those that he saw playing.

Ger Cunningham
(Cork)

Joe Hennessey	Brian Lohan	Sylvie Linnane
(Kilkenny)	*(Clare)*	*(Galway)*
Pete Finnerty	Ger Henderson	Brian Whelahan
(Galway)	*(Kilkenny)*	*(Offaly)*

Ciaran Carey   John Fenton
(Limerick)   *(Cork)*

Martin Storey	Tomás Mulcahy	Jamesie O'Connor
(Wexford)	*(Cork)*	*(Clare)*
Eanna Ryan	DJ Carey	Nicky English
(Galway)	*(Kilkenny)*	*(Tipperary)*

Connacht Team of the Century

(all Galway, except where indicated)

John Commins

Sylvie Linnane	Conor Hayes	Ollie Kilkenny
Pete Finnerty	Tony Keady	Gerry Mcinerney

Steve Mahon   John Connolly

Michael McGrath	Brendan Lynskey	Martin Naughton
Eanna Ryan	Adrian Kelly	Joe Henry
	(Roscommon)	*(Mayo)*

3 – Ray Cummins

We hear a lot nowadays from some players, prompted by unenlightened journalists or people with a different agenda from outside the Association of the 'sacrifices' inter-county players have to make to wear their county jerseys. This attitude is propagated as if dedication to training or playing GAA games was a recent phenomenon. It would be well for those people to take a look at the commitment required from players in previous decades.

Ray Cummins was unique. A superb footballer, and a lethal full-forward in hurling, he was in heavy demand from his club, his college and his county. Ray told me that he remembers one particular year when there was only one Sunday that he had not a game of hurling or football, and that was the Sunday before Christmas. On top of that, he had many mid–week matches and training sessions with his club and county during the course of the twelve months. Cummins loved sport, he loved games and as a young man brought up in a strong tradition of Gaelic games, he regarded it as an honour to wear his club or county jersey whatever the occasion.

Ray Cummins

Ray's achievements on the field of play are mind-boggling. Apart from his successes with his beloved Blackrock and UCC at local level, he wore the Cork county jersey in hurling and football at minor, under–21 and senior levels. Between 1966 and 1982, he collected two All-Ireland under–21 hurling medals, nine Munster hurling and three football medals, one All-Ireland football and four All-Ireland hurling medals, and had the honour of receiving the McCarthy Cup as captain in 1976. He won two National Hurling League Medals, two Railway Cups in hurling and one in football and three AIB All-Ireland club medals with Blackrock.

In the first ever All-Star Awards presentation in 1971, he won an award in both hurling and football, and added two more hurling awards and one football award in subsequent years. More recently Ray's achievements on the field of play were honoured by his selection as full-forward on the An Post/GAA Team of the Millennium.

To watch the tall, slim Blackrock man walk into Jury's Hotel in Cork for our meeting, it was hard to imagine how such a modest quiet-spoken man could be so honour-laden. It quickly became clear that when Ray did not recall matches, incidents or his own achievements, it was because he modestly saw himself as merely part of a team trying to achieve something. The greatest pleasure he got was from wearing his club or county jersey and from the many friends he made over the years through the games. What a role model he is for the young and not so young players of today, and for the GAA in general.

Ray Cummins was born in Ballinlough in the parish of Blackrock in Cork City in November 1948. His father, Willie played minor hurling for the county in 1938 and 1939 and won two All-Ireland medals at that grade. In 1938 he played at left half-back, and on the opposite wing was a young man called Christy Ring. Willie and Christy became life-long friends although they played for different clubs. His mother, Mae Walsh played camogie and was related to the famous 'Bowler' Walsh who was chairman of the Cork County Board for a number of years.

To say that their three sons, Kevin, Ray and Brendan were steeped in GAA tradition is an understatement. Kevin was captain of the Cork minor team that won the All-Ireland in 1964, while Brendan played centre-forward on the senior All-Ireland winning side of 1976.

When I asked Ray if he remembered getting his first hurley, he replied, 'I never remember being without one.' He then brought me on a nostalgic trip down memory lane to life on the Ballinlough Road in the 1950s and 1960s. Croke Park for the Cummins brothers was their back garden that measured all of 30 feet by 30 feet, not a place to practise the long puck, but it certainly taught them to hit the ball in a confined space, a skill that stood to a six foot, three inch full-forward in later years. When Ray was on his own, he spent hours practising his skills against the side-wall of the house.

Another game they played across the road with neighbours was a form of 'handball'. They made a ball of paper wrapped with twine and tried to score between the gate-posts, hitting with the hand. It is no wonder that the poor unfortunate goalkeepers of later years had no hope of stopping the many palmed goals that Ray put away when it was legal to score with the hand. In looking back on those years, Ray was lavish in his praise for the many dedicated club officials who unselfishly gave so much of their time to looking after the young people of the area, none more so than the late Derry Cremin who he referred to as 'Mr Under-age' of Blackrock. Derry injured himself playing soccer, of all things. He was paralysed from the waist down, but devoted himself to coaching and organising the under-age hurling teams in the area.

After Benediction in the local church on a Sunday evening, all the youngsters met on the Ballinlough road for the big weekly game. Derry would be there on his crutches sorting out two teams for the match which was played on the road. He would then sit on the wall at O'Driscoll's shop refereeing and shouting advice and encouragement to the exuberant young hurlers. I am sure that the young people now living in the area will find it hard to imagine how a game of such intensity could be played there now. In those days, the only possibility of an interruption was the sight of a Garda on his bicycle who sometimes wandered into the area, but often turned a blind eye to the proceedings. The gardai were well aware that where boys were engaged in the manly sport of hurling, there would be no serious police duty to be done.

The other aggravating interruption was from a local man who used to go into the city on a Sunday evening by horse and butt (a cart to you and I) to drink. He usually left the pub footless and climbed up on the butt and the horse took him home, arriving back at the Ballinlough road at about 9.30 when the light was getting dim, and the match was at fever-pitch. The game had to halt while the horse and butt slowly weaved its way up the road. By the time he got to his house it was invariably too dark to finish the match.

Ray also recalled that an old man who was permanently ill lived in a cottage on the road. Derry was friendly with the man and more or less had the run of the cottage. He used go in there to repair the boy's hurleys in the kitchen, and the old man used to listen to the hammering and the banter in the kitchen from his sick bed. The old man died and Derry inherited the cottage and it became the local 'clubhouse.' The youngsters loved going down there at night, when it was too dark to hurl to listen to all the stories of the great hurlers of the past from the older men. There was great 'craic' and banter while John Farnan from Kilkenny and some others of Wexford heritage tried to keep the Leinster flag flying amongst all the Corkonians. It was there that they heard of the Mackeys, Lory Meagher, the Rackards and even the words of 'Boolavogue'.

Later on in the night when the lads called into the 'clubhouse' on their way from the pub, the revelry got a bit more boisterous and the youngsters were sent home. Ray has fond memories of Derry and that little cottage where they learned much about hurling and the glorious tradition surrounding the game in Cork, and where they were inspired to try to emulate the heroes of the past.

The endless practising on the Ballinlough Road, and the astute coaching of Derry Cremin paid dividends, and they were highly successful at under-age level in both hurling and football.

They graduated from the road to playing street leagues in the Blackrock club grounds. There was fierce rivalry between the areas for these competitions, and these games sharpened the competitive edge which stood to them when they represented their club in the county championships.

The under-age structure was very strong in Cork City, and the games were very well organised. The only problem was that they had to walk to the 'away' games. Ray remembers walking across the city to Fairhill to play a match and walking home afterwards which was a round trip of 20 miles (the lads in the country were spoiled, they usually had lorries to take them that distance). The Blackrock youngsters assembled at the club grounds and then walked together with their hurls and gear over their shoulders. Following their success at under-15 level, seven of the Blackrock team were sent to a trial for the county under-15 team. Six of them were picked for the team, and there was one very disappointed youngster, Ray Cummins. As it turned out, none of those six players reached inter-county level in the higher grades in latter years and it was the one left behind who made it to the top. Ray often uses that story when he is coaching young players to give them encouragement to stay with the game.

There were no games played at Ballinlough National School. The Blackrock Club looked after the games for the boys of primary school age. For his secondary education, Ray went on to Coláiste Chríost Rí which was located about three miles from his home. Chríost Rí was traditionally a gaelic football school, having won the All-Ireland colleges senior title on four occasions.

When Cork won their first All-Ireland minor football title in 1961, nine of that team were Chríost Rí players. Famous senior All-Ireland-medal-winning past pupils included Billy Morgan, Jimmy Barrett and Frank Cogan, but past pupils of the school won All-Ireland senior hurling medals too. Apart from Ray himself, John O'Halloran and Martin O'Doherty got their hands on the McCarthy Cup. Ray was on the team that won the Munster junior colleges hurling final in 1962.

However, a big disappointment for Ray was the year he was picked as captain of the college senior hurling team and to discover later that they had to withdraw from the Harty Cup competition because they could not get enough hurlers to put a team together. But he felt that his sporting horizons were broadened during his years in the school in that it was the first time that he had the opportunity of playing with players from other clubs.

Brother Denis, who in later years did wonderful work for hurling in Offaly had been laying foundation stones for the school's success on the Gaelic fields before Ray arrived in Chríost Rí. Dick Tobin was another teacher who did Trojan work in those years. Dick arrived as a young teacher fresh from UCC having won a county championship medal with the university and unselfishly put hours of committed work into preparing and coaching teams.

When Ray entered UCC to study for his engineering degree, the unwritten rule that students played for the college team meant that Ray, along with five or six of his colleagues, had to break their allegiance with their beloved Blackrock. UCC won the county championship in 1970, beating Muskerry in the final. The only consolation was that they did not meet up with Blackrock on the way to the final. Looking back at his sporting life in college, he realises that it was a period when he learned most about the games.

Ray got his first experience of playing to inter-county standards in the university hurling and football competitions. He won a Fitzgibbon medal in 1967 and added a Sigerson Cup medal in 1969. He also feels that he learned a lot about the running of a club, because the teams had to be organised by the students themselves.

When Cummins qualified as a civil engineer, he returned to play with the Rockeys in 1970. The college experience certainly stood to the UCC players from Blackrock as they won the county championship that year and added another four titles before the end of the decade. That was a phenomenal achievement considering that they had to compete with star-studded teams from St Finbarr's and Glen Rovers to win through. They also won five AIB Munster club finals in those years and three AIB All-Ireland club championships. In the 1971–1972 All-Ireland, they beat Rathnure by one point in Waterford in a high-scoring game, 5–13 to 6–9. Ray played at centre-forward that day marking Teddy O'Connor.

Two years later, they met the same team and drew, 2–14 to 3–11 at Croke Park. The replay was fixed for Dungarvan and Ray remembers it as a particularly tough game. Ray played at full-forward and was marked by Jim Quigley who was one of the five Quigley brothers playing that day. Blackrock emerged victorious with a score of 3–8 to 1–9. His third AIB All-Ireland club medal was won against Ballyhale Shamrocks of Kilkenny in the 1978–1979 final. The game was played in Thurles and they won by two points, 5–7 to 5–5. In the 1975–1976 final they were beaten by James Stephens of Kilkenny, 2–10 to 2–4. Ray played at full-forward that day and was marked by Phil 'Fan' Larkin. The photographers had a field day, with the newspapers carrying pictures on the following day of the towering Ray Cummins standing beside the diminutive five foot, four inch Kilkennyman. Ray found Fan very difficult to get away from. 'He was all the time stuck under me rather than shoulder to shoulder as I was used to with other opponents,' he recalled.

It was a great decade for the club, and Blackrock produced many stars that made a huge contribution to winning All-Ireland titles for the county. John Horgan, Dermot McCurtain, Pat Moylan, Eamonn O'Donoghue, Tom Cashman and Brendan Cummins wore the red jersey with distinction. While one of the best midfielders of all time won eight All-Ireland medals with Kilkenny, 'Frank Cummins was totally committed to Blackrock Club,' said Ray. 'He was incredibly strong and a tower of strength when playing for us either in the half-back line or at mid-field. I never saw him play a bad game and he was hugely influential in all our successes.'

During our conversation, Ray came back time and time again to shower praise on the unsung heroes of their club at Blackrock. 'The amount of time and energy those club officials and mentors gave us was incredible,' he went on. 'They lived for the club, and if we were beaten, they just could not go to work on Monday. They took everything about the club so much to heart.'

He was lavish in his praise for the former county coach and team manager, Joe McGrath. 'We did have a strong panel of players, but that would have counted for nothing but for Joe. Joe was the icing on the cake. Even though he had to travel from his place of work in Shannon to the training pitch, he was always there first, even during the winter when roads were bad. He was a perfectionist, a great organiser, a great speaker and motivator. He was on a different plane altogether than what we were used to. He succeeded in bringing the team together to play as a unit. But he was practical too in that he spent a lot of time with us practising the basic skills, something we had not done since we were under-14. He improved my hurling no end with his methods,' Ray concluded.

Ray's brother Kevin was the first of the brothers to wear the Cork county jersey when he was captain of the All-Ireland-winning county minor team of 1964. Ray followed, being selected at wing-back on the minor team of 1966 who were beaten by Wexford in a replay. They drew in the first game 6–7 each and Wexford won the replay with the unusual score of 4–1 to 1–8. 'They scored ten goals in the two matches,' Ray laughed, 'so much for the defence!'

He continued as a defender at under-21 level and was selected at wing-back for the All-Ireland final against Kilkenny in 1968. They won by 2–18 to 3–9. Frank Cummins was on the Kilkenny losing team that day.

'During that period, I was at UCC,' recalled Ray. 'I could not get my place on the UCC team at wing-back, and someone suggested that I be thrown up to full-forward,' he joked. As they say in the best circles, the rest is history.

By the time that the 1969 under-21 championship got under way, Ray Cummins had established himself as an outstanding full- forward, and he played in that position in the All-Ireland final of that year. He won his second under-21 All-Ireland medal against Wexford in a high-scoring game, 5–13 to 4–7.

Ray was now well and truly caught in a whirlwind of GAA activity. He had been selected for the Cork senior football team in 1968, and following his performances with the under-21s, he was drafted on to the senior hurling panel in 1969. He was now playing under-21 and senior hurling and football for his club and county. He was brought on as a sub in the 1969 Munster hurling final when Cork beat Tipperary by 4–6 to 0–9. 'I don't remember touching the ball in that match,' laughed Ray. But when centre-field star, Justin McCarthy was injured in a motorcycle accident in the lead-up to the All-Ireland final, the team was re-shuffled, and Ray was selected at full-forward. 'Things were happening for me so quickly then, I have very little recollection of that game against Kilkenny,' said Ray 'but I did think that it was one that got away from us.'

I hadn't the heart to tell him that it was an All-Ireland final that was very special to me in that it was the first and only time that I had the honour of accepting the McCarthy Cup as captain of the Kilkenny team. Cork were superior for long periods, but there were two turning points that I recall. The first was a Kilkenny goal by Martin Brennan just before half time, which brought us to within striking distance against the run of play. The second was a bad injury to Kilkenny's Pat Delaney in the second half that had the effect of unsettling the Cork team and inspiring the Kilkenny players. We ran home comfortable winners by 2–15 to 2–9.

That game was historic in that it was the first time players wore the now familiar hurling helmet. 'It was really introduced in UCC by Micheál Murphy who had had a serious head injury, but wanted to continue playing the game', said Ray. 'He imported an ice-hockey helmet from Canada to protect the injury. A number of us then started to wear them then, and Donal Clifford and myself continued to do so when we played for the county.' The brightly coloured helmets caught the imagination in that 1969 final, and they became popular with many players since then. I asked Ray what he thought of the face guards that were added in later years. 'I could not see myself wearing one,' replied Ray. 'I did try a face guard once, but I found that there was no way that you could see a breaking ball through the wire. I see players on the field now in difficulty after a clash. They are always late in picking out the flight of the ball after a close encounter. It also makes me wonder if they pick up more injuries by being unable to see the flight of their opponent's hurley. Is it possible that players could lose the skill of avoiding injury, which is an intrinsic part of the game of hurling?' he wondered.

1970 was another historic year in many ways. The 80-minute game was foisted on the unsuspecting players within a week of the commencement of the Championship. To increase the length of the game by 20 minutes was dramatic to say the least, and it gave the players very little time to prepare physically for Championship encounters of that duration. For the record, the duration of Championship games were reduced to 70 minutes in 1975.

Cork beat Wexford in the All-Ireland final in 1970, to win Ray his first All-Ireland senior medal. Wexford were short a number of key players for this game due to injuries, but they still managed to score 5–10. The Cork men scored an amazing 6–21 to win comfortably and establish a record for the number of scores in a final. Ray remembers very little about the game itself other than the fatigue he suffered for days afterwards. It was naturally a great thrill to win his first senior medal, and he recalls the reception the team got on returning to Patrick Street with the McCarthy Cup.

After beating Clare by 6–18 to 2–8 in the Munster final, Cork established themselves as firm favourites to beat Kilkenny in the All-Ireland final of 1972. Many people regard this game as being the best ever final for entertainment, thrills and great scores. I can still recall vividly the performance of the Cork forwards that day and particularly Ray Cummins who scored two magnificent goals, and three glorious points, as well as laying off some scores for his colleagues. We had to make a number of attempts at a comeback during the second half before the Cork team succumbed. I scored a rather fortunate goal at one point, only to see Ray bursting through shortly afterwards to rattle the net. Only for Noel Skehan in the Kilkenny goal, Cork would have amassed an unassailable lead by the time we got to grips with the game. Con Roche sent over a magnificent point from 80 yards with 18 minutes to go, and amazingly that was Cork's last score. The Kilkenny backs closed ranks superbly at that stage, and we managed to break through for some scores to which the Leesiders were unable to respond.

Ray remembers Frank Cummins' goal particularly when he broke through from centre-field and went on a run all the way before sending in a low pile-driver from 35 yards to Paddy Barry's left-hand side and all the way to the net. Kilkenny eventually won by seven points, 3–24 to 5–11. Although it was great to be part of such a magnificent final, it was understandably no consolation to Ray when he ended up on the losing side. He felt that the team played so well and had the potential to beat Kilkenny, they should not have let it slip. I have to concur. I thought that it was the best display I ever saw from a losing side.

Although beaten in the Munster hurling championship the following year, Ray created his own bit of history by winning his first and only senior All-Ireland medal in 1973. It is somewhat ironic that for a man whose first love was hurling, he described the 1973 All-Ireland football final as the game that gave him the most pleasure.

Cork accounted for Kerry in the Munster final and that was the first time that Ray had ever seen or been involved in a pre-match plan. He was playing at full-forward, and his immediate opponent was the solid, teak-tough Paudie O'Donoghue. He was instructed to take the Kerry man out of the square and to play out on the left wing between the full and half lines. The plan worked a treat and Cork got through for five goals while Kerry were trying to grapple with the open space in front of goal. The final score was 5–12 to 1–15.

In the All-Ireland final, he was given the same instruction when marking the great Jack Cosgrove of Galway. I was at that final myself and Ray's play was most unusual and unique for that era. He operated out as far as the 40 and opened up the backs most effectively and created some great scores for his colleagues and scored some lovely points himself. I remember him particularly collecting a great ball and sending in a huge fisted pass to Jimmy Barry Murphy who finished it to the net with superb skill.

Ray recalls an unusual fact from this game. He described Declan Barron as the very best natural footballer that he had ever seen. Declan was the free-taker, but was strangely off-form with the placed balls that day and Ray was given the job. This came as a complete surprise to him as he had never taken frees before, but he felt in great shape, was at peak fitness and his mind was right. He took over the task and had a successful day in his new role. He said that he often woke up in a cold sweat afterwards wondering what would have happened if he had known the night before the game that he would be the free-taker in an All-Ireland football final.

In 1974, the Leesiders defeated Kerry again in the Munster football final, but were beaten by Dublin in the semi-final. Kerry came through Munster in 1975, which brought about the great confrontations between Kerry and Dublin for the remainder of that decade.

1974 was a very special year for Ray when he married Bernadette Allen who was from a well-known Cork family steeped in GAA tradition. Bernadette was one of ten Allen sisters, one of whom married Billy Morgan and another married Frank Cogan. Ray and Bernadette have three children, Cara (25), William (20) and Cliona (16). William made the Cork minor hurling panel three years ago, but when he joined the Air Corps was not allowed play hurling during the initial training period. He is now back playing the game. The Cummins family now live in Kinsale where Ray works with the Kinsale-based pharmaceutical company, Eli Lilly. He has been with the company for the past 20 years, and his work takes him frequently to the continent visiting the company's European plants.

In 1976, Ray was building his house by direct labour which put enormous pressure on him. He recalls on one occasion stacking blocks at 3 a.m. in the morning for a block-layer, who was arriving the next day. That was after a hard day's work, followed by training and work the following day. It was at that point that he decided to give up football and concentrate on his first love, hurling.

1976 proved to be another highlight in the illustrious career of Ray Cummins. As county champions, Blackrock nominated him as captain of the county team and he led his county to the first of a magnificent three-in-a-row All-Ireland title wins, but not before some heart-stopping moments.

Wexford were their opponents in the final, and the Slaneysiders got off to a whirlwind start with Martin Quigley slapping in two goals in the first few minutes. After six minutes the score was Wexford 2–2, Cork 0–0. Ray remembered that for the first time, as he stood helpless at the other side of the field, he began to wonder about his captaincy. I remember the game as one of tremendous anticipation with the two best full-forwards in the game, Tony Doran and Ray Cummins playing on the field on the same day. The question on everyone's lips was how Pat McDonnell and Willie Murphy were going to cope with the fielding and hand-passing ability of these two goal-poachers. I can still remember the hush of expectation every time the ball landed in the goal mouth at either side of the field.

Cork clawed their way back, helped by a point from their captain and a super, kicked goal after Ray had lost his hurley following a tussle with Willie Murphy. His team mate and colleague from the Ballinlough Road, Pat Moylan was also on song, sending over points from play and frees. The teams went in at half time level at 1–11 to 2–8.

Wexford started the second half with a goal from Tony Doran, but that was followed shortly after by a Charlie McCarthy goal from a great ball sent in by Ray's brother, Brendan. The game ebbed and flowed for the remainder of the half and Ray contributed to two crucial points before full time. For the first, he had to call on his football skills again to kick over the bar when he lost his hurley in a tackle. The second was when he sent out a beautiful pass to Jimmy Barry Murphy who raised the white flag. Cork held on to win by four points, 2–21 to 4–11 and Ray had the honour of accepting the McCarthy Cup on behalf of his county.

Cummins collected his third All-Ireland hurling medal against the same team the following year. It was close to the end in that game, and it took an incredible last-minute save by Martin Coleman from Christy Keogh to save the day. Martin had to dive to the top right hand corner of his goal to keep out Christy's powerful drive. The final score was 1–17 to 3–8.

To achieve the three-in-a-row, they had to beat Kilkenny in 1978. Having been beaten by the Noresiders in 1969 and 1972, Ray said that this Cork team felt that they had to beat Kilkenny in an All-Ireland to prove themselves. They did by 1–15 to 2–8 and gave themselves a special place in the history books. Although the elusive 'double' has been achieved by Galway, and twice by Kilkenny since then, it is most unlikely in today's game that any team will ever again record a three-in-a-row.

Ray's last hurling game with club or county was the All–Ireland final of 1982 against Kilkenny.

He was playing in his usual position at full forward, marking Brian Cody and he remembers Brian taking off up the field on a solo run to which he had to give chase. He remembers being exhausted as they passed the middle of the field and not a Corkman in sight to challenge the Kilkenny man. Brian almost scored a point, but as Ray dragged himself back to his position, he recalls saying, 'that's it, I'm 34 years of age, it's time to go.'

That was the last time that he played hurling at any level. He threw in his lot with his adopted club in Kinsale but concentrated on coaching youngsters. His travel commitments have prevented him in recent times, but he enjoyed coaching the Kinsale under–12s for many years.

'To be with those young boys and watch how they listen to advice and learn is as enjoyable as playing,' he enthused.

Ray's early heroes were Mick Cashman and Jimmy Brohan. They were members of the Blackrock club, and he loved to watch them training in the club grounds. He stood behind the goal with his hurley hoping that the ball would go wide so that he could puck it back to them. It was a great thrill to hit the ball back to these inter–county stars. He still remembers the electricity that Christy Ring generated in the crowd when he played for Cork in a Munster final. 'Ringey was magic, and it is great to say that I saw him play, my father had told me so much about him,' Ray said proudly.

Jimmy Doyle was another hero and Ray recalled going to the great matches in the 1960s between Tipperary and Cork and watching the stylist from Thurles sending over some magnificent points. He met Jimmy on the first All-Star trip to the USA in 1971, and they became great friends. He was thrilled to meet his idol and find that he was such a lovely fellow and so modest. Jimmy and Ray still exchange letters at Christmas.

Ray spoke also of Pat Hartigan who he described as a gentleman on and off the field. He was a magnificent full-back and they played against one another for over ten years and he never remembers getting a bad stroke or an unfair challenge from the Limerick giant. 'Pat and I remain great friends to this day,' he went on. 'I can't remember details of games, or scores or wins or losses, but I remember the great friends I made through the games with the club, college and county,' he concluded.

Ray spoke about the modern game and is of the view that the game is much faster now and that there is a greater emphasis on physical fitness then in his own day. He is not sure, however, if the skill level has kept pace with the running qualities. 'There is a lot of running and short passing in today's game,' he went on, 'but I would prefer to see the hurlers playing more hurling in training. I believe that if a training session is properly structured, players will become perfectly fit by using the ball and hurley and playing "backs and forwards" and other hurling routines.' He admires many of today's players – 'too many to mention.' But he singled out Brian Corcoran, DJ Carey and Trevor Giles as having something special.

Ray has mixed views on the structure of the Championship. He senses that some of the bite is beginning to go out of the provincial finals, but that the quarter-, semi- and All-Ireland finals have given us great matches since the system was introduced. He would consider having a way back for first-round losers as a better alternative. 'A team can be put out of the Championship in the first round by a poor refereeing or umpiring decision, or just by bad luck on the day. It could be a long year then.' But Ray admitted that his proposal would also have its drawbacks, and said that he was not sure if he could come up with a better alternative.

Like most people, Ray is very much in favour of players being treated well with perks such as 'gear,' good meals after training and matches, and holidays away together. He believes that they should be adequately compensated with reasonable travelling expenses and not be 'out of pocket' through playing the game. 'But I'd leave it at that,' he said. 'I'd never play hurling or football professionally. I would hate to see it. It would take from the camaraderie and the spirit that is inherent in our Gaelic games. There isn't the same spirit in professional games as in amateur sport. In any event, this country could not support professional sport. That has been proven in soccer and rugby.'

On the subject of the formation of the GPA, Ray was very sad to see two groups now representing the players. 'Many players will want to be loyal to the GAA, and having an outside group mustering support can only cause unnecessary friction amongst players and will lead to trouble within county teams. It is good that players are represented, but on balance I feel that it should be by one group and from within the GAA itself. I do hope, however, that neither of the groups have as their ultimate aim that players should be paid.'

Ray Cummins has made a huge contribution to Gaelic Games on the field of play at all levels. He was an example to everyone with his sportsmanship qualities during his long and distinguished career. He still has a lot to offer the Association on the administrative side, and when travelling abroad is no longer part of his daily work, I feel sure that he will be persuaded to become involved at that level of the GAA in Cork and maybe further afield.

4 – Tony Doran

Tony Doran

'Boolavogue,' 'The Boys of Wexford' 'The Croppy Boy' 'Kelly, the Boy from Killane'. Why did they have to have such rousing songs in Wexford to inspire them. I can still remember standing under the stage in the old hall in Adamstown in Wexford in the 1960s listening to Brendan Bowyer belting out those songs. For a few short moments, we were all from Wexford. But you couldn't get carried away, they were our rivals, the opposition! We had the beautiful 'Rose of Mooncoin,' and Brendan threw it in when the Royal Showband were performing in the Mayfair in Kilkenny. But that was a love song: great for the last dance of the evening when a fellow should be making a move, but not the sort of stuff to listen to on the morning of a Leinster final. Listening to those Wexford songs on the morning of a match must be worth at least two goals to them, I often thought, so we had to start early in the game to make up the deficit.

As young Kilkennymen, that was not the first time that Wexford inspired us. When we were growing up in the 1950s, Kilkenny was going through a lean patch. We were living off the memories of the 1947 All-Ireland, and the pictures that I cut out and pasted carefully in a book were those of Kilkenny heroes, Jim Langton, Terry Leahy, Paddy Grace, Jimmy Kelly, 'Diamond' Hayden, Shem Downey and others. It was a long ten years before we won our next Championship. In the early 1950s, our hurling heroes were gone past their best, and we looked to our neighbouring county for inspiration.

Wexford had emerged as a hurling force and they boasted of players with names like Wheeler, Morrissey, O'Donnell, Kehoe and English. How those names rattled from Micheál Ó Hehir's lips as he gave the line-out before an All-Ireland. But Rackard, RACKARD, how rousing that sounded, and where did he come from? KILLANE. There were of course three outstanding Rackard brothers, Bobby, Billy and Nicky. But Nicky was the one who started it all. He was big in heart and big in stature. He was our hero when he took on backs and thumped the ball to the back of the net and we heard Micheál Ó Hehir roaring over the Croke Park crowd 'and Nicky Rackard, the boy from Killane has put Wexford right back in this game.' John Kelly is dead, long live Nicky Rackard!

It took another decade or more for Micheál Ó Hehir to have an opportunity to grab a line from another of the Wexford rebel songs. The Rackards were gone. There were no 'Boys from Killane' as inspirational as the Rackards. Then along came another inspirational figure. I can still hear the great commentator's voice ring out as Tony Doran crashed through with the whole Tipperary defence on his back to score the goal that put Wexford ahead in 1968. 'And the red-headed Tony Doran, the man from BOOLAVOGUE has given Wexford the lead,' he roared. What a way to introduce that inspiring name, 'Boolavogue' when Wexford were making one of their most famous comebacks ever in an All-Ireland final, fashioned by a 22-year-old from that famous place of song and story, who would continue to raise terror in many defences over three decades.

But Tony was quick to point out to me when I called to see him, that although he now lives in the parish of Boolavogue, he was born in Monamolin which, with the other side of that parish, Kilmuckridge, formed the team that Tony made famous – Buffer's Alley. To complicate matters further, there is no place called Buffer's Alley, but he did say that there was a crossroads nearby which is known as Buffer's Alley Crossroads.

The Doran household is steeped in GAA. The lovely dwellinghouse, neat outbuildings and well kept garden is indicative of a progressive dairy farmer. Tony's wife, Mary, came from Ballygar, only a few miles away, and she herself was no mean camogie player and an outstanding athlete. As we spoke, Tony junior, age 17 and Pat, aged 15 were hurling out front. They both attend Good Counsel College in New Ross who have had reasonable success on the college's hurling fields in recent years. Terese (20) is studying Business Studies at Carlow IT. She was just getting over a defeat in the Purcell Cup, a third-level camogie competition. Tony and Mary had travelled to Galway the day before, and were there to console. Noelle (19) was also been beaten in the Ashbourne Cup when playing for UCD. She is studying first-year Commerce there. When later I asked Tony if he had any other interests or pastimes, he smiled and said, 'no, only GAA!' Tony, Mary and family spend all their spare time either coaching young hurlers and camogie players, going to support their own family playing, or merely going to club or inter-county matches.

Tony's own father was a dedicated GAA man too. One of his fields was always made available to the local hurling club, and Tony and his brothers played their early hurling there. Four of his five brothers were very keen on the game, but the real 'All-Irelands' were played in a little park, which used to be an orchard at the back of the house. As Tony described those youthful games where he said he insisted on being Nicky Rackard, I could not help thinking how many similarities there was with my own early hurling days in Inistioge. I'm sure that there are thousands of hurlers of our vintage who could identify with that scene. The fact that there were still odd apple trees in the orchard that had to be dodged and negotiated while trying to control the ball did not take away from the game. This was still their Croke Park, and the All-Ireland had to be won. The neighbouring boys, of course, joined in to make the two teams.

In Inistioge, our Croke Park was on The Square in the village, and we hardly noticed either that there was a large fountain surrounded by chains, and also a historic monument in the centre that had to be played around.

Tony recalled how our club, The Rower Inistioge played a part in the development of Buffer's Alley's lovely pitch and clubhouse in the 1970s. We had been invited to play in the Monamolin tournament, which was a fund-raising event each year for the club. We had four inter-county players on our team at that time, and proved to be very popular competitors when faced with Buffer's Alley, but particularly Rathnure. Our games with the Quigley-powered Wexford team always seemed to end in a draw and the crowds flocked to every game for more. We were never sure if it was that a certain Joe Doran was referee on each occasion that the games ended level, but the money kept rolling in as the crowds got bigger and bigger. Seriously, these games are still talked about in our parish, and the trips to Monamolin are recalled with great affection.

Tony graduated from the old Orchard Park to the Monageer/Boolavogue school team, where he attended national school. His first big game was as a ten-year-old when he was brought in as a sub on the school under-14 team who were playing neighbours, Oylgate, in the Nick Rackard Schools League. He played corner forward that day. This League was set up initially for rural schools to which the Wexford hero of the 1950s more than lent his name. Tony's greatest thrill was in 1956 when they got into the quarter-finals of this competition, to find that the great Nicky himself was refereeing the game. 'Nicky was a God in Wexford,' said Tony, and he recalled how excited he was when he was brought to Croke Park in 1955 for the first time to see his hero in action. The far-seeing organisers put up a set of hurleys for the teams getting to this stage of the competition, so, with regular success, the Doran household was never short of camáns.

His stories of up to a dozen youngsters being packed into Fr Hartley's VW Beetle, brought back memories for me too. The good curate in Boolavogue along with Master Doran (no relation), the teacher in Monageer, made sure that every boy got to the match. In our case, Master Walsh usually called on local GAA enthusiast, Pat Foley, and they both filled their cars with budding hurlers to transport them to similar games. This was the 1950s when it wasn't easy to get a pound to put petrol in a car. Nowadays it is good to reflect on the work these men did for the games in times of hardship. The Celtic Tiger is roaring now, and there are noises from some sources that people should be paid for playing our games! Fr Hartley is now back in Tony's parish as parish priest in Kilmuckridge, and is president of their club.

The well-built youngster with the flaming red hair was now coming to the notice of the county selectors, and in 1962, as a 16-year-old almost made the Wexford minor team. The following year, however was his first big breakthrough.

Tony won his first All-Ireland medal when the Wexford minors defeated Limerick in the 1963 final. He remembers watching the senior game that day from the front seat, upper deck of the old Cusack Stand, and seeing Kilkenny defeat Waterford in the senior game. We both won our first All-Ireland medals that day, but there were more coincidences in the lead-up to that game.

After a number of minor trials for the team in April of that year, Doran was very much in the running for a place on the team. However, before the final trial, which was a challenge game against Waterford minors at New Ross, Tony twisted his ankle in a junior football championship game. He was in severe pain, and early in the week thought that he had no chance of playing. The honour of playing for his county seemed to have been lost, but his father made some enquiries, and he was quickly lifted into the car and brought to a bone-setter. 'Guess where?' said Tony with a twinkle in his eye. 'Inistioge, of course,' I replied.

Mrs Hogan was a sister of a famous bone-setter in the area widely known as 'Nail of Myshall' The O'Neills still carry on the tradition there. Mrs Hogan, her husband and son Pat moved to Inistioge in the 1950s and she was gifted at repairing injuries with the family's traditional methods. Cars came from far and wide to the house on the Square and there was a continuous procession of injured people and animals brought for treatment. Meanwhile, Pat, who never hurled before coming to the village, soon took part in the hurling 'All-Irelands' played on the Square, and became one of the best under-14 goalkeepers in the county. He amazed us all with his skill and bravery in being able to catch a ball blasted at him from the 14-yard line. He confidently showed us how it was done, a skill that stood to us all in later years. Pat was often called in to assist his mother, and I couldn't help wondering, as Tony told his story, if Pat was standing with him as he got strapped up and showed him how to catch a ball. Tony's skill at fielding a ball was to become legendary in his career.

However, whatever skills we in Kilkenny might be able to impart to our Wexford neighbours, catching was certainly not one of them. This skill was really introduced by the great Wexford team of the 1950s, and the Rackards and Nick

O'Donnell confounded hurling followers at that time by showing how a ball could be caught amongst a forest of hurls clashing, and without getting injured. This evolved as an integral part of Wexford style of hurling and was adopted by other counties at a later stage.

Getting back to the story, Mrs Hogan strapped up Tony's ankle, and he came through the trial game with flying colours and earned his place on the team. They brushed aside Laois in the first round and defeated Kilkenny, who had Kieran Purcell playing in goal, in the Leinster final.

The team, which included clubmate, Mick Kinsella, Vinnie Staples, Joe Murphy, Pat Quigley and Con Dowdall grew in confidence. Powered by Tony on the 40, they edged out a great Limerick team, which included Eamon Cregan and Eamonn Grimes, in the final. It was a proud day for Wexford and Buffer's Alley.

It was the bones of this team that brought home under-21 All-Ireland honours to Wexford in 1965. They had been defeated by Tipperary in 1964 by 8–9 to 3–1, a game which Tony missed through injury. But they were back, a year older and wiser in 1965 and, with the addition of Dan Quigley and Jack Berry, they avenged that defeat at Nowlan Park in Kilkenny. Tipperary still had the services of Babs Keating, Francis Loughnane, Len Gaynor and Noel O'Gorman, but Wexford turned the tables with a 3–7 to 1–4 victory.

Tony was too modest to tell me how much he scored on that day, but that, in fact, was the first time I really saw him in action. He was operating at full-forward, and I can still see him fearlessly careering through the stout Tipperary defence to finish the ball to the net, a feat that was to become his trademark in the years ahead. In 1966, they met Cork in the final, and it took three games to decide the issue. After two exciting draws, Cork came out easy winners, 9–9 to 5–9 in the third encounter. Gerald, Justin and Charlie McCarthy from that team played an important role in Cork's defeat of a fancied Kilkenny team in the senior final that year.

Young Doran's displays with the under-21s brought him to the notice of the senior selectors in 1965 and the 21-year-old played a few League games in the autumn of that year. However, he did not make the Championship selection in 1966, but was recalled at the end of that year for the 1966–1967 League campaign. By that time, he had firmly established his position, and made his Championship debut in 1967. Wexford suffered defeat at the hands of Kilkenny in the Leinster final that year.

1968 was a historic year for Buffer's Alley, Wexford and Tony Doran. The club's progress over the previous years was very similar to that of many other rural clubs including my own, The Rower-Inistioge. The team was built around a number of sets of brothers including Bill, Joe, Colm and Tony Doran, Joe and Liam Murphy and three Butlers. Being a young team they opted to move out of junior to intermediate grade where it was felt they could perform better. After a few Final defeats at intermediate grade, they won the Championship in 1966 and were promoted to senior level. They reached the county final in their first year to be well beaten by the experienced Rathnure team.

However, the Alley were on the move, and, in their second year at that grade, won the county final against Willie Murphy's Faythe Harriers. Tony was to play his part in ten further Championship wins, but he singled out a few that were of particular significance. The team's best display ever was in the 1970 county final against Shamrocks, Enniscorthy, but it was to be a very sad day for Tony when he learned after the match that his father had died at the game.

In 1975 they defeated neighbouring parish, Oulart-The Ballagh in a local derby. Another highlight was winning the 1985 final to equal Rathnure's and St Aidan's great record of four-in-a-row. Ironically, it was Rathnure who stopped them in their bid for the outright record of the elusive five-in-a-row. Rathnure, in fact, had been their bogey team, and with all their success, it took until 1988 to beat them in a final. The victory was all the sweeter by the manner in which it was achieved. Rathnure were nine points up at half-time, and it looked as if the Alley were going to fail again. However, a tremendous Tony-Doran-inspired rally in the second half forced a draw, and they well and truly smashed the bogey in the replay with an easy win.

That win qualified them to contest the AIB All-Ireland club championship in 1989 and they went all the way to beat Ciaran Barr's O'Donovan Rossas who boasted several Antrim inter-county stars. They had to beat Seir Kierans of Offaly and Ballyhale Shamrocks of Kilkenny to get out of Leinster before defeating Four Roads from Roscommon in the semi-final. This was a marvellous achievement for such a rural club with a relatively small pool of players to select from, but Tony thought that it was also very praiseworthy that they continued that year to retain the county title beating their neighbours Oulart in another 'crunch' match. The first game was a draw, and the teams were level at full time in the replay. Extra time had to be played, and it was felt that the younger Oulart team would have the advantage, but it was Buffer's Alley that came out on top and were well ahead at the end. The older players were now on the wrong side of 40, and Tony regarded that win as a 'dying kick' from this great team.

The highlight of Tony's illustrious career must surely be the winning of his one and only All-Ireland senior medal with his beloved Wexford in 1968. We talked at length about that game. Tony said later that he could remember every puck of the game, but remembers nothing of the aftermath. It says something of what made Tony so great – total focus on the game. I put it to him that I always marvelled at his dedication and his tremendous will to win, and asked him how he motivated himself. He replied 'I never had any difficulty in motivating myself, I suppose because I am a bad loser' – but a very sporting one, I must add.

Ned Power and Padge Kehoe prepared the 1968 team very diligently. They prepared the team very well for the traditional, tight-marking Tipperary defence. Tony told me that all the training sessions involved tight-marking 'backs and forwards'. He was usually pitted against Dan Quigley or Eddie Kelly, and it was full-blooded stuff with no prisoners taken. He believes that these sessions hardened them up and served them well when they had to try to haul back

Tipperary's eight-point half-time lead. When they trooped off to the dressing room at the break, they just couldn't believe that they could have played so badly. Padge Kehoe got them around the table at half time, and with a good rousing speech, told them that all was not lost, and that they could still win this game.

Tony remembers saying to Christy Jacob as they took the field for the second half that if they could get an early goal, they would be well there with a chance. Another factor played an important part in the comeback. The selectors had made a number of positional switches for this game, moving Tony to centre-forward and Paul Lynch to the wing. Tony felt that this move had not been successful, and the selectors reverted to the old combination for the second half. They probably thought that Doran would have a better chance of holding Mick Roche, but it had not worked. When Paul Lynch returned to the 40, his quick pulling unsettled Mick Roche for a time and more balls came quickly in to the full-forward line which had telling results. Tony was now operating in his favourite full-forward position.

I watched that game from a front seat in the upper deck of the recently demolished Hogan Stand. I was on the 21-yard line at the Railway end with a fantastic view of Wexford's second half rally. It was vintage Wexford, vintage Tony Doran all the way.

Jack Berry was the first to score with a good point, followed quickly with the first of Doran's spectacular goals. Now they were only four points down. Another point and it was three between them. The rampant Buffer's Alley man careered through again only to be taken down by a frustrated Tipperary defence who conceded a 21-yard free. Everyone expected Lynch to take a point, but he crashed an unstoppable shot past the surprised Tipperary men to the net to leave the sides level. Tipperary tried to rally, and there was nail-biting stuff up and down the field with no scores from either side.

Then, with ten minutes remaining, Tony got through again for that never-to-be-forgotten goal that put them three points ahead. Wexford were dominant from then on, and they tagged on a brace of points before Jack Berry really buried Tipperary. I can still remember him getting possession and angling himself out to send a pile-driver to the far side-netting of John O'Donoghue's goal. Tipperary staged a late rally, but could only narrow the gap to two points before the final whistle.

It is amazing to think that after such an earth-shattering performance, and many more similar performances in his career, the 22-year-old Doran would never again be on the winning side on All-Ireland day. He felt that he was a little unlucky that the Kilkenny team was building again into a great side that won four All-Ireland titles between 1969 and 1975. Wexford and Kilkenny fought great battles in the early 1970s in Leinster finals, and there was only a puck of a ball between them in any of those games. He felt that if they had got through any of those matches, they would surely have won another one or two titles. When they finally beat Kilkenny in 1976, they were gone past their best, but even at that, he was of the opinion that they should have beaten Cork that year but for a number of factors that affected them.

Kilkenny were going for an unprecedented, six-in-a-row Leinster titles, and had performed well up to then in winning the League. Wexford pulled out all the stops to beat them, and peaked for that game.

They had two gruelling games with Galway in the semi-final in full view of the Cork players and mentors at Pairc Uí Chaoimh before putting the Tribesmen away. These two games, under brilliant sunshine. drained the now ageing side, and they had only two weeks to recover before the final. They got off to a great start, but the fresher Cork team clawed their way back, and the Model County could not respond. Nevertheless, only for a brilliant last-minute save by Martin Coleman, they could have still won the day.

Tony, however, got great enjoyment from beating Kilkenny in the Leinster final that year. Kilkenny had also come through a gruelling year, with a number of draws in the final stages of the League, a draw in the final against Clare, a trip to the west coast of America and the replay of the League final. They turned straight into the Championship to meet a hungry Wexford in the Leinster final. Kilkenny collapsed and were hammered. Tony enjoyed particularly his second-half goal when he grabbed a loose ball in a ruck of players, turned and ran through to palm the ball past Noel Skehan. This put them about eight points in front and killed any chance of a Kilkenny rally.

He tells a good story about an incident late into the second half when Wexford had an unassailable lead. Fan Larkin came out to take a 65 near the sideline, and called to the Kilkenny dug-out to ask 'How long is left?' Before the reply could come, the witty Henry Butler shouted out from the nearby Wexford dug-out 'twelve months for you boy!'

Another score that Tony got great pleasure from was that last-minute goal in the 1984 Leinster semi-final against Kilkenny. Strange that he seems to have got most pleasure from scoring against Kilkenny! The Noresiders had won two All-Irelands in a row and looked to have this game won, but Wexford made a late charge and drew level with a few minutes remaining. The sides were still level at full-time when the Buffer's Alley man fielded a long ball, rounded Dick O'Hara and sent a left-handed 'rasper' to the net. Unfortunately, I remembered that incident too well, as I was a selector that year with Kilkenny. The slow-motion action replay of that score was fixed in my mind for some time afterwards.

While Tony and I generally played against one another, and on opposite ends of the field, I still appreciated every move the great man made. I can still recall the tingling feeling of how he raised the temperature of the Croke Park crowds, and the air of anticipation he created for both sets of supporters every time a ball was sent soaring into the square. Tony always battled fairly for possession, and brought the best out of his marker. He played a huge part in creating the atmosphere that made the Kilkenny-Wexford clashes of the 1960s and 1970s so great.

I did get to play with him, of course in the Railway Cup, and we recalled the great run Leinster had in the early 1970s against great rivals Munster when we won five-in-a-row from 1971 to 1975. We were barely beaten in 1976, but came back to win in 1977 again to complete a great spell. He was wonderful to play with, as he had the ability to draw backs to him, which made room for the rest of us.

Tony won the coveted Texaco Award for 'Hurler of the Year' in 1976, and made the 'All-Star' team in the same year. While he made three trips to the USA with the All-Stars, he confessed that he did not like flying, and was happy to get his feet back on the ground. I had the feeling that, for Tony, playing the game gave him the greatest pleasure.

We talked about great players that he played on, and he had no hesitation in saying that Mick Roche of Tipperary was the finest hurler he had seen. He had great clashes with Pa Dillon of Kilkenny. 'You'd earn your crust off Pa,' he said, but he always found him fair. Pa and himself struck up a great friendship, and regularly meet. Nickey Orr of Kilkenny was another difficult opponent, unspectacular, but very tight and effective. He found Eugene Coughlan of Offaly very hard to hurl on. Eugene had developed a great skill of tipping the ball away just when you thought you had control of it. He said that he only played directly on Pat Hartigan of Limerick on a few occasions. 'He was very spectacular, and when he was on his game, he could make you look very poor' said Tony.

On the current state of Wexford hurling, he was concerned that they had very little success at minor level for some time. They had limited under-21 success in Leinster, but the players are finding it hard to deliver at senior level. Wexford had developed a style to suit the big men of the 1950s, 1960s and 1970s, but they have not been producing the big men in recent years, and they held on to the old style for too long. They should have changed their style to suit the new crop of players. However, he felt that the game was never as strong throughout the county as far as numbers playing is concerned, but he was not sure of the quality.

Tony and his family took great pleasure from the county's great All-Ireland success in 1996. The win was long overdue, and it gave a much-needed boost to hurling. When I spoke of Liam Griffin, the glint came back into his eye. I hadn't realised that they were related, but I soon gathered that they were quite close friends as well, and that most of their discussions were about hurling, and that they enjoyed a good argument. 'I didn't always agree with some of the things he did,' said Tony, 'but I have to give him full marks for the way he prepared Wexford that year. He took some chances that came off for him, and it must be said that he played a major part in the victory. His commercial management skills were brought into hurling management,' he went on, 'and every angle was covered from start to finish: training, match-day and even the homecoming.' He liked the way that Liam insisted that the players behaved themselves during the celebrations. He told them that they were ambassadors of hurling, representing Wexford, and should show an example to the youth. I must say that they lived up to Liam's expectations, and they were a credit to their county at the few receptions that I attended.

Tony had mixed views on the back-door system. At first he thought that it was not a good idea, but the quality matches that he has seen in the quarter- and semi-final stages have convinced him that it has worked. 'It has not impacted on the provincial finals as I thought it might' he said. 'It appears that players are still as keen to win provincial medals.' He is glad that there are moves to give the weaker counties more games with a preliminary 'round robin' competition.

So I left Boolavogue, and the friendly homestead of the Doran family with many great memories rekindled. The memories of Tony I had before our meeting were of a player who was skilful, fearless, determined and tough, but a gentleman on and off the field. These were the memories I also took with me as I drove home on that February afternoon.

Tony Doran's team selections do not include any Wexford players. The Ireland team is picked from the period 1967 to 1984, and the provincial team is picked from players with whom he played from 1968 to 1980.

Tony Doran's Team of the Century

Noel Skehan
(Kilkenny)

Fan Larkin   Eugene Coughlan   John Horgan
(Kilkenny)   *(Offaly)*   *(Cork)*

Iggy Clarke   Mick Roche   Martin Coogan
(Galway)   *(Tipperary)*   *(Kilkenny)*

John Connolly   Frank Cummins
(Galway)   *(Kilkenny)*

Jimmy   Pat Delaney   Jimmy Doyle
Barry Murphy   *(Kilkenny)*   *(Tipperary)*
(Cork)

Charlie McCarthy   Ray Cummins   *Eddie Keher*
(Cork)   *(Cork)*   *(Kilkenny)*

Leinster Team

Noel Skehan
(Tipperary)

Fan Larkin   Pa Dillon   Pat Dunny
(Kilkenny)   *(Kilkenny)*   *(Kildare)*

Joe Hennessey   Pat Henderson   Martin Coogan
(Kilkenny)   *(Kilkenny)*   *(Kilkenny)*

Des Foley   Frank Cummins
(Dublin)   *(Kilkenny)*

Liam O'Brien   Pat Delaney   Eddie Keher
(Kilkenny)   *(Kilkenny)*   *(Kilkenny)*

Mick Brennan   Kieran Purcell   Mick Bermingham
(Kilkenny)   *(Kilkenny)*   *(Dublin)*

5 – Jimmy Doyle

Jimmy Doyle

On 4 December 1999, at Thurles Sarsfields GAA Club, beside the famed Semple Stadium, a low-sized, dark-haired man stood on the stage beside Micheál O'Muircheartaigh listening to the story of his life. As the story unfolded, former hurlers from many counties queued behind the stage to be called upon to pay tribute to one of the most admired hurlers of his own, or any other era. All of these hurlers had played against him. Some had had the task of directly trying to curb the will o' the wisp with the deft ball control, the neat side-step and the clinical finish. Others had stood helplessly on the other side of the field watching in awe as Jimmy Doyle weaved magic with his hurl, drawing gasps of admiration from the crowd. The Thurles man may have been the reason why all those former hurlers had few or no Munster or All-Ireland medals, but they all travelled distances on a Saturday night in December to be part of this celebration of the greatness of the Tipperary legend.

With typical shyness, Jimmy stood with his head bowed wishing he was somewhere else, or that some other star was being honoured. The organisers knew that this wouldn't be Jimmy's scene and he was brought there on the pretext that Thurles Sarsfields was celebrating the 35th anniversary of the great run that brought them 10 county finals in 11 years. 'Otherwise he would not turn up,' they said. The function room was full of club and county colleagues and friends. Every accolade that was heaped on him by friend and foe was cheered to the rafters. 'Jimmy Doyle, this is your life,' said Micheál, and as hurlers and hurling were discussed into the small hours of the morning, the hero of the night slipped into a quiet corner to enjoy the chat.

The first time I saw Jimmy Doyle in action was in Kilkenny's Nowlan Park in 1954–1955. In those years, there was no All-Ireland colleges competition. The colleges played out their provincial competitions, which was then followed by an Inter-Provincial Colleges Railway Cup Final. The All-Ireland was not revived until 1957.

I had just started as a boarder in St Kieran's College, Kilkenny, and we were allowed out to Nowlan Park to see Leinster play Munster in the final. Some of the St Kieran's players had been selected on the Leinster team, but as young 'first years', we were not too familiar with the rest of the Leinster players. We were even less familiar with the Munster team, but we were aware of Tom McGarry of Limerick, who was a star handball player as well as an outstanding hurler. We picked him out early on in the game.

Munster was far too strong, and as the game went on, we lost interest in the score and began to admire the individual performances. I became fascinated with this black-haired youngster operating at right half-forward. We had been told in coaching sessions from a very young age that, if we wanted to be any good at hurling we had to hold the hurl 'right hand on top'. This lad was playing left hand on top, but he was different, he was a natural. His left hand was also his strong side, and what a swing! I still remember the grace and style as he swept in behind the centre-forward and onto the breaking ball, and with one sweet movement gathered the ball and swept it over the bar. This happened time after time, and on each occasion, every movement was the same, and the stroke was finished with a beautiful follow-through as the ball went straight over the black spot! Who was this guy? There were no programmes for the match. Eventually, the most knowledgeable of the first years, Dick Somers from Clogh, was able to tell us, 'that's Jimmy Doyle from Thurles, and he has three more years as a minor.'

Jimmy was two years my senior, which is a lot when you are 14. Travel was not easy in those years, and I did not get any other chance of seeing him in action in those early years, although I kept a close eye on the sports pages to read about his exploits at minor level. He inevitably ended each game as top scorer. The next time I saw him play, I was playing against him in the 1957 All-Ireland minor final. My first All-Ireland final in the black and amber jersey in front of 71,000 people was not a time to be gazing down the other side of the field. We had a job to do but we didn't do enough. We scored 3–7, but the Jimmy-Doyle-led Tipperary scored 4–7 and he appeared to have been involved in most of them. There was some consolation that day when Kilkenny seniors overcame Waterford in a thriller. I also took some comfort from the fact that I had two more years left as a minor and that we might have some chance now that Jimmy Doyle had graduated from that grade.

Hurling was tough and robust in those days, and it was generally accepted that senior hurling was no place for a young, small player. But Jimmy Doyle was exceptional and he was selected to play with the senior team in the 1956–1957 National League final against Kilkenny while still in the minor ranks. He had just turned 18 in March of 1957 and had earned his place after a Tipperary trial game between Possibles and Probables. That trial game was his first chance to realise his dream of playing senior hurling for his county, and he lined out at corner-forward for the Possibles. To be landed in 'Hell's Kitchen,' as the Tipperary full-back line was later called, was one thing, but to be marked by Mickey 'The Rattler' Byrne was something else altogether. The teak-tough corner-back did not go easy on his clubmate in the early stages of the game, and Jimmy's father, Gerry, was quick to see that his son had no chance in close. He ran in and told Jimmy to wander out the field, which he did, and ended the game with a tally of 2–11! He had proved to the selectors that he could display the same mastery at senior level and against the toughest of opposition. Tipperary beat Kilkenny in the League final that year by 3–11 to 2–7, and Jimmy won his first major senior medal and a trip to New York before a ball had been pucked in the minor championship.

When the Championship came around, both minor and senior selectors had a problem for their first outing against Cork at Limerick's Gaelic Grounds. The minor selectors agreed to 'rest' Jimmy for the senior game, but they had to spring him off the bench in the last quarter to save the day when the game was all but gone from them. He took control of the game immediately and popped up everywhere to spray well placed balls for his forwards to finish as well as contributing himself to the score sheet. He turned the game in Tipperary's favour.

Doyle then had to line up immediately afterwards with the Tipperary seniors, only to be beaten by a dogged Cork squad. A strong Paddy Dowling kept a tight reign on the minor star, but Jimmy did enough to justify the selectors' faith in him and he was an automatic choice for the 1958 Championship.

The 1958 All-Ireland semi-final between Kilkenny and Tipperary was the first time I saw the now 19-year-old in a senior jersey. He was picked at left half-forward and would be marked by the sweet-striking Paddy Buggy, later to be president of the GAA. Jimmy enthralled the crowd, scoring 1–8, which equalled Kilkenny's total score that day. His goal from a '21' could be described as cheeky in the circumstances. Here was a 19-year-old playing in an All-Ireland semi-final in Croke Park and faced with a packed Kilkenny goalmouth including Ollie Walsh. He had intended to take a point, but he spotted a gap away from Ollie and decided to have a go.

He won his first senior All-Ireland medal that year in the final against Galway where he scored 0–5 of Tipperary's 4–9. Galway scored 2–5 in a disappointing game. Jimmy was not happy with his performance that day and felt under pressure from the excessive media attention after the Kilkenny match. He took it as part of the learning exercise that hurlers have to go through.

In the manner of his arrival Jimmy Doyle became an inspiration to young hurlers. You did not now have to be in your mid-twenties to be considered for a senior county team. If you trained hard enough, practised enough, there was always a chance that you could go straight from minor to senior. It happened for me one year later, thanks to Jimmy for leading the way.

It seemed appropriate that Jimmy and I should arrange to meet for the interview at the back of the old stand at Semple Stadium. The stadium held so many memories for both of us, victories, defeats, good days, bad days. We were standing beside the best hurling sod in Ireland, where it is said by hurling folk, 'if you couldn't hurl in Thurles, you couldn't hurl anywhere.' Located in the centre of the hurling world, surrounded by all the strong hurling counties, it has an atmosphere that can inspire greatness. Even on that Friday afternoon in March, the deserted stadium made you want to take deep breaths to inhale the magic that surrounds the place. Back in Jimmy's home, which is only around the corner from Semple Stadium, we talked of his young days, and as the enthralling minutes turned into hours, I learned how the genius with the camán honed his skills in the shadows of the hallowed ground.

Gerry Doyle, a brother of the more famous Tommy Doyle had two All-Ireland medals as sub goalkeeper for Tipperary in 1937 and 1945. A shoemaker by trade, he was skilled with his hands and made the young Jimmy Doyle his first hurl as soon as he was able to walk. The young Doyle grasped it firmly with his naturally strong left hand and very soon, that beautiful left-handed swing began to develop as he belted a ball around the house and front garden.

As he grew up, the stadium began to beckon, and the youngster could be seen climbing over the wall of the outside pitch with his hurl and ball, and the rat-tat-tat of a tennis ball being belted against a green door could be heard from morning 'til nightfall. If you listened closely, you might have heard the Micheál Ó Hehir commentaries of the many games that were played against that green door. There was one thing sure, Mrs Doyle knew where to find her son, and on most nights as darkness fell, she would have to go up to the wall and wait for a break in the noise to tell Jimmy that it was time to come home. She then knew how far to stand back as the hurl and ball soared over the wall followed by her perspiring son. It was no problem to get him to bed, because the morning would bring more light and there were more matches to play against that door. Later, Mrs Doyle would quietly remove the hurley and ball that Jimmy clutched close to him as he slept.

As Jimmy grew up, he continued practising against that door. When the other young boys of the neighbourhood came to hurl, they organised little matches on the street. The Guards had to do their duty on occasions, but the lads would scatter quickly along well used escape routes before resuming later on. These games paid dividends, and when they were old enough to take part in the under-16 street league with the local team 'Bothar na Naomh', they were well prepared. Jimmy won his first ever medal in this local competition.

Thurles CBS Primary School had one attraction for Jimmy Doyle. They played hurling! He won a Rice Cup medal (under-14 Tipperary county competition) with the school. He spent six years in the primary section, and knew that he would have to get into the secondary section if he were to progress to play in the Croke Cup, the Dean Ryan Cup or indeed the Harty Cup. But Jimmy's life was hurling and not studying.

On the morning of the Primary Certificate examination, Brother Boland addressed the boys and wished them luck. 'Ye're all ready now boys, but I have to say that there is one boy here who will not pass.' Turning to Jimmy he said, 'Jimmy, I'm afraid that boy is you. I am saying this so that you won't be worrying, but I will also make a prediction. You will play for Tipperary and you will be captain of a winning All-Ireland team.' That was worth 20 Primary Certificates to the budding hurler.

Jimmy fulfilled that prophecy in 1962 when he was captain of the team that overcame Wexford in the All-Ireland final. Unfortunately, Jimmy fractured his collar-bone in a clash with one of the Wexford backs and was carried off on a stretcher. The team and mentors wanted him to go up to receive the cup tied to the stretcher, but he felt that it was not practical to do that, so he gave the honour to his club-mate Tony Wall. Brother Boland was at the game and was disappointed not to see his protegée climb the steps of the Hogan Stand. But in 1965, Jimmy Doyle was again captain of the winning side against the same opposition. As he was coming down from the stand with the cup, he saw the excited Brother at the back of the milling crowd and he made his way to him.

Back to his teenage years: Jimmy, of course, did move to the CBS Secondary School and won all the honours including that Harty Cup Medal when they defeated North Monastery of Cork in the final. At 15 years of age, he had already come to the attention of the Tipperary minor selectors as a goalkeeper. One of Doyle's heroes was the legendary Tony Reddin, the star Tipperary net-minder of the 1940s and 1950s who, in 1984, was selected on the GAA Team of the Century, and in 2000 on the Team of the Millennium. Tony took him under his wing and they used to practise together. Tony had told him 'I'll make a goalkeeper out of you.' and he did. Jimmy was selected in goal for the Tipperary minors in 1954 and won the first of his four Munster minor medals. However, they were beaten by Dublin in the All-Ireland final of that year, and coming back in the car to Thurles the next day he told Brother Dooley, 'I want to get out of the goal, I don't want to play there any more.' Brother Dooley said that he had hoped that Jimmy would stay in goal but he would try him out-field against Nenagh in the Dean Ryan Cup in two weeks. Jimmy 'starred' in that game at half-forward, and so began the forward career of one of the most lethal attackers that game has ever known.

Jimmy admits that, during those years, hurling was his god. He studied all the great hurlers of that era, and because he lived beside Semple Stadium he had a great opportunity to see them in action. Christy Ring was his idol, and he told me how he used to go down to the hotel where the Cork team dined just to see Ring eating his dinner. But he got closer than that as the years went by.

In his teenage years he continued to use all his spare time practising against the green door in the outside pitch of the stadium. But now he had his personal trainer, Billy. It was Billy who made sure that he went to the field every day. It was Billy who ensured that he could rise the ball into his hand first time, and in double-quick time too. It was Billy who made him develop the feint and the side-step that was to leave many a back stranded as the ball shot over the bar. It was Billy who made sure that he hit hundreds of frees every evening over the bar, and saw to it that the ball was returned for the next one. Billy has never been mentioned as one of the outstanding coaches of the Tipperary teams, nor indeed was he listed as a possible candidate in the 'Ireland on Sunday Manager of the Millennium' competition. But he played a big part in fashioning and honing the skills of the future Tipperary scoring machine. Billy was the red collie sheepdog who used greet his master as he came home from school with Jimmy's hurl in his mouth and his tail wagging excitedly. It was up to the field every evening until tea time, and back again until nightfall. When I asked Jimmy what was the end of Billy, a tear came to his eye as he told me that he just died of old age. He loved that dog. 'He was the most perfect dog I ever met,' he said. Thoughts of Elvis's 'Old Shep' came to my mind, it was time to move on the conversation.

It always seemed that Jimmy Doyle used a short hurley, so I asked him how that arose. He said that he got used to that type of stick, and found it easier to use. He used Ollie Walsh hurls or O'Brien's from Cahir, but his father would then shorten the handle for him by cutting it and re-splicing it.

He recalled a story of when he had just made the senior team and had broken his hurl before an important match. The county secretary's wife, Mrs Phil Purcell, called to the Doyle household to see his mother. She heard the conversation going on about the hurl, and she said 'get on your bike immediately and go up to Phil, he has just got in a load of hurls'.

The secretary was in discussion with the renowned Paddy Leahy when Jimmy called and looked at him suspiciously over glasses perched on his nose. 'I heard you got in some hurls', said the boy timidly. He was brought into a room and there lined up around the wall was the biggest selection of hurls that he had ever seen. The two senior administrators went on talking about their business as Jimmy examined each hurl carefully. After some time he narrowed his selection down to twelve. Then he went through each one of those several times and after another period he had six hurls left out which he regarded as ideal. He kept going over and over these half dozen sticks, feeling them, testing the spring, examining the grain, and starting again. Eventually Phil looked across at him over his glasses, 'You have a problem, young man?' he said.

'I have' said Jimmy, 'these six are all ideal and are all lovely, I can't make up my mind.'

'I'll tell you what, my good man,' said the genial county secretary, 'you pick up those six and run out of here. I won't look at you, and I'll tell you, I won't miss them either!' That was probably one of the best investments that Phil Purcell ever made.

After four county minor medals, three minor All-Ireland medals, and a host of other medals in under-age competitions, Jimmy had now moved on to be a star senior player with the Tipperary. His six All-Ireland wins were all very special to him in different ways. Doyle regards 1964 as the highlight of his career. To my mind, and that of most hurling followers, it was the greatest display by that great Tipperary team of the 1960s. What a pity that it had to be against Kilkenny! Jimmy had the game of his life that day marking Martin Coogan whom he regards as one of the greatest left half-backs of that era. Jimmy did pay tribute to the Kilkenny team that defeated them three years later, and went on to get their own good run in the late 1960s and early 1970s.

Newspaper and television commentators are persuading today's players that they are making too many 'sacrifices,' giving too many hours to the game without any rewards. I know that we are in a different era, but it is worthwhile reflecting on the hours put in by Jimmy Doyle for the honour of playing for his county, which was all he looked for in return. Apart from his private sessions against the door and playing and training with his successful club, Thurles Sarsfield, he was training with the county team three nights a week. If that was not enough, for six Sunday mornings before the 1964 All-Ireland, Doyle and John O'Donoghue, the Tipperary goalkeeper trained for two hours in Semple Stadium. They arranged with the caretaker to have nets on the goals and the dressing rooms open.

In his series of previews of the match, John D. Hickey wrote in the *Irish Independent* about these sessions, how he had watched Jimmy curving the ball in all directions to deceive the goalkeeper. Knowing that the wily John D's roots were in the Premier County, we wondered if this was a ruse to unsettle Ollie Walsh in the Kilkenny goal, but it was true. Jimmy had practised this skill during his workouts against the green door, and perfected it on these Sunday mornings in August 1964. By spinning the ball a certain way when throwing it up to strike, he could hit the ball straight at John O'Donoghue to have it curve away at the last minute to the angle of the upright and crossbar. He could also send a ball in about a foot higher than the crossbar and make it dip under the bar at the last minute. That was Jimmy Doyle at his peak.

The fact that he took the field at all in the 1961 All-Ireland against Dublin is not alone a miracle, but proof that this elegant ball-player also had the guts and determination to overcome any setback. In the Munster final against Cork in that year, he contested a ball with Jimmy Brohan and they both ended on the ground. He was carried off, and next day he went to Pat Stakelum who took him to Nenagh Hospital to find that he had a double fracture of the ankle. The All-Ireland was six weeks away, and the surgeon told him he had no hope of playing. He said that he would have to put the ankle in plaster of Paris for at least two months. Jimmy told him that he would not allow him to do so unless he would undertake to remove it in four weeks to give him two weeks to train. After four weeks, the surgeon took off the plaster and asked him to walk down the room. He couldn't move and the surgeon said that he would have to plaster it again, but

Jimmy would not allow him and he went home and worked on it himself. He did exercises, walked on the straight and up hills until he could go without pain.

The team doctor told him he would have to have a fitness test on the Friday before the game. With two other injured players, Tony Wall and Kieran Carey the test began. In a sprint, Jimmy got a dart of pain and had to pull up. The doctor told him that he couldn't play, and that he should put on his clothes and go home. Wall and Carey passed the test. Jimmy wept in the dressing room and went home to bed when the doctor called to give him another option. He said he could give him an injection before the game and at half-time to 'deaden' the leg, but there would be a danger in that he would not know if the leg broke again. It could finish him for all time. After consulting his father he decided to take the chance.

He got through the first half and almost to the end of the second half when the leg gave in. He went to the sideline to come off to find that Tipperary had already used their quota of substitutes. Wall and Carey, who had already left the field, told him to get back on. As he returned, Des Foley was just ahead of him catching the ball, and as Des hit it down the field the final whistle blew. The record shows that Jimmy Doyle scored 0–9 that day!

That was surely a triumph of mind over matter, but it was at a price. Although he continued to thrill the hurling world for the rest of that decade, the ankle always gave him some trouble and had to be strapped up before every game and training session. It probably also contributed to the back problem he later developed. This meant that he only appeared late in the 1971 final to earn his sixth All-Ireland medal.

During his illustrious career, Jimmy Doyle won eight Railway Cup medals with Munster. He regarded it as a great honour to play for his province, but it was even a greater honour to play in the same forward line as his boyhood hero, Christy Ring. He won his first medal in 1958 playing at left half-forward with Ring at full-forward. I remember reading the newspaper reports the next day that said that the youthful Jimmy Doyle seemed to be obsessed with feeding Christy Ring when he was in a scoring position himself. It would appear that Jimmy just wanted to see the Master perform at close range. For the record, Munster won 3–7 to 3–5.

In the following year, Munster met Connacht in the final, and Jimmy recalls a funny incident with his hero. Ring received a blow to the head from the full-back as the ball was being cleared by the Galway defence. Christy was lying motionless on the ground facing the Munster goal with the St John's Ambulance men trying to stop the blood flowing. Jimmy came in from the half-forward line to see how he was, when suddenly the Munster backs send up a clearance. Ring leapt to his feet, scattered the attendants in the process, caught the ball and stuck it in the net. He threw himself down again for further attention, and as he did so, he looked up at Jimmy and said 'Doyle, I bet you never did that!'

He was thrilled to be accepted by Ring as his travelling companion, and he remembers a Railway Cup game in Belfast when they sat together on the train journey and talked hurling all day. When they arrived at the station in Belfast, Christy pulled out a cap and pulled it down over his eyes. 'Hey Jimmy,' he said. 'I don't want to be known up here at all!' He also recalls another occasion when they shared a room in Barry's Hotel in Dublin on St Patrick's Eve.

There were three single beds in the room, and Ring was in the middle bed. They went to bed early, and Christy spent most of the night lying on the bed, hurl in hand hitting the ball against each wall and doubling on the return. As the ball whizzed back and forth over his head as he lay in bed, Jimmy knew that he was safe and that he wouldn't get a belt of a stray ball when the Maestro was the one with the hurl.

Doyle is also a deep thinker on the game of hurling, an attribute that helped him later when coaching teams. His wife came from Castlecomer, Co. Kilkenny which meant that Jimmy was a frequent visitor to the town. One evening, he met Fr Johnnie Kearns who was a passionate hurling man and trainer of the local team. He asked Jimmy if he would go down to the local field where the team was training. Jimmy said that he didn't have time, but Fr Kearns didn't listen and said, 'go on down then, the lads will be delighted.' Anyone that knew the late cleric will also know that he never took 'no' for an answer. Jimmy went down, and noticed that Martin Coogan was playing at right half-back instead of his usual position on the wing on the left. He also noticed that Martin was not nearly as effective at that side. That incident occurred a short time before Tipperary were to play Kilkenny in the 1964–1965 National League home final for a trip to New York.

They went to Dublin the night before the match and Jimmy was sharing with Donie Nealon in Barry's Hotel. 'I want to win this match and get a trip to New York,' said Jimmy, 'but I think that Kilkenny are too good. We have a chance though if you swap wings with me.'

'I couldn't do that,' said Nealon, 'I couldn't hurl Coogan.'

'Well I can't either on that side, but I think if I move across he will follow me, and I'll handle him there.' replied Doyle. He could not get Donie to agree, so Jimmy went to Paddy Leahy's room to tell him his plan. Paddy was horrified to see him still up, but he listened, and agreed. 'But,' he said, 'ye start as selected, and as soon as the ball is thrown in, ye can change.' The move was made, and Jimmy had four points on the board before Kilkenny made the change. Martin did his best to stop the gap but was unhappy at right half-back, and his influence on the other wing was missed by the Kilkenny forwards who could always depend on a good supply of ball from the Castlecomer man. Tipperary ran out easy winners by 3–14 to 2–8.

Jimmy's last outing in the blue and gold was in the first round of the Munster Championship in 1973. He had retired from the game due to his injury problems. He came home one night to be met by his father who warned him that the selectors would be calling to him to ask him to play in goal. 'How could I do that,' said Jimmy, 'I haven't played in goal for twenty years.' The selectors did arrive and told him that they had a problem. Their goalkeeper, Tadgh Murphy had gone to America and they would like Jimmy to step in. He reluctantly went to the training sessions and played against Waterford and won. He continued to train for the next game, but one night Murphy appeared in the field having returned from the USA. Jimmy immediately approached the selectors and told them to give the position back to Tadgh as his own sight was not as good as it used to be. The selectors agreed and Jimmy bowed out with dignity. He had answered the call when he was needed.

When he finished his playing career, Jimmy continued to give back something to the game he loves. His late sister was married in Portlaoise, and through her he was approached to manage the Portlaoise team. Although mainly a football club, an interest in hurling was developing and Jimmy met the players and was pleased with their response and their enthusiasm. Camross were the kingpins of hurling in the county at that time. In Doyle's first year as manager, Portlaoise met them in the county final and were pipped by a last-minute goal.

However, Jimmy was convinced that they had potential, and he helped them to win the county final in the following four years 1981 to 1984. He was approached during that period to manage the county team, but despite his best efforts, he could not get the clubs to unite and train together as a county team. He withdrew as soon as Laois were beaten in the Championship after six months at the helm.

Jimmy Doyle now lives quietly in his Thurles home. He loves to socialise and talk about hurling. He particularly loves to meet players from his own era and reminisce about games from the past. He is enthusiastic about the present-day hurlers, and loves to watch skilled players such as DJ Carey and Brian Whelahan.

His dedication to the development of his own particular skills are a model for all budding hurlers to copy. His sportsmanship on the field was outstanding and he can look back with pride on a career that was without blemish. Jimmy was loved by colleague and foe alike, and when men are gathered to pick great players of the past, the name of Jimmy Doyle will always be pencilled in as one of the forwards. It was no surprise that he was selected on the 1984 Team of the Century, and more recently on the Team of the Millennium. He has left a legacy to the game of hurling that should be emulated, but will never be equalled.

Jimmy Doyle's Team Of The Century

Tony Reddin
(Tipperary)

Jimmy Brohan	Nick O'Donnell	John Doyle
(Cork)	*(Wexford)*	*(Tipperary)*

Jimmy Finn	Tony Wall	Martin Coogan
(Tipperary)	*(Tipperary)*	*(Kilkenny)*

Frank Cummins   Theo English
(Kilkenny)   *(Tipperary)*

Eddie Keher	Mick Mackey	Christy Ring
(Kilkenny)	*(Limerick)*	*(Cork)*

Frankie Walsh	Ray Cummins	Philly Grimes
(Waterford)	*(Cork)*	*(Waterford)*

Munster Team of the Century

Mick Cashman
(Cork)

Jimmy Brohan	Michael Maher	John Doyle
(Cork)	*(Tipperary)*	*(Tipperary)*

Tom McGarry	Tony Wall	Larry Guinan
(Limerick)	*(Tipperary)*	*(Waterford)*

Theo English   Seamus Power
(Tipperary)   *(Waterford)*

Jimmy Smyth	Tom Cheasty	Frankie Walsh
(Clare)	*(Waterford)*	*(Waterford)*

Christy Ring	Ray Cummins	Phil Grimes
(Cork)	*(Cork)*	*(Waterford)*

6 – Pat Fox

Pat Fox

Pat Fox was born in July 1961 two months before the start of another glorious era of Tipperary hurling. On the first Sunday in September in that year, Tipperary defeated Dublin to win their eighteenth All-Ireland title and went on to record three more titles in that decade. They started the next decade on the same note by defeating Kilkenny in 1971 to bring the number of All-Ireland titles for the county to 22.

A ten-year-old, who had been used to seeing his native county appear in All-Irelands almost every year of his life and winning so many of them, could be forgiven for assuming that this was the natural way of things and that the pattern would continue. Little did he know that it would take another 18 years for the Premier County to record their 23rd title, and that he would play a major part in that achievement while entering the twilight of his hurling career.

Pat was born in Annacarty a small parish in West Tipperary. Eire Óg Annacarty had won the west divisional title for four years in a row in the early 1940s, and went all the way in 1943 to win their one and only county final. In his youth, Pat heard of the exploits of the heroes of that great team, Bill O'Donnell, Philly Ryan and Mikey Ryan of the Castle. Bill O'Donnell RIP, a native of Golden, was the local teacher in the primary school and played with the

Tipperary senior team in the 1940s and 1950s. There was no primary schools championship in the area, but Bill had the boys out hurling in the school twice a week, and as an All-Ireland medal holder, was a great inspiration to them.

Pat's father, Tom Fox had played as far as minor level with the club, but the five Fox brothers were passionate about the game. As farmers, there was plenty of space, and hardly a day passed without a game being played in the back field where they were joined by neighbours, Whites and Hanleys to make up the two teams.

At the age of eight, the young Pat Fox was regularly called on to puck in the ball from the middle of the field while the senior went through their 'backs and forwards' training routine. With his left-hand-on-top style, the seniors used call him 'Jimmy Doyle' which gave him a great surge of pride. Doyle, one of the greatest hurlers of all time, was in his prime then.

Due to the small population in the parish, they had no success at juvenile level, but when they joined with Cappawhite for the minor championship, they won the west division finals of 1977 and 1978. In 1977, Eire Óg Annacarty played in the junior championship on their own, and at the age of 16 Pat won his first and only county medal at that grade. In that same year, a Cappawhite/Eire Óg amalgamated team won the county under-21 title, defeating Holycross in the final. Pat's brother, Kevin was on that team, as was Fr Pat O'Neill who had a great hurling future ahead of him until he got a greater call in life.

By the 1980s, these two teams were contesting the senior championship on their own, and when they met in the west division senior championship final in 1981, fireworks were expected. In fact, it turned out to be a damp squib when hot favourites, Cappawhite froze on the day and Annacarty ran away easy winners.

But they came up against a powerful Borrisoleigh side in the quarter-final who had ten of the county panel in their team and they went down badly. They had no answer to the likes of Bobby Ryan, Noel O'Dwyer, John McGrath and the Stapleton brothers, Gerry and Timmy. Borrisoleigh went on to win the county final. Eire Óg Annacarty won the west final again in 1986, but failed again in their bid for county glory.

Pat Fox began his working life as a mechanic with the Kilkenny firm, Mahon and McPhillips and was based in their Hollyford plant. As he became more prominent in the hurling scene, he moved into sales with O'Dea and O'Dea Car Sales in Cashel. By the end of the 1980s he was a national figure, following Tipperary's resurgence on the hurling fields, and the names of English and Fox were on everyone's lips, as the dynamic duo struck fear into every hurling defence in the country. It was during that period that Pat decided to go into business on his own, and he took the major step in 1993 when a well located public house on the main street in Cashel came on the market. Fox's Pub is now a Mecca for hurling enthusiasts from within and without the county.

Pat is married to Marita, who is from Dundrum and they have two lovely young children, Rianne and Tracy. It was not the first time I found myself on their friendly premises, but we had to adjourn to a comfortable sitting room upstairs for a bit of privacy to do the interview for this book.

After winning the under-21 county final with Cappa-Eire Óg, he came to the notice of the county minor selectors, and took his place at right full forward in 1977. Cork defeated them by two points in the first round and went on to the All-Ireland that year to be beaten by Kilkenny in a replay. The following year, Fox was playing at centre-forward only to be beaten by Cork by two points again in the Munster final, 1–14 to 3–6. Pat felt that they were very unlucky in that game not to win, and Cork went on to take the All-Ireland title. Although he had no success in the county minor jersey, Pat was thrilled with the honour of wearing the blue and gold for the first time.

In 1979, Pat went to see Tipperary play Cork in the under-21 Munster final. He was thrilled to see them defeat the Rebel County by 1–13 to 2–7. He remembers coming home from that game wishing himself onto the team. When the 18-year-old looked at the line-out which included Michael Doyle, Gerry Stapleton, John Ryan, Bobby and Pat (Flowery) Ryan and Brian O'Shea, he acknowledged that he hadn't a hope. However, fate was to play a part in the saga. Pat was asked in to Semple Stadium to play in a few trial games, where he obviously impressed. His chance came when regular centre-field player, Pat (Flowery) Ryan found that he could not play in the All-Ireland final due to a prior holiday arrangement. He couldn't believe his ears when selector, Danny Morrissey called to his door to tell him that he would be playing at centre-field in the final. He had never played in that position before, but he would have played anywhere to have the honour of walking out in an All-Ireland final wearing the blue and gold. The game was played in Portlaoise and they defeated Galway by 2–12 to 1–9. Pat Fox had won his first All-Ireland medal. He was happy with his game that day, noting that he was the only centre-field player on either team not to be shifted during the hour.

He was, at this time, regarded as a 'play anywhere' utility man, and when the under-21 team set out to defend their title in 1980, Pat found himself in the half-back line in the first round of the Munster Championship. They drew with Cork in the Munster final, and the versatile Mr Fox was brought back to corner-back to mark star Cork attacker, Tony Kilcoyne for the replay. He held him well, and they won the replay by 3–8 to 2–9. They went on to meet Kilkenny in the final. Fox was retained at corner back to try to cope with the free-scoring Noresider's full forward line who had put away more than five goals in the Championship up to then. The dogged Tipperary full back line held their Kilkenny opponents goal-less and they went on to win 2–9 to 0–14. However, Pat felt that Tipperary did well to hold out to win that match. He remembers playing with their backs to the wall for long periods in the second half while Kilkenny put them under relentless pressure to try to snatch victory. In 1981 they got to the final again and had a more comprehensive win over the Noresiders by 2–16 to 2–10.

I asked Pat what kind of game he played at corner back and if the experience helped him in later years when he was trying to outwit men in that position. 'If I was a selector on those teams, I wouldn't like the way I played. I played too much from behind,' he confessed, 'and I let the forward get the ball and then tried to block or hook him.' He described his style as a pusher, a shover and a stopper. Those of us who saw Pat Fox the stylist, the dramatic goal-scorer in later years would not recognise him from that description.

Because Tipperary had been making first-round exits from the senior championship during the 1970s and when Pat started playing on the team in the early 1980s, I had not really seen him in action until that famous drawn game with Cork in the Munster final of 1987. On that occasion, he scored ten glorious points, three from play. He scored seven points from frees, but everyone remembers the last two from which they snatched a draw.

Pat Fox and Ger Loughnane compete for possession in the Munster Championship, 1987. Tipperary's Bobby Ryan also gives chase.

'We were very lucky to get to the final for a start' said Pat. 'We got through Clare in a replay and faced Cork in Thurles with not a lot of confidence. But we played above ourselves and led them for 67 minutes and had them for the taking, but we allowed them back to draw level from a Kieran Kingston goal with three minutes to go.' Cork went ahead with two John Fenton points and it looked all over for the inexperienced Tipperary team. 'With two minutes remaining we were awarded a free about 60 yards out, and Theo English ran out to me to tell me to drop it in, but I felt that we would never get a goal against those backs and I decided to take the point.'

I remember seeing Pat standing over that free and admiring how he stroked the ball over the bar under such intense pressure. On the call of time, Nicky English was fouled on the 20-metre line and the point to level the game was only a matter of form to the inspired Annacarty man.

My next outstanding memory of Pat Fox came in the replay which was fixed for Killarney on the following Sunday. Anyone who had been in Thurles and had experienced the fantastic atmosphere there had to travel to Killarney to see it out. Huge crowds made the long journey to Fitzgerald Stadium, and I recall getting a seat near the sideline very near the end line.

Pat Fox scored a memorable goal that day, but it was never registered on the scoreboard. Michael Ryan drove a massive clearance from the full-back line in the second half, which deceived the Cork backs. The alert corner forward sprinted past his man, brilliantly gathered the ball on the run and took off across the face of the goal. He sent a bullet past the helpless Ger Cunningham, which hit the stanchion at the back of the goal and bounced back out to be scrambled away by the Cork goalkeeper. I still remember how Pat carried on his run over the end line with his arms raised in triumph knowing that he had scored his best goal ever in the Tipperary jersey. 'When I looked back out the field,' he recalled,' I saw Pat Fitzelle sending the ball over the bar, and I looked at the scoreboard to realise that there was no goal registered! I rushed in to the umpire to protest, and I may have questioned his ability to see. But it was fruitless.' That match ended in a welter of excitement with the sides level again, and extra time had to be played. The records will show that the younger Tipperary team outpaced the Leesiders in the extra period and went on to win comprehensively by 4–22 to 1–22. The famine was over.

Tipperary were drawn against Galway in the semi-final, and as if to make up for the disappointment of the 'unrecorded' goal in Killarney, Fox put away two beauties in that game. One was a well-taken penalty that hit the ground ten yards from the goal line and careered to the roof of the net. The other goal sticks in the mind more for the build-up than the goal itself. Pat had been moved out to the half-forward line and he collected the ball and went on a solo run in by the Cusack Stand. The part I remember most was the way he ducked under Sylvie Linnane's challenge to avoid being beheaded, and continued on towards goal. 'I was expecting that Conor Hayes would leave Nicky to come to meet me, and I intended sending in a pass to English to finish,' he recalled. 'But Conor stayed with his man and I had no option but to keep going, and I finished the ball to the net on my right side.' Those two great goals were not enough to see Tipperary through, and they lost on a scoreline of 3–20 to 2–17. 'It was disappointing to make our exit in an All-Ireland semi-final,' Pat declared, 'but we had made some progress that year, and we were not downhearted.'

Fox had first got his call-up to wear a Tipperary senior jersey in a challenge match against Limerick in 1979, 'just to make up a team.' In 1980, he was brought on the team for a few League games and he was thrilled to be named in the starting side for the Championship in that year in their first outing against Cork. He was selected at centre-field and was marking John Fenton. He recalls that John got his usual quota of nine or ten points from frees, but did not score from play. He remembers the frustration of his first seven years on the team before the breakthrough in that there was never a settled team. Tensions were high in Tipperary, and almost every year there was a change of manager and/or selectors in a fruitless effort to achieve success.

But now, as they faced the 1988 Championship, there was a new optimism. Apart from the confidence gained in winning the Munster final for the first time for 16 years, the impact of Babs Keating's new management style had given a whole new impetus to the team.

Pat was high in his praise for the role played by the manager. 'He brought a whole new dimension to the scene,' he declared. 'The first days he took over, he had boots, hurleys, tracksuits for all the panel, and we had the best of meals after training. He arranged holidays for the team, and brought in the best expertise available for the physical aspect. Phil Conway ensured that any injuries got the proper treatment for early recovery, and he brought the team to a level of fitness that we had not experienced before. Babs did the skills and team-play coaching. He was brilliant with the forwards, and devised patterns of play for us that worked a treat. He coached the backs and centre-fielders to play to deliver good quality ball to the forwards, and in the "match" situations in training, the backs improved dramatically from constantly trying to counteract our moves'.

With their new-found confidence, they had no fears when they faced Cork in the Munster final of 1988. They also took heart in the fact that John Fenton would not be playing that year which would reduce Cork's scoring power. They had a convincing win by 2–19 to 1–13.

They had an easy win over Antrim in the semi-final before facing Galway in the All-Ireland final. Pat has no pleasant memories of that game. He was very disappointed in his own performance. His marker, Ollie Kilkenny, stuck to him like a leech, and maybe got away with a lot of pulling and dragging from a lenient referee. 'He did his job well,' Pat conceded.

1989 was to be their year. The breaks that seem to come when your name is on the cup came that year. The draws came right for them. They had a big win over Waterford in the Munster final. 'There were some unsavoury incidents in that game, but they were very isolated and maybe over-hyped by the media,' Pat recalled.

Now, for the third time in as many years, they had to face that great Galway team of the 1980s in an important game. The Tribesmen were All-Ireland champions as well as semi-final specialists, and had the self-belief that they could beat the Premier County. The Tipperary supporters were uneasy. They had been satisfied that their team had made the breakthrough in Munster, but now they wanted All-Ireland success. Tipperary got their next 'break' in their Championship campaign. The media focused on Galway as the famous or infamous 'Keady affair' erupted. Tipperary quietly went about their preparations as, day after day, headlines appeared as each new twist developed in the story. The end result was that Tony Keady was suspended for playing illegally abroad and could not take his place on the team. That was a big blow in itself to Galway, but it was the uncertainty that the whole affair created in the Galway camp that unsettled them with their preparations for the game. Nevertheless, the Westerners came out fighting and made it difficult for Tipperary right to the end. Pat had learned his lesson from his encounter with Ollie Kilkenny the previous year and kept away from him. He succeeded in breaking the shackles enough times to score 1–5 from play.

However, Pat conceded that Galway would have won again that day if Tony Keady had been playing. The game did have its share of 'incidents' as the rivalry that had built up over the previous years spilled over, and two of the Galway players were sidelined for heavy tackles.

The surprise defeat of Offaly by Antrim in the other semi-final, ensured that they would not be meeting an experienced team in the final, and it really looked as if the gods had finally smiled on the Premier County after their 18 years in the wilderness. 'It was not that easy' said Pat. 'In fact it was much harder to keep our composure in training while the Tipperary supporters were almost celebrating the All-Ireland for the weeks before the game. This put awful pressure on the players, and we developed a real fear of losing. When we won, the emotion I had was relief rather that joy.' Fox does not think he played well that day, but he contributed 1–2 to the scoreboard. The highlight of that one–sided game was the score of 2–12 that Nicky English amassed. His second goal was a real 'gem'. Pat felt that his friend Nicky reserved the peak performance of his distinguished career for that day.

1990 was the year that the Cork manager, Fr Michael O'Brien used all his guile to get his team on to the high ground in the build up to the Munster final. Babs was aware that, as All-Ireland champions, they were going to be favourites for the clash with Cork. He was also conscious that the hype and celebrations had barely died down in time for the Championship, and that it would be difficult to get his team properly focused to beat Cork. In one of his colourful interviews during to build-up to the game, he tried to 'play down' his own team. He had a number of injuries and had to play a few untried players, and when asked about the prospects, he used one of his racing analogies by saying, 'you can't train donkeys to win the Derby.' The statement made good paper headlines, and the cute Corkman saw it as an opportunity to use it against them. Fr O'Brien pretended that Babs was referring to the Cork team and gave some colourful responses himself that delighted the media. Babs made some efforts to clarify, but he found himself digging himself into a bigger hole.

The end result was that Tipperary entered the game a beaten team, while the highly motivated Corkmen took the field like thoroughbreds. Cork won easily by 4–16 to 2–14. That was one of Pat's very few bad days, and he was replaced at half time. The year had started badly for the Annacarty man. He had been dropped for the first round against Limerick, but won back his place on the team in a way that Michael Cleary will not let him forget. They were pucking the ball around in training a couple of evenings before the game when Pat connected on a ball and hit the Nenagh man 'below the belt.' Michael was unable to play in the game and his place was taken by ... Pat Fox, of course! To add insult to injury, Pat went on to get the 'Man of the Match' award on the day. One way of getting your place back, I suppose.

By the time the 1991 Munster final came around, the Tipperary batteries were recharged, and they were anxious to avenge the 1990 final. They played a thrilling draw with Cork at Pairc Uí Chaoimh, 1–18 each, and Thurles was again the venue for the replay. Pat regards this game as his best ever in the county colours. He scored 1–5, and the goal he scored that day was the favourite score of his career. Tipperary were trailing by nine points when a long ball was sent in behind Fox and his marker, Denis Walsh. Ger Cunningham started to come off his line, but hesitated when he saw Denis chasing close behind Fox. He started to come again as Pat flicked it 'tennis style' past him from about 20 yards. The two Corkmen collided, and an alert photographer captured the final moments of the collision with the Tipperary man running clear. This goal started the revival, and Michael Cleary and himself added a few more points before Declan Carr flicked the ball to the net for the equaliser. Tipperary went on to win 4–19 to 4–15.

After disposing of Antrim in the semi-final, they were set to face Kilkenny in the All-Ireland final. Another meeting with the Noresiders after a lapse of 20 years renewed all the great rivalry that exists between these two counties. 'I never found that fierce rivalry between the two counties where I lived,' said Pat. 'I always had the utmost respect and admiration for Kilkenny hurlers. There was no bitterness as far as I was concerned, I think that was confined to the border areas.'

They had major worries though with injury problems for English, Cormac Bonner and Bobby Ryan. He considered that they were lucky to go in level at half time after Kilkenny's first-half dominance all over the field. Christy Heffernan was causing havoc at centre-forward, but he believed that he should have gone for scores himself rather than wasting possession by passing to his colleagues, when on some occasions the chances were lost. Richie Power was also devastating at centre-field. Tipperary got a somewhat lucky goal from a mis-hit free by Michael Cleary that was deflected to the net by a Kilkenny defender. Not ones to look a gift horse in the mouth, Tipperary went on to win the game by 1–16 to 0–15. Pat Fox scored several vital points in the game and was responsible for others that came off frees which were conceded by his marker. The Tipperary man felt that Liam Simpson showed him too much respect that day by playing him from behind, which enabled him to get possession of the ball first. He said that it was a 'different kettle of fish' when they met on subsequent occasions, when Liam knew how to play him.

The Munster final of 1993 turned out to be a bad day for the Bannermen, but in a strange way, may have been the spark that lit the fuse that exploded the Claremen on to centre stage in the years to follow. Just like Fr O'Brien used an incident to motivate his charges in 1990, the Clare mentors used an incident in that game to stimulate their team in subsequent meetings of the teams.

Nicky English was injured for that game, but Tipperary were coasting to victory and the selectors decided to introduce the Lattin-Cullen man to test the injury. The forwards were already well on top, so they began playing the ball to English to re-establish his confidence. He missed a few early chances, but he knew what his colleagues were at, and when he eventually found the target, he smiled back at his team-mates in acknowledgement. The clever Claremen thought or pretended to think that he was laughing at them, and they didn't miss the opportunity of reminding their players of the incident when they faced Tipperary in subsequent years.

Pat Fox's last game in the blue and gold jersey was in the 1996 Championship against Waterford. He had broken his collar-bone and two ribs in a League game against Laois some months previously, and at 35 years of age was finding it difficult to make a recovery. He came on as a second-half substitute, but struggled with the injury. 'It was not the way I would have liked to finish, but I had a great time playing for the county, and I have no regrets.'

Annacarty is located close to the Limerick border, and as a youngster Pat frequently went to see Limerick championship games – Limerick championship games that involved South Liberties, that is. His hero was Pat Hartigan, and every chance he got to see him in action with club or county, Pat Fox was there. 'There was nobody like him,' he recalled. 'He looked massive on the field, and was strong and skilful and played fairly. He was a great sportsman and a model for all budding hurlers.' Of the present-day players, he admires Brian Whelahan who he describes as a 'class apart'. 'He has great vision, and lovely skill and ball control, and is great to pick out forwards with his clearances. Everything he touches turns to a score.'

Pat has not been won over by the success of the back-door system. He would favour a 'first-round losers group' who could play off and enter the championship at a later stage. He considers it very unfair that the Munster or Leinster champions might have to meet up with the defeated team again in an All-Ireland final, and could lose.

He is also behind the new Players' Association. He feels that the players need professional support to get what they deserve. 'The players should be very well looked after with good expenses,' he declared. 'I think that they will eventually get paid, but not a lot, and the GAA may as well face up to it and follow the trend in other sports.'

Pat plays golf for relaxation nowadays, and has worked his handicap down to 15, but he is still involved in the game of hurling. He was asked by Borrisoleigh last year to coach their senior team, and he was delighted to do so. He had coached the Annacarty team to win the intermediate championship five years ago, but that was the first time that he got involved with a senior team. They had moderate success in his first year, but did not qualify for the championship from the preliminary league matches. 'I learned a lot in my first year,' he said. 'It takes time to get to know players. Some mediocre players will give it everything, while the good players sometimes will do the opposite. All the players are responding well this year, and I am confident that we will do well'.

Pat Fox can look back on a glittering hurling career. Extremely popular in his own county, he won the 'Tipperary Hurler of the Year' on two occasions in 1981 and 1989. He is also hugely admired throughout the hurling world. 1991 was his golden year. He won his third All-Star Award, but also 'Man of the Match' on All-Ireland day, 'Players' Player of the Year,' 'Texaco Player of the Year,' 'Texaco Supreme Sportsman of the Year,' and 'Ballygowan Sports Star of the Year'.

Pat Fox's Team of the Century

Ger Cunningham
(Cork)

Denis Mulcahy
(Cork)

Pat Hartigan
(Limerick)

Paul Delaney
(Tipperary)

Brian Whelahan
(Offaly)

Mick Roche
(Tipperary)

Tom Cashman
(Cork)

Frank Cummins
(Tipperary)

John Fenton
(Cork)

Nicky English
(Tipperary)

Joe Cooney
(Galway)

DJ Carey
(Kilkenny)

Joe Dooley
(Offaly)

Joe McKenna
(Limerick)

Eddie Keher
(Kilkenny)

Munster Team of the Century

Ger Cunningham
(Cork)

Denis Mulcahy
(Cork)

Pat Hartigan
(Limerick)

Paul Delaney
(Tipperary)

Dermot McCurtin
(Cork)

Mick Roche
(Tipperary)

Tom Cashman
(Cork)

Ollie Baker
(Clare)

John Fenton
(Cork)

Nicky English
(Tipperary)

Gary Kirby
(Limerick)

Jamesie O'Connor
(Clare)

Tony O'Sullivan
(Cork)

Joe McKenna
(Limerick)

John Fitzgibbon
(Cork)

7 – Len Gaynor

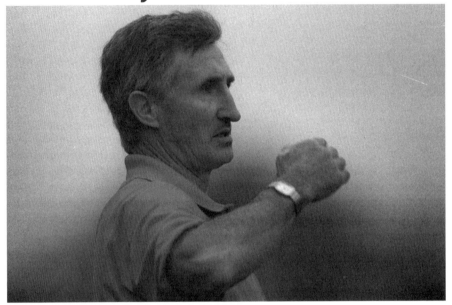

Len Gaynor

I am sure that many red-blooded Tipperary and Kilkenny hurling supporters who lived through the tempestuous era of the 1960s are wondering how I could be doing a chapter on Len Gaynor. Tipperary certainly ruled the roost in the early part of that decade with a team that is rated as one of the best ever to wear the blue and gold, and many would claim to be the best of all time. Kilkenny were biting at their heels and had beaten them on a few occasions, but Tipperary had gained the upper hand in the important games. It took until 1967 for Kilkenny to beat the Premier County in an All-Ireland final, and Tipperary left the decade with four All-Ireland titles to Kilkenny's three.

It is not surprising that the rivalry between the two neighbouring counties grew to intense levels during that era. Len and I found ourselves in direct opposition during a few of those highly charged games. The ironic thing was that Len and I lived nowhere near the Tipperary/Kilkenny border. In in his area of Tipperary, Limerick and Cork were the teams to beat while I lived on the Wexford border and it was the Model County who were our great rivals. But when we went into our respective dressing rooms on the day of a match, we were left in no doubt by the players who lived near the border who our enemies were.

The rivalry reached fever-pitch for the 1967 All-Ireland final, and in the heat of battle, a number of Kilkenny players including myself were injured, some more seriously than others and an unsavoury bitterness replaced the sporting rivalry of previous years. The1968 League final was the watershed, and the first half of that game was as tough, and many would say dirty, as was ever seen in Croke Park.

I was playing right full forward that day had been 'stretched' on a few occasions before Len and I got involved. Although not marking one another, we got into a bit of a tangle following which he raced into the centre to meet a ball arriving behind the centre-back. I came in late to tackle and as I was arriving I saw that he was going to strike directly off his hurl rather than take it in his hand. I pulled from behind, catching Len behind the ear with the lower handle of my hurl. This resulted in one of the many scuffles that took place in that game. He arose bloodied and bandaged to play a stormer.

I suppose, at that moment, I would never have thought that I would one day be sitting in Len's house in Kilruane recalling such incidents, being treated royally by his lovely wife, Eileen and two of his daughters, Fionnula and Sinead. It was ironic also that when I called for the interview, Len was in severe pain from a muscle injury having taken a kick from a cow while on AI duties that morning. The familiar spray and ice-pack was being put to use. 'Worse than 1968, Len?' I enquired. 'Ah. I was hardier then,' was the reply. The truth of the matter is that Len and I have always been good friends, and we had many interests in common, not least a passion for the game of hurling or that we were both life-long members of the Pioneer Total Abstinence Association.

For a man who has contributed so much to hurling on the field of play and as a coach, it is extraordinary to think that but for a quirk of fate, Len Gaynor could have been a star Australian Rules player. His father was deeply involved in the War of Independence with the local brigade of the IRA, and later in the Civil War. When the conflict ended, there was little left in this country for him and, in 1923, he emigrated to Australia. Later, he spent some time later in San Francisco in the USA, before returning to settle in Melbourne where he met and married an Australian lady with the Irish-sounding name of Eileen Murphy. They had five children and were well settled there, when he received a letter from his uncle asking him to come home to take over his farm. This was a major decision for the Gaynor family and particularly Len's mother who was being asked to leave the modern luxuries that they had become used to in Melbourne, and come to a rural farm in north Tipperary with no running water or electricity. The only source of heat was an open fire on which the cooking was also done.

However, in 1939 they took the big step and made their home in Rapla, Kilruane where Len was born on 2 January 1944, followed later by Melissa and Imelda. The 'Australians,' Mary, Kevin, Julia, Ned and Des, and of course, Len's mother Eileen quickly adapted to the Irish way of life and soon were immersed in the running of the busy dairy farm.

Hurling was the big pastime in the Gaynor household, and the farmyard was the scene of many a thrilling encounter. Mother dreaded that 'dangerous' game, and the clash of the ash sent shudders down her spine, while a roar could be heard from his father whenever a stray ball went up on the roof 'mind those bloody slates!' The barn door was the goal, and 'three goals in' was the usual contest until the neighbours Michael Aylward, and the Slattery and Gleeson brothers joined in. They had to move to the back field for those games where coats and bits of sticks improvised for goalposts. Brothers Des and Kevin hurled afterwards for the local club, Kilruane, while Kevin went on to St Flannan's College in Ennis where he won a Harty Cup medal.

As his brothers and sisters started going to the pictures and dances, Len spent hours in the summer evenings hurling a sponge or wind ball in the yard. He devised games to play alone by sending the ball around the walls and meeting it again or using the wooden window of the barn as a target. He realised later that, with these games he had been building up a repertoire of skills that would serve him well in the future.

Len met his own Eileen (O'Donoghue) in 1965 and they married in 1968. They moved to their present house and farm in that year. Len had milked cows by hand for years at home and realised the time required to run a dairy farm. He was in the middle of an outstanding hurling career at that time and they made a conscious decision not to start a dairy herd but to concentrate on tillage, cattle and sheep, which would give more free time. 'It might have cost me money,' he said, 'but I'll never regret that decision.'

Their first child, Fionnula arrived on a very special occasion. Eileen was 'due' the day of the 1971 All-Ireland final, but after consulting with Dr Joe Stuart, former president of the GAA and gynaecologist at the Coombe Hospital, they were assured that she could attend the game. Fionnula obliged and waited until the day after the match to make her appearance and so Len celebrated his last All-Ireland victory and the birth of his first child in the Coombe Hospital. Eileen later met a Kilkenny priest who told her that he had noticed this 'large' woman squeezed into a seat in the Hogan Stand and said he felt that she should be elsewhere. He realised later who she was when the papers carried a photograph of the happy family.

By coincidence, my own wife, Kay, was in the same position when Kilkenny and Tipperary contested the 1967 All-Ireland final. Our first child was also due that day as Kay watched the match from the Hogan Stand. The only difference was that, instead of me sitting in the Coombe Hospital while the celebrations were going on, Kay was sitting in the Mater Hospital where I had to spent the night following an injury in the match. As it turned out, our son Eamonn conveniently waited until the end of the week to make his appearance.

When I was moving house some years ago, I came across a letter from a very young Brian Gaynor from Kilruane looking for an autograph for his collection. He told me in his letter how much he loved hurling and that his father had played for Tipperary and had won All-Ireland medals. How well I knew that. I was thrilled later on to see him starring for the Tipperary minors winning a Munster medal, only to go down to Kilkenny in the All-Ireland of 1991. He showed the same tenacious and skilful defending qualities of his father at centre half-back that day. He also made the Tipperary under-21 team and had a short run on the senior team until injury hampered his career.

Ciara won two All-Ireland minor camogie medals before winning national recognition as one of the stars of Tipperary's first senior camogie All-Ireland success in 1999, retain the title in 2000. Her sisters play with the local club team.

Len Gaynor clipped the briars in the ditch with his hurl as he went down the road to the local school for the first time. He was a little disappointed that there was no playing pitch at the school. The local teacher was not a great hurling man, but turned a blind eye when the boys went out on the by-road that went past the school to hurl at break time. If the teacher was not that interested, the senior boys were, and they had great matches on the road whenever they could. When he was 10 years old, one of the older boys came to him one day and said, 'we're playing Ballinree School next Sunday and you're on the team.' Len was thrilled, but immediately wondered how he would get there. He said he would have to ask his parents,' to which the older boy replied: 'Oh God, what sort of parents have you!' He went on his bike to Ballinree and that was his first 'big' match. Because he was small, he was selected at corner-forward and did reasonably well. The match had been organised by the lads themselves, so they had no jerseys, just played as they were. Ballinree won the match with their star player, Frankie Ryan, who ran through the Kilruane lads. A replay was arranged in Kilruane, and the cry was 'who's going to mark Frankie Ryan?' Like the youngest shoved first into the dentist, Len was detailed to do the job, and he remembers seeing the Ballinree lads arriving for the match led by Frankie on a bike. He looked huge and he carried another player on the bar. Len cannot recall how he got on in the game, but they won the replay.

At the age of 11, he was selected on the Kilruane McDonaghs juvenile under-14 team in 1955, and was honoured with the captaincy in his final year in 1959. That was a marvellous year, and a great experience for a young player. Most players of that era would identify with the transport system. Secretary, Con Heffernan RIP would pack a load into his Hillman Minx, as would Fr McNamara, the local curate and the rest of the selectors. They won the northern championship to the delight of the people of the parish, and got to the county final where they would meet Ballybacon-Grange at Semple Stadium in Thurles. The selectors were very well organised to the extent that they were far-seeing enough to go to the other semi-final to see the opposition perform. They came back to announce that Ballybacon had one great player, and if they could hold him, they would win the final. The player was Michael 'Babs' Keating! Len was playing at centre half forward, but he was told that if the Kilruane centre-back was not able for Babs, he would be moved back to do the job.

A bus was arranged to bring the team to Thurles and Len remembers the good curate going around to the team in the bus giving them sips of pure orange juice which he had carefully extracted and bottled the day before. This was to give them energy for the game! Babs scored 1–2 in the first five minutes, and the switch was made. Len succeeded in holding him scoreless for the rest of the hour and they won the match. It was a great honour to be presented with the Dean Ryan Shield, and he has one abiding memory of the presentation. He can still see the beaming face of Jack Reddin as he stood in the crowd during the presentation. Jack had worked on the Gaynor farm he was obviously proud to see Len accept the trophy.

In the autumn of 1956, it was time for Len to go to secondary school. He was given the choice by his parents to go to either the CBS in Nenagh or St Flannan's in Ennis. His older brother Kevin had attended St Flannan's, and Len had been inspired by the atmosphere at the college matches when Kevin won his Harty Cup medal. It was an easy choice for a young boy with a passion for the game.

He watched the college senior team win the Harty Cup that year, but still recalls the disappointment when they went down to St Kieran's, Kilkenny in the All-Ireland final played at Easter in 1957. St Flannan's were ten points ahead going into the last quarter, 2–5 to 0–1. Then the Kilkenny boys started to move. In an extraordinary 15-minute spell, they turned the game around to come out winners on a score of 4–2 to 2–7. That was the day I won my first All-Ireland medal, while a small dark-haired youngster from Kilruane returned dejected to his alma mater in Ennis.

But disappointments pass quickly and Len was out hurling within days with ambitions to get his place on the college teams. They hurled every day at the school and twice on Sundays. He believes that the games he played there gave him a wonderful grounding for his hurling career.

He was captain of the victorious team that won the Dean Ryan Cup (junior), and in the same year, he was captain of the senior team that went down to St Finbar's Farranferris in the Harty Cup final.

While still a minor, Len was selected at wing-back for his first senior match with Kilruane McDonaghs in 1962. It was a tournament final against the kingpins of Tipperary hurling at that time, Thurles Sarsfields. The winners would be presented with transistor radios which was a big prize in those days. He remembers someone saying to him in the dressing room, 'you'll be marking Jimmy Doyle!' He wasn't as it turned out. Jimmy was playing at centre forward that day and Thurles won in a very good match.

It took them until 1965 to make any real impression when they beat Toomevara in the northern championship. Len was captain of the side, and they also had other county stars in Tom Moloughney and Gerry McCarthy. They were defeated in the semi-final by a controversial Sean McLoughlin goal for Thurles Sarsfields, who went on to win the county final.

By now Len had attended the National Coaching Courses in Gormanstown. He learned a great deal there, particularly about organisation and man-management. He began coaching the under-age teams, starting with the club minor team in 1970. In his second year, they won the county final for the first time. He coached the under-21s to four county titles, before moving on to the senior team. By 1977, they had a good, well-organised squad. They had great heart and came back from certain defeat on occasions to show their mettle. That senior team won their first county title in that year and followed on to win three in a row beating all the top teams, Borrisoleigh, Roscrea and Thurles Sarsfields in the process.

They did not have great success in the Munster club championship in that period, being beaten by Sixmilebridge, and Blackrock twice. He felt that they had a chance the second time that they played Blackrock, but they were unlucky that the bus company gave them a hopeless vehicle that chugged its way all the way to Cork. While they left in plenty of time, they arrived as the Blackrock team was going out on the pitch. They had no time to get organised or get mentally tuned in to the game. A lesson learned for the future.

After that they went through a lean period, but his proudest moment for the club was yet to come. By 1985, he had retired himself from the senior club team, but continued to coach them. They won the county final that year and defeated Blackrock in the AIB Munster club final in a replay. They reached the AIB All-Ireland club final and had a marvellous victory over Buffer's Alley by 1–15 to 2–10.

Len always places great emphasis on discipline when coaching a team. He enforces it in training and he believes that it paid off for his team on many occasions. He remembers that a lack of discipline in a player from Buffer's Alley on that day caused them to lose the game. Kilruane were behind coming towards the end when Len went right around the back of the Wexford goal to give an instruction to the corner forward. As he was about to return to the dug-out, the ball went wide at his feet and he returned it to the Alley goalkeeper so that he would not waste time with the puck-out. The keeper recognised him and proceeded to call him a string of unmentionable names. He subsequently missed the puck-out which went to a Kilruane forward who sent it back over the bar. They scored another two points to win the game in the dying seconds. Len's dream had been fulfilled, Kilruane McDonaghs were the AIB All-Ireland club champions, the best club team in the country.

Len recalls with pride the first time he wore the Tipperary colours when he was called up to play with the county minor team in 1962. He felt that he had really made it when, for the first time, a taxi called to the door to bring him to Cork to play Limerick in the first round. He climbed into the taxi to the envy of the neighbours as Paddy Burke from Roscrea guided the car carefully down the road. A far cry from the bike journey to Ballinree! He played his first match at centre field, but reverted to centre half-back for the Munster final against a Gerald-McCarthy-led Cork team. They won their way to the All-Ireland final to meet Kilkenny. 75,000 people were crammed into Croke Park that day to see if Tipperary could retain their All-Ireland senior crown against Wexford.

The young minor from Kilruane could not believe the atmosphere in Croke Park that day. Naturally the Tipperary supporters vastly outnumbered those from Kilkenny, and he recalls the huge roar reverberating in his ear drums as he sent over a point from a '70' as Tipperary drew level, having trailed for most of the hour. But Tom Walsh almost immediately got a goal for Kilkenny and victory went to the black and amber. Gaynor marked Tom Walsh that day and he regarded him as one of the most outstanding hurlers of that decade.

Len caught the eye of the Tipperary senior selectors following his great display for the under-21 team in the Munster semi-final against Clare in 1964. He was immediately promoted to the senior panel, but he had his wrist broken in the under-21 Munster final, and he feared that he would lose his chance with the seniors. He never knew how bad his wrist was, or indeed if it was broken at all. When he went to hospital, he was told by a rather over-zealous young doctor that it would require a plaster and he came out from the theatre with a huge plaster cast from his hand right up to his collar bone.

Not wanting to lose his place on the panel of the senior team, he turned up at Semple Stadium for training on the following Tuesday evening sporting this huge plaster. He eventually succeeded in fully togging out. He made his way to the sideline unnoticed and waited until the team had finished the hurling routines and started to jog around the field. As the group of players passed him, he jumped in to join them until he heard trainer, Paddy Leahy roar after him 'Young Gaynor, young Gaynor come back here!' He explained to Paddy that he wanted to take part in the running was allowed to join in that part of the session for the following two weeks, after which his plaster was removed and he was passed fit.

Tipperary won the All-Ireland under-21 championship that year, beating Wexford by 8–9 to 3–1 in the final. While a directive had been issued by Croke Park to the county boards that year to limit the panel of players for All-Ireland day, he was delighted to have been retained in the senior panel to contest the All-Ireland final against Kilkenny. Len feels that his efforts to train while injured swung it for him. History records that the Tipperary display on the first Sunday in September in 1964 was probably one of the best seen at Croke Park, and Len was proud to have been part of the panel. He recalls that he was awe-struck by the range of skills that he saw from the likes of Jimmy Doyle and Liam Devaney. He knew that he had to practise harder to match that standard.

He got his first chance of lining out with the senior team in an Oireachtas final in Croke Park three weeks after the All-Ireland. He came in at right half-back for the injured Mick Burns. Those were the great days of that competition when the crowds almost matched those of All-Ireland day. That was the first time Len and I came into direct opposition on the field. I remember him as strong, tenacious and possessing great vision. It was very hard to get away from him.

Kilkenny broke away from Tipperary early in the game led by 11 points at half time. Len remembers trudging off with his head down expecting that the team would be devoured by the trainer in the dressing room. He felt that there would be wholesale changes and substitutions. He was surprised that no panic was evident. Not a word was said, there were no changes and everyone was completely calm. Before they left, Theo English stood up and said 'come on now lads, we'll go out and beat them in the second half.' They did, and Len remembered that experience which he put to good use many times later both as a player and coach. Players should always try to relax when things are going against them. He remembers hitting a sideline ball that day that went all the way to the net. That started the Tipperary revival and they hauled back Kilkenny to win by five points. He remembers the thrill of going home with his first senior medal that night. The Oireachtas medals were always presented after the match, whereas the All-Ireland senior and under-21 awards would not be presented until the end of the year. Michael Murphy was the left half-back on that great team and he picked up a long-term knee injury around that time. Len fitted in to his place and made the position his own until he retired in the early 1970s.

Gaynor won his second All-Ireland medal the following year when Tipperary beat Wexford 2–16 to 0–10. He felt that he did not play well that day and blamed it on the fact that he had overdone the relaxation tactic by reading books before the game. The edge was not there when he took to the field. Another lesson learned! He did succeed in making one spectacular catch in the second half, from which a point was scored from his clearance. A long, high ball was delivered from the Wexford backs that left himself and Wexford's Jimmy O'Brien back-pedalling to get under it. It appeared that it would go over their heads, so the Wexford man turned to run on to it. Len kept going backwards, lost sight of the ball in the sun and just stuck up his hand where, to his amazement, the ball landed. He thought he might have been taken off had O'Brien got through for a score.

He was on the losing side against Kilkenny in the All-Ireland final of 1967, although he regards that game as his best display in the blue and gold colours. He was totally 'geared up' as he felt that that great team was coming to an end, and he would have loved to see John Doyle get his ninth All-Ireland medal. It was a day that the ball seemed to follow him. He remembers kneeling on the ground to get his wind after a heavy bout of play, and the ball coming into his hand for another clearance.

1968 was another big disappointment. After cruising to what looked like certain victory after a strong first-half performance over Wexford, the Model County struck back to snatch victory in an amazing second half.

Len won his last All-Ireland medal in 1971 against Kilkenny. He does not have a great recollection of the game, but remembers well their great victory over Limerick in the Munster final in Killarney that year. It was a spilling wet day, and he had the foresight to bring a second pair of boots and socks. He remembers the weight of his boots at half time as he trudged through the mud to the dressing room. He dried his feet and changed into the fresh boots and socks at half time and felt like a new man taking the field. The sun came out as they lined up for the second half which they won in a thrilling game.

I asked Len to describe Tipperary hurling: 'stubborn, resourceful, direct, strong-minded, fierce, resistant, a fair sprinkle of skill and a strong back line that could be relied on to keep scores to a minimum.'

He described Kilkenny and Cork as more skilful, 'classier' on the ball, handling the ball more often than Tipperary. Their strategy in playing Kilkenny was to close them down as quickly as possible. He admitted that they always feared that if they gave Kilkenny room they would destroy them. So that's how they did it! He said that they always admired Kilkenny for their manliness in that they could give and take a wallop on the field, and no grudges would ever be held.

Len Gaynor gave as much and more back to the game as he received from it. Much of his life was, and continues to be spent coaching teams at all levels. As well as coaching his own club, Kilruane McDonaghs, teams, he has guided five other club teams to county honours. He told me that his first loyalty lies with his own club followed by his county. But if he can help anyone else, he is more than willing to do so. 'The game of hurling is bigger that any of us,' he said with passion.

I asked him if it was difficult for him to agree to take on the management job in Clare, knowing that there was a strong possibility that they would come up against Tipperary in the Championship. He conceded that it was, and he agonised over it for some time. But the Clare County Board was very forceful and he agreed. A deciding factor was his five good years in St Flannan's College in Ennis where he learned a great deal of his hurling. He felt that he owed it to the county to give something back.

As it turned out, Clare did meet Tipperary in the Munster final of 1993 and his native county destroyed them, 3–27 to 2–12. Clare turned the tables the following year in the Munster semi-final only to go down to Limerick in the final. At that stage, Len felt that he had given them all that he could and he resigned. He considers that he did make some contribution to the successes that Clare enjoyed in the subsequent years. He enjoyed very much his two years with Clare and the cooperation he got from the county board and his selectors, who included Bishop Willie Walsh. A foundation had been laid, and when he gave in his resignation to the county board, he told them that they would win a Munster final in the near future. Little did he imagine that they would go on to win the All-Ireland in 1995!

Gaynor was manager of the Tipperary senior team from 1984 to 1986, and from 1997 to 1998. He gave it his best, but like Kilkenny and Cork, Tipperary are impatient for victory. 'It takes time to build a panel, and find out what players are really like,' said Len. 'You never know the mettle of players until they have taken part in a Munster Championship, and if you're beaten, and they have failed the test, you need another year or so to find the right guys. They won't wait in Tipperary, and they'll bring in someone else to do the job who will have to start the same process and who will be faced with the same problem.'

Len's first hero was the great Mick Mackey. He was inspired by a photograph in his brother's scrapbook which showed the Limerick man being carried off the field with the McCarthy Cup, and beads of sweat on his brow. He remembers his brother saying: 'will you look at the head of Mackey, he's still sweating!' Len wanted to be like that, and it happened to him after Kilruane McDonaghs had won the Munster club final. After the AIB club All-Ireland, he carried his daughter Sinead off the pitch and a picture of that appeared in the paper.

He also had great admiration for Tony Wall. He knew that Tony had to work hard at his game and he developed some lovely stickwork. He regarded him as a true Tipperary hurler, and he had the honour of playing beside him when he came on the team first. He thought out the game very well and always gave Len good advice on his play. Although Tony had to drive from Cork to Thurles to training, he was always first on the field, pucking the ball by himself.

The story is told that Tony lived beside a fanatical Cork supporter. Cork had been out of the frame for a few years, but this particular year the Corkman was sure they would beat Tipperary in the Munster final. On the day before the game, he was all worked up, had his colours ready, and couldn't wait for the next day to come when they would hammer Tipperary. On Saturday evening, it was wet and he went out in the garden and saw his next-door neighbour with his cap and coat and wheelbarrow working away in his garden. He couldn't believe that the centre half-back on the Tipperary team could be so relaxed on the day before the game. He slunk back into his house. 'We're bet!' he moaned to his wife, 'you should see that fellow out there and not a care in the world on him.' And they were the next day!

Declan Ryan is one of the present-day hurlers Len admires. He described him as a powerful, honest player with good hands. He is good to win the ball and he brings his colleagues into the game with deft passes.

Len is very pleased with the way that the back-door system has provided the public with excellent matches during the hurling season. He would like to see a way to bring more teams into the frame at that time of the year without diluting the championship fervour that exists at present. 'With more games, the weaker counties would have a better chance of improving,' he suggested.

On the subject of professionalism, Gaynor would not like to see players being paid, but he does thing they should be better looked after. He believes that they train harder and more often nowadays than in his time. 'In some ways, times are harder now. There's more money around, but people have to go out and earn it!' He believes that playing games and having a job at the same time is good. The job can help to take the mind off a bad performance, and hurling is a great antidote to the pressures and stresses of work.

He also believes that media pressure is very hard on players and managers now. In his time, the commentators knew more about the game and wrote a good analysis or preview of a game. Nowadays, they are looking for headlines and negative stories which can be very hurtful to players and their families.

Len Gaynor finished his hurling career playing at full forward with the Kilruane McDonaghs junior team while well into his 40s. He told me of a player on that team who was a marvellous athlete but not a very experienced hurler. He came to Len one day and said, 'Len, I can get the ball all right, but I don't know what to do with it when I get it.'

'I'll make it very simple for you now,' replied Len. 'When you get the ball, hit it in to me high or low. I'll know what to do.' It worked and Len Gaynor, former great defender became top scorer in his final years of hurling.

I got a kind invitation to Cloughjordan this year to present gold and silver Pioneer pins to the year 2000 recipients. I had the honour of presenting gold pins to two outstanding Tipperary hurlers, Tom Moloughney and Len Gaynor. What an example these men have been in their parish, and what a contribution Len, in particular has made to his parish, his county and to the game of hurling in particular.

Len Gaynor's Team of the Century

Tony Reddin
(Tipperary)

John Doyle
(Tipperary)

Nick O'Donnell
(Wexford)

Bobby Rackard
(Wexford)

Jimmy Finn
(Tipperary)

Tony Wall
(Tipperary)

Jackie Power
(Limerick)

Lory Meagher
(Kilkenny)

Joe Sammon
(Galway)

Jimmy Doyle
(Tipperary)

Mick Mackey
(Limerick)

Eddie Keher
(Kilkenny)

Jimmy Smith
(Clare)

Martin Kennedy
(Tipperary)

Christy Ring
(Cork)

Munster Team of the Century

Tony Reddin
(Tipperary)

John Doyle
(Tipperary)

Brian Lohan
(Clare)

Tony Shaughnessy
(Cork)

Jimmy Finn
(Tipperary)

Tony Wall
(Tipperary)

Jackie Power
(Limerick)

Philly Grimes
(Waterford)

Mick Roche
(Tipperary)

Jimmy Doyle
(Tipperary)

Mick Mackey
(Limerick)

Frankie Walsh
(Waterford)

Jimmy Smith
(Clare)

Martin Kennedy
(Tipperary)

Christy Ring
(Cork)

8 – Pat Hartigan

Limerick's mighty No. 3, Pat Hartigan rises to fetch a ball in their unsuccessful bid to retain their All-Ireland title in 1974. From left to right, Eddie Keher (Kilkenny), Jim O'Brien (Limerick), Willie Moore (Limerick) Mick Brennan (Kilkenny) and Pat Hartigan.

'He was a Giant of a man that the miners knew well. Broad at the shoulders and narrow at the hip, and everyone knew that you didn't give no lip to Big John.' The words of the 1960s Jimmy Dean hit song/monologue spring to mind when trying to find words to describe the Giant from the South Liberties club.

Pat Hartigan didn't win an All-Ireland senior medal until 1973, but his outstanding performances for Limerick in the three historic National League clashes with Tipperary in 1970-1971, and his heroic efforts in their narrow defeat by the same county in that never-to-be-forgotten championship clash in Killarney in 1971, made him an unanimous choice for the full back position on the first ever Carrolls All-Star team in that year.

Although I met him, and stood with him for the official photograph on the night of the All-Star Banquet that year, I didn't realise how enormous his physique was until I saw him at close quarters, togged out in the blue number three Munster jersey in the Railway Cup Final of 1972.

While he stood six feet four inches in height, with huge muscular arms and shoulders, he was fleet of foot and carried his huge frame with the nimbleness of a flyweight boxer. That day he was pitted against the experienced Tony Doran, and it was an amazing contest. Both players were superb fielders of the dropping ball, and there was an extraordinary buzz of anticipation every time the ball dropped in the square, with the balance of superiority shifting between one player and the other as the game progressed. It was a confrontation that brought the crowd to their feet on a number of occasions, and, although the Leinster team emerged victorious in the end, the Leinster players and hurling supporters got their first real 'close-up' of the man who was to dominate, and make his own the number three jersey for the remainder of the decade.

The 1970s rule changes had a very significant impact on the progress and development of the game of hurling. While many traditionalists still bemoan the loss of the 'Hell's Kitchen' activity in front of the goal under the old rules, I strongly believe that the opening up of play in front of goal by the introduction of these rules, made hurling more appealing and attractive to all sports followers, and particularly television viewers, who were introduced to the game in that way. For the younger readers, the main changes in the game brought about by these rules were the elimination of the 'third man' tackle, and the tackle on the goalkeeper in the small square. An infringement of these rules within the large square by the backs resulted in the 'new' semi-penalty, which, with only three men in the goal, was always very scoreable.

Many of the traditional full-back line players found it difficult to adapt to their new role in the game, which necessitated a complete change in their style of play. A full-back could no longer merely stay at all times between the forward and the goal, keeping the forward out by any means at his disposal. Under the new rules he risked fouling, which would inevitably end in a goal for the opposition. These 1970s rule changes, one would almost think, were designed with Pat Hartigan in mind. Here was a full-back, who had the physique of a traditional number three, but who loved to hurl the ball. The way I remember Pat's style is of a colossus, sprinting out in front of his man (which would be heresy under the old rules), fielding the high ball and sending a huge clearance to the other end of the field.

The Limerick and Tipperary supporters who packed into Fitzgerald Stadium in Killarney for that historic championship clash in 1971 still talk about his efforts to regain Limerick's early supremacy after they had let Tipperary back into the game to take a commanding lead in the second half. Tipperary's comeback, inspired by Babs Keating's controversial 'dry ball' free, started a run of scores that took them four points in front. Normally, Championship specialists Tipperary would surge ahead to a comfortable win at that stage of the game, but Pat Hartigan was not reading that particular script. Disregarding the driving rain, and the reputation of the opposition, he caught a high ball in the square, and burst his way out, leaving a trail of Tipperary bodies on the ground. He drove a huge clearance to the other end of the field where Eamonn Grimes was on hand to double on it to send to the net. Limerick had now reduced the deficit to a point, and inspired by Hartigan's example were back in the driving seat. Limerick supporters will claim to this day that, but for the fact that the advantage rule was not applied for Willie Moore's follow-up goal shortly afterwards, they would have been victorious. Tipperary held on to win by a single point.

Heads still turn when Pat walks into a public place, as they did when he walked into the Castletroy Park Hotel in Limerick on 11 February 2000 where we had arranged to meet. Although he confesses that his physical activity is now reduced to walking and playing golf, he still carries his huge frame athletically, and looks almost as fit as when he set hurling fields alight back in the 1970s. He greeted me warmly and as we adjourned to a quiet spot to do our talking, I knew that we had a great few hours of reminiscence in store. Pat and I go back a long way.

Married to Kate for 21 years, they have two children, Sally Anne and Faye. Sally Anne works in a bank in Dublin and is now 20, while Faye, aged 17 is in boarding school in Thurles. Basketball is her game and she was looking forward to playing in the League A Final in Tallaght (the Croke Park of basketball) at the time of our meeting. Kate had no knowledge of hurling when she met Pat in 1977, having been born and raised in the traditional rugby stronghold of Garryowen. Pat jokingly recalled how she took some time to come to understand why the two opposing hurling teams were 'mixed up together' rather than occupying their own side of the field.

They live in Corbally, a residential area on the north-east side of Limerick city. When describing the location, Pat reverted to hurling terms and said 'a puck of a ball away from Clare' and with a glint in his eye 'close enough!' A puck of a ball, perhaps, for the former Cooley mountains long-puck winner, but five or six for the rest of us. It was the first sign of the healthy rivalry that exists between these two neighbouring counties, and, of course with Tipperary, a rivalry that is the life blood of hurling and the GAA in general.

Ironically, it was a Kilkenny man, Phil Maher of Paulstown, who approached Pat in 1974 to join Grassland Fertilizers Ltd, who at that time were owned by the Walsh family of Irishtown in Kilkenny City. The company was later taken over by the Avonmore Group, and in 1990 became part of Greencore. A Pat-Hartigan-inspired Limerick had defeated Kilkenny in 1973, and were to meet again in 1974 when the result was reversed. Pat admitted that his hurling prowess was a help to him in his job, as he covered mainly the counties of Clare, Limerick, Cork, Tipperary, and Kilkenny at that time. He dealt with the farming community in those counties, who were invariably hurling fanatics. It did not always mean automatic sales. He had to work at that too, but doors were always opened for him. He now holds the position of area sales manager for the south and west from their premises in Cork and Limerick.

I always regarded South Liberties GAA Club as a city club, but Pat informed me that it was really a rural club on the outskirts of Limerick City. Like many rural clubs, players were drawn from three parts of the parish consisting of Donoughmore (where Pat was born) Knockea and Ballysheedy (Eamonn Grimes' birthplace). One of the oldest clubs in Limerick, formed shortly after the foundation of the GAA in the 1880s, they won the senior championship in 1972 after a lapse of 87 years. Eamonn Grimes, who came across many times in our conversation as a man of outstanding leadership qualities, from Ballysheedy and Pat himself from Donoughmore helped to get the various sides of the parish to work together to make a serious challenge for the title. Another ingredient was the presence of a number of brothers in the panel, Grimes, Shanahans and Hartigans. Pat's older brother Bernie, however, despite all their efforts did not play with Liberties. Bernie, an established member of the Limerick team since the 1960s had been a member of a senior team, 'Old Christians' (effectively a team comprising past pupils of Limerick CBS). He lived in Coonagh near the Gaelic Grounds, and it was easier for him to train with the Old Christians team.

South Liberties went senior in 1967, and lo and behold, who were they drawn against in the first round – Old Christians! This almost caused a split in the Hartigan family! with their father, for his own good reasons I am sure, siding with the eldest brother and Old Christians for the match. This, of course increased the tension in the Hartigan household, and, although only 16 years old, and playing left half back in a senior championship, Pat was totally fired up for the game. He remembers that very early on in the game, Bernie tore through him on his way to goal before burying the ball in the net. On his way out, he scoffed at Pat, 'keep out of my way young fellow.' Pat went to strike him and had his name taken – for the first of two times in his distinguished career, and the first time was for a foul on his own brother.

However, Liberties won the game and reached the county final that year, only to be beaten well in a replay by the more experienced Kilmallock. They had the drawn match almost sewn up with minutes remaining and two goals up, but Kilmallock crashed two balls to the net in the dying minutes to snatch a draw.

A Cregan-powered Claughan beat them in the 1971 county final, but they reached the final again in 1972 and had to face the Patrickswell team boasting the talented Bennis brothers, Richie and Phil, Tony O'Brien and the Careys. It appears that the 'leave no stone unturned' Patrickswell mentors rang up the Met. Office on the morning of the game to get a detailed weather forecast for Limerick city. 'Very professional for 1972,' said Pat. However, there was a twist to the tale. The Met. Office told them that there would be gales that would increase to storm force later in the day. Patrickswell won the toss and decided to play against the wind in the first half in the knowledge that the ferocity of the wind would increase in the second. Unfortunately for them, the forecast was incomplete in that it did not say that, as well as increasing, the wind would change direction. Liberties had the luxury of playing with a strong wind in both halves and ran out easy winners for the first time in 87 years. Pat won two other county finals in 1976 and 1978, which together with an unbeaten run from 1971 to 1979 in the east Limerick senior championship amounted to a healthy haul of county senior medals.

His only regret was that they never won an All-Ireland club championship. They were beaten by a powerful Glen Rovers team in the Munster Club Championship, and Tipperary's Kilruane on another occasion.

Pat regarded Joe McKenna as a great hurler for Limerick and for the Liberties, and was very influential in the club's break-through. Although an Offaly man, he lived in the diocese of Killaloe and was educated at St Flannan's College in Ennis. Pat would have played against him during the 1960s when St Flannan's and Limerick CBS met. The Ennis hurling stronghold was going through a lean period at that time and, although the Sexton Street boys feared them because of their tradition, they were able to beat them during those years. Joe was stocky and spike-haired in those days, but shot up to be a six foot, four inch giant by 1971 when he came to work in Limerick. Fate works in mysterious ways, and by chance, Pat was driving through Limerick that year and was stopped at traffic lights when he noticed an athletic figure crossing the street. Although a foot taller, and with a 1970s hair-style, he was sure that it was Joe from St Flannan's. He made enquiries and discovered that the Offaly man was in town working with Vincent Byrne, a Liberties clubman. Pat approached him to join their club, and the rest is history. However, there was a slight difficulty to overcome. Joe needed to be living in the parish to be eligible and his flat in town was outside the parish. Joe's address became 'c/o Vincent Byrne' from then on!

Many a farmer's son who grew up in the 1950s could identify with Pat Hartigan's early childhood days working hard on a traditional style mixed farm with his father and brothers. So too, many hurlers could identify with his introduction to hurling. His early days were spent trying to learn the skills of the game during breaks in haymaking or sowing or milking cows under the critical eye of a father whose main concern was to get through the heavy daily workload. 'Give up that bloody hurling, for God's sake and do a bit of work!' was a regular call from a weary father trying to keep a busy farm ticking over. He was 58 years old when Pat was born in 1950. It was understandable that he took a nap after dinner before the afternoon work commenced. This gave Bernie, Seamus and Pat an opportunity to 'sneak' out to the yard to have their little 'All-Ireland.' As the game grew in its intensity, they forgot to keep quiet, and inevitably a careless stroke of the ball brought it crashing against the kitchen window to wake up the father. Game over, back to work.

Hurleys were hard to come by in those days and, being the youngest, Pat had to make do with the fireside shovel until more coal was needed for the open fire and his mother came looking for Pat's hurl. When the eldest, Bernie, became involved with the club, hurls became a little more plentiful and Pat could have the luxury of Bernie's broken ones. The farmyard games had a decided influence on Pat's hurling career. As the youngest, and the smallest, he inevitably found himself 'stuck in goal' while Bernie and Seamus battled it out in the middle of the field. This position, however gave him an 'eye' for the fast incoming ball, and, with only a fire shovel in his hand, taught him to catch the ball in flight, a skill that was to become the outstanding hallmark of his game in later years.

Pat's mother came from fisherman stock in Northern Ireland to work as a butter-maker in the local co-operative. There she met his father, who was a supplier. She made occasional trips home and once arrived back with an old fishing net that was to transform the farmyard to Croke Park standards. The net was placed over the half-door of one of the many sheds surrounding the farmyard, and so began the many accuracy contests between the brothers.

Kilkenny's Ollie Walsh was his hero in those days, and like all heroes of a nine-year-old, he believed that Ollie was invincible. He remembers listening to Micheál Ó Hehir's broadcast of the 1959 drawn All-Ireland final between Kilkenny and Waterford. Kilkenny had scored 5–5 and Waterford 0–17 with a minute to go. Ollie had made miraculous saves and had a clean sheet, when Seamus Power's dying effort was deflected by Kilkenny's full-back, Jim 'The Link' Walsh to the corner of the net and out of Ollie's reach. Ollie had conceded a goal, Pat's dream was shattered.

Another boyhood hero was Tipperary's John Doyle. He remembers being brought by his father to the 1960 Munster final between Tipperary and Cork in the Gaelic Grounds that attracted a record crowd of over 60,000. They arrived at 10.30am to get a seat on the sideline, and an announcement was made at 11.30 to say that the sideline was full. He made sure to get a seat beside the tunnel so that he could get a close view of his heroes. He still has a vivid recollection of John Doyle, with his shock of black hair, and his collar turned up running out beside him and on to the field. He remembers a row during the game when Doyle and Ring were locked in combat rolling around the ground.

Mick O'Connell was another boyhood hero. Mick's exploits on the field of play were told in graphic detail to a receptive class of nine-year-olds by their teacher Tom Johnston. The Kerryman used every opportunity to talk about his own hero. Geography lessons were often about the Kingdom, and Valentia Island was full of finger marks on the school wall map. Hartigan remembers a gasp from the students as they were told how O'Connell, after collecting the Sam Maguire cup as captain in 1959, had rushed out of Croke Park, leaving the cup in the dressing room to catch the train home. He showed them on the map the stretch of water that the Valentia man had to row across to reach his beloved island home before the tide changed.

The young Hartigan had little success by way of medals at under-age level but as an 18-year-old, with his brother Seamus, Pat got a trial for the Limerick seniors in 1968. As Pat had succeeded in playing minor, intermediate and under-21 hurling and football with Limerick in that year, he forfeited a South Liberties Divisional Match for the opportunity to represent his county at all grades in the same season.

He was positioned at right half-forward and scored five points and was selected on the panel to play a strong Clare team in a League match. Due to his age, he did not expect to get a place on the team. But, because of a dispute that was taking place between St Patricks Club and the county board, they were missing some established players and he found himself at right half-forward marking one of the best defenders of that era, Eamonn Russell. He was again happy with his game, scoring 1–1. From that day, he held his place on the Limerick senior team until his enforced retirement in 1979 following an accidental eye injury in training that year.

In 1970, he was played at full-back, marking Ray Cummins in a tournament game. He did well, and the selectors were happy that they had now found a man for the troublesome position.

Pat felt that he 'came of age' following the three tempestuous games against rivals, Tipperary in the National League of 1970–1971. They were somewhat in awe of the 'big-name' players including Jimmy Doyle, Mick Roche, Len Gaynor, Babs Keating and others who had starred in the 1960s. Having beaten them in the first round of the League, they had to beat them again in a play-off, before meeting them yet again in the National League Final in Cork. To say that 'aggro' had developed was an understatement. He remembers that he was marking Babs Keating in that final, and before the ball was thrown in, he said to Babs, 'I suppose you have a bet on this game, or a bet on how much you'll score on me today. We'll see before this game is over.' As the world knows, Babs liked to have a bet, but Pat felt immediately that his remark was very immature and said in the tension of the occasion. They had a tough game, but afterwards, Babs came over to congratulate Hartigan and made a remark that stung Pat deeply: 'I hope that you'll be a better sportsman the next time we meet.'

The next time they met was in that famous Championship clash in Killarney in 1971. The first ball came between them, Babs pulled a little early and caught his opponent on the chest. 'Are we square now?' said Pat. 'We are' was the reply. They both went on then to play hard and fair, and both had outstanding games. Pat remembers meeting Donie Nealon some time later who told him how he got the idea of the 'dry ball' from a club game he had refereed the Sunday before. A dry ball was slyly substituted by an astute mentor for a '65' in the dying minutes on an atrocious day. The taker was well able to get the distance to equalise. He found out that the dry ball was brought in a towel which was dropped to the ground.

Pat had a high regard for Joe McGrath and felt that he was way ahead of his time when he took over the Limerick team as coach in the early 1970s. He claims that he played a big part in their 1971 League victory and Oireachtas win of the same year. They were unlucky not to beat Tipperary in the 1971 Championship, but he also feels that he sowed the seeds for the 1973 All-Ireland success. Joe's methods, and his demands from the county board did not endear him to that conservative body, and when Limerick went down badly to Clare in the 1972 Championship, Joe was dumped without explanation. The Hartigans, Grimes and Jim Hogan lodged a protest, and refused to play in the early League games. 'I was young then' said Pat, 'and I probably would have handled it differently later on, but we felt strongly that Joe was at least entitled to be given a reason.' The protest was short-lived following Joe's approach to the players. The point was made, business as usual.

Mick Cregan, an army man and brother of Eamon, did the physical training for the 1973 campaign, and like Clare's approach in the 1990s, felt that hard physical training was the only way to help them make the breakthrough. It worked, but, as Pat said, 'he nearly killed us.' They went all the way in 1973, but they may have been burned out the following year.

He was also very complimentary towards Jackie Power, their coach. Jackie felt that Limerick teams were living under the shadows of the great men of the 1940s, the Mackeys, Timmy Ryan, Dick Stokes and, of course himself. When demonstrating a skill, he would say 'look, you are better than I ever was, or

Mackey or any of those players you heard about.' That gave them great confidence in themselves.

While luck was not on their side in 1971, Pat felt that they did get a few fortunate breaks in 1973. Ned Rea had being playing in defence for a number of years, but was then beginning to lose his pace. Rea was an experienced player, and looked up to by the other players. Jackie Power felt that he was needed on the team, somewhere. He put him at full-back for a League final and moved Hartigan to the corner. Ned had little success there against Tony Doran. He was dropped for the first round of the Championship when they scraped home against Clare. Power told Rea, when Rea called to see him in hospital, that he was too important to the team to be left off, that he would bring Hartigan back to full back and try him up in the forwards. Ned had never played up front in his life, but he was selected at full forward for the Munster final showdown against Tipperary, and his size caused problems for his opposite number, John Kelly. Limerick scored six goals that day, and Rea had a hand in all six, apart from finishing a few himself. The Faughs man was to be a thorn in Kilkenny's side too in the All-Ireland.

Apart from those well-timed goals, Limerick also got a number of other breaks in that match. A disputed '65', and the subsequent point went their way, but they felt that they were due some luck after Killarney in 1971. Donie Nealon is on record as saying that Richie Bennis' effort was inside the post, but Pat mischievously responds to questions from Tipperary men that it was 'not only wide, but two feet wide.' They do not know that the full-back, in fact, turned his back when Bennis was taking the shot, only to look when he saw Seamus Horgan dancing with excitement in his own goal. That is known as 'rubbing salt into the wounds!' The twinkle is back in his eyes, the Limerick/Tipperary rivalry is alive and well.

Limerick did not fear Kilkenny coming in to the All-Ireland that year. He did say, graciously, that it was doubtful if they would have beaten a fully-fit Kilkenny team that day, but they were the 'luck team' that year, and they were not going to let the opportunity pass. I told him that I am on record as saying that it was Limerick's year, and nothing was going to stop them against any team in 1973.

He has many happy memories of that day. Eamonn Grimes was an inspiring captain who led from the front. His half-time speech had them crying in the dressing room. He felt they had it won when Seamus Horgan made that reflex save from a hand-passed effort by Mick Crotty. If the ball had been blocked out, there was every possibility that an incoming forward would finish it to the net. But Horgan safely deflected it over the bar. Pat's opposite number that day was Jim Lynch, who had been recalled as a replacement for the injured Kieran Purcell. Jim was substituted late in the second half, and shook hands and said: 'Pat, ye have it won, enjoy the victory.' Very sporting, Pat thought.

While the high-profile players on the team got much of the glory, he believes that, it was players like Phil Bennis, Willie Moore, Jim O'Brien, Liam O'Donoghue and Frankie Nolan who 'ground' away for the 70 minutes in atrocious conditions who played the biggest part in forging that famous victory.

The reception the team got from their supporters was unbelievable. Everyone wanted to be part of that great occasion. So much so that the reception at the Crofton Airport Hotel never took place, as the hotel could not serve meals or drinks due to the 'milling' crowd. The players ended up in their rooms with County Secretary, Tom Boland eventually getting to a piano to lead a sing-song. The homecoming to Limerick was chaotic too, but equally enjoyable. The crowds came out to Castleconnell in their thousands to greet them, but they also crowded into the hotels and bars, so that the hoteliers were unable to serve them a meal! The players dispersed to various pubs only to be followed by thousands of excited fans. Players had to be hidden inside and the fans told that they had gone elsewhere. Limerick came to a standstill for this joyous occasion.

If they did get the 'rub of the green' in the 1973 Championship, Pat felt that Lady Luck was not with them the following year. In the Munster final against Clare, the Liberties man had his best game ever in the green and white jersey. Gus Lohan, father of Brian and Frank Lohan had given him a turbulent time in the 1973 meeting of these teams. It was the old-fashioned pushing game between the full back and full forward. This time, Pat, basically a hurling full back, decided to avail of the new rules and play his own game from the front. Lohan got dragged out the field, and his lack of mobility out there gave the Limerick man the advantage. Eventually the speedier Enda O'Connor was brought in at full forward, with Lohan moving to the corner. Then the first bit of ill luck struck. As Pat went out to rise a ball, Gus shouldered him and he fell on O'Connor's boot and dislocated his shoulder. He had to leave the field, but the game was well and truly over at that stage.

Apart from making him a doubtful starter for the All-Ireland final against Kilkenny, the injury had perhaps a more profound effect on their bid to retain the title. South Liberties were due to play a championship match the following Sunday, and Pat was told by a prominent official when he visited him in hospital that they would postpone the game. The county board went ahead with the fixture, and Liberties refused to play, and were thrown out of the Championship. This left a sour taste in the mouths of the county players from the club. During training Grimes, McKenna and himself were taken aside, and their attitude to training questioned.

Hartigan himself, was, in any case was fighting a fitness battle, but felt strong enough to line out for the final. He laughingly reminded me that I hit him early on in the chest when he turned into me to hit a ball. I couldn't recall the incident, but maybe it is just as well, as I might have had second thoughts about our meeting on his own ground. Seriously, I did recall the next incident that he had thought had been engineered to test his shoulder. A sideline cut was taken by Pat Lalor, and Hartigan saw that the ball was hit into an open space, where he was amazed that he was left all alone to catch it. All of a sudden, that human tank, Frank Cummins appeared in the space to give him a shoulder that lifted him two feet off the ground. 'It was the hardest belt I ever got,' confessed Pat, 'but I picked myself up and hurled on in the knowledge that there definitely was nothing wrong with that shoulder after.' I assured him that nothing had been planned in that regard before the game.

Pat Hartigan joins the fray in the All-Ireland final 1973. From left to right Mick Crotty (Kilkenny), Eamon Cregan (Limerick), Pat Hartigan (Limerick), Jim Lynch (Kilkenny).

Limerick got off to a great start, and were leading six points to one, before Kilkenny got through for three goals which Pat feels were a little against the run of play. He argues strongly that he did not foul Pat Delaney in an incident which resulted in the semi-penalty that brought the first goal. Mick Brennan's kicked effort barely got inside the post, he said. The third goal, from Pat Delaney, from out the field he went to catch but he missed and it trickled all the way in under Seamus Horgan's legs. He can still vividly recall every roll of that ball as he watched it cross the line. He said that they had a chance to silence the doubters by beating a full Kilkenny team in 1974, but they blew it. The circumstances of the build-up certainly did not help. Hartigan acknowledged that the Kilkenny team of the 1970s was one of the best teams he had ever seen, and also had great praise for the Cork team of the late 1970s.

I asked him about great players he played against, and he named Ray Cummins, whom he found it hard to outwit in front of goal. The names of Tony Doran, Babs Keating, Roger Ryan and Pat Delaney and Kieran Purcell rolled off his tongue. But what was more interesting was he was able to recall their contrasting styles, and how he attempted to mark each one. 'It was always difficult playing Kilkenny where he had to cope with the different styles of Purcell and Delaney as they switched frequently from centre to full forward during the game.

He felt that the 1990s saw the best hurling of the century. 'Modern equipment, a lighter ball, better training methods for players, and a more scientific and better knowledge of diet for athletes has to make better hurlers.' He is very much in favour of the back-door system. Top class matches, televised have increased the popularity of the games in many traditional rugby and soccer strongholds in Limerick and the rest of the country.

Pat is also very much against any move towards professionalism. 'There are thousands of people at club and county level working hard for the Association in a voluntary capacity,' he said. The GAA is dependent on those people to survive. The inter-county players are the only people that are getting anything by way of recognition, local and national. Ireland hasn't the population to afford the cost of paying players. And if they tried, what would happen to the clubs? Would the inter-county players play for their club for free?'

Hartigan strongly favours the retention of the Railway Cup competition. He felt that it was 'hounded' out by the media. When he started playing, there were 30,000 at these games, and the media were already writing them off. Social changes, with St Patrick's Day Parades all over Ireland stopped people from travelling to Dublin to the games. 'The GAA should have acted earlier,' he said, 'but the players still love the competition, and it should be retained even if it means that there are no spectators there to watch.'

I asked him about his good friend, racing magnate, JP McManus who had recently announced that he would be giving a personal donation of £50 million to the new National Stadium. McManus was very involved in the South Liberties club in the 1970s, and was the youngest chairman of the club as a 19-year-old. He was way ahead in his thinking, even at that time. In his early 20s, he donated a set of jerseys to the club, and Pat said that it was probably a greater financial strain on him to make that gesture then as it is to make that £50 million donation now. Hartigan felt that he had a lot to offer the GAA and should be brought on to some of the GAA 'think tank' committees as soon as possible.

He thought for a while when I asked him if he would be interested in the Limerick coaching/manager's job. He eventually said that he would not be interested and gave me a detailed set of reasons why he thought that he would not be qualified for the position. His in-depth analysis of a hurling manager's job led me to believe that he was an ideal candidate.

Pat has great memories of the All-Stars trips and games in the early 1970s. A chance to travel to the west coast of America in those days was like a dream come true. I was appointed captain of the first All-Star team to play All-Ireland champions, Tipperary in San Francisco in 1971. Pat remembers me coming to him a day or so before the match when I must have felt that the team was losing sight of the forthcoming game with all the excitement of sunny California. He credited me with this statement: 'Pat, we are having a great time, but the people at home will only want to know who won the game. When you arrive back in Shannon, I want you to be able to say "we had a great time and we won the match." I want you and all the lads to remember that.'

We swapped many great stories from those trips until well past midnight. It was great to renew friendship with this great Limerick man, a gentleman on and off the field. We vowed to meet again later on in the spring to renew our friendly rivalry, but this time we will be forced to do so on a golf course, somewhere in Kilkenny or Limerick.

Pat Hartigan's Team of the Century

Noel Skehan
(Kilkenny)

Fan Larkin	Conor Hayes	John Horgan
(Kilkenny)	*(Galway)*	*(Cork)*
Denis Coughlan	Pat Delaney	Colm Doran
(Cork)	*(Offaly)*	*(Wexford)*

John Connolly   Mick Roche
(Galway)   *(Tipperary)*

D.J. Carey	Babs Keating	Eddie Keher
(Kilkenny)	*(Tipperary)*	*(Kilkenny)*
Nicky English	Ray Cummins	PJ Molloy
(Tipperary)	*(Cork)*	*(Galway)*

Munster Team of the Century

Seamus Durack
(Clare)

Jackie O'Gorman	Martin Doherty	John Horgan
(Clare)	*(Cork)*	*(Cork)*
Denis Coughlan	Sean McMahon	Pat McGrath
(Cork)	*(Clare)*	*(Waterford)*

Mick Roche   Gerald McCarthy
(Tipperary)   *(Cork)*

Babs Keating	Noel O'Dwyer	Jimmy Barry Murphy
(Tipperary)	*(Tipperary)*	*(Cork)*
Nicky English	Ray Cummins	Jim Greene
(Tipperary)	*(Cork)*	*(Waterford)*

Both teams are confined to the years 1970 to 2000 and Limerick players are excluded.

9 – Fan Larkin

The city of Kilkenny has a long and proud history. The once capital city of Ireland was principally developed in the thirteenth century, and most of the historical buildings that were built by the Anglo-Normans during that extraordinary period still remain today. The planning and careful regulation of the ancient city continues to bring thousands of tourists to Kilkenny to enjoy its wonderful history. The walls of the old city extended across the top of Patrick Street where one of the city gates existed, and the subsequent residential development outside those gates of the city became known as 'The Village.' That name still remains to this day, and the famed James Stephens GAA Club, which was formed in 1887 in that location continues to be known as 'The Village.'

Fan Larkin watches intently with Noel Skehan to his left.

It was in that area on the Kells road that Philip 'Fan' Larkin was born on 5 October 1941. His father, Paddy was a hero of the famous Kilkenny team of the 1930s. Paddy won four All-Ireland medals in 1932, 1933, 1935 and in the famous 'thunder and lightning' final of 1939. He usually played at right full-back, the position his son filled in later years. Indeed, Fan surpassed his father's record, winning five All-Ireland medals in the 1960s and 1970s.

There were no televisions and very few radios to distract or hinder conversations as the young Larkins were growing up, and with his brothers Paddy and Michael, young Philip listened at meal times as their father told them about the great games of the past.

'I heard all about Kilkenny's three great games with Cork in 1931', Fan recalled, 'how they recovered from eventual defeat to win two-in-a-row. He told me about all the great players such as Neddy Doyle, the Byrnes, Peter Reilly, Peter Blanchfield, Mattie Power and his friend Mattie White, who is alive and well to this day. Lory Meagher was a wonderful "stick" man with an abundance of skills and a lovely overhead striker of the ball. In those days, even up to the start of my own career, the players didn't run all over the field as they do today. The centre-field players commanded the middle and contested every high ball in the air. Overhead striking is the one skill I miss in today's game,' Fan said ruefully. 'I saw Ned Wheeler, John Sutton, Mick Brophy, Sean Clohosey, Theo English, John Hough and Bill Walsh who were all great overhead strikers. They wouldn't be let hurl today because the referees would blow for a free every time they pulled!' His father's assessment of Lory Meagher and Paddy Phelan bears out their selection on the 'Team of the Millennium.'

Fan regrets that he never saw his father play, but Jimmy Walsh of Carrickshock, Mick Neary, Jim Langton, Paddy Grace and his uncle Jack McGuinness told him of his exploits on the field.

Paddy Larkin saw his son win four of his five All-Ireland medals before he passed away in 1976.

Paddy was a great reader of the game and advised Fan as he progressed through minor to senior ranks. His father used to say, 'the golden rule is be first to the ball. If you haven't the ball, you can't hurl. Rule number two, practise, practise, practise. When you get to the ball first, you must have the skill to either control it into your hand, or double on it down the field. It's as simple as that.'

'The Village' in the 1950s was like any rural village community. There was a green in front of the houses where the youngsters played. Hurleys were thrown down in two bunches to pick teams. The goalposts consisted of coats. As matches progressed, proud fathers came out to watch, leaning on the walls, chatting. The competition was keen and the players developed to such an extent that, of the James Stephens team, that won the county minor final in 1957, ten learned their trade on the green on the Kells road. Fan lived next door to Mickey 'Socks' Dunne who was as good a minor as ever hurled, according to Larkin. Others who later starred for James Stephens and Kilkenny at various grades were Florrie and Lou McCarthy, Sammy Kirwan, Nick Morrissey, Paddy Maher, Dixie Brennan and Coley Dunne. As a close-knit community, they all had their nicknames to distinguish the different families. Young Phil Larkin had a cousin with the same name, so his middle name of Francis was abbreviated to 'Fan' to avoid confusion. Before and after the matches on the green, Fan used every minute to follow his father's advice to practise and he spent hours with the Dunne brothers hitting the ball to one another. When on his own, he used the high wall of the old sanatorium, which was located opposite the green to hone his skills by hitting a sponge ball and catching or doubling on the return. It would not have been a surprise if the sanatorium had to be converted to a mental hospital as the patients lay in their beds listening to the rat-tat-tat of the ball against the wall.

Brother Finney and Brother Cyril coached the school's under-14 team at St Patrick's Primary School in the parish. It was not long before they recognised the skills of the diminutive young Larkin, and, at the age of 11, he earned a place on the substitutes' bench for the county final against Thomastown in 1953. He was brought in during the game at wing-back to try to counteract the influence of Tony 'Tuts' Hayes, who was causing all sorts of problems for the St Patrick's defence. Thomastown went on to win the game by two points, 5–1 to 3–5.

Fan won his first hurling medal when St Patrick's won the county under-16 final in 1955, beating Johnstown by nine points in a replay. They also won the under-16 football in the same year. His next medal came in 1957 when a star-studded James Stephens minor team won the county final defeating Coolroe in emphatic fashion, 4–10 to 1–1.

His displays for the club earned him a trial for the county minor team in 1958, but he failed to make the panel. However, the following year he performed well in a trial when he marked Tom Murphy who was one of the Rower-Inistioge stars. Fan was selected, but Tom had to wait another year to get his place. Fan admitted that the Village selector, Bill Leahy might have had something to do with it. He was thrilled that he would be wearing the black and amber with the county team, but he was in for a big shock when Laois nearly beat Kilkenny in the first round at Birr. St Kieran's College star, John Alley almost won the game for Laois on his own. Kilkenny hung on to win by a point.

They beat Wexford fairly easily in the Leinster final and went on to play Tipperary in the All-Ireland final. 'It was every young man's dream to play in an All-Ireland, and I was delighted to walk out on Croke Park before 77,000 people to fulfil that dream,' Fan said. But that dream was shattered when he was unable to resume after half time due to an injury he received late in the first half. 'It was a game we should have won,' he said, 'but Tipperary came with a late surge to beat us 2–8 to 2–7. But we were winning when I left the field,' he added with a glint in his eye. Johnny McGovern, who was injured in the senior game against Waterford, ended up in the same room with Fan in hospital that night. I remember that day well too, as it was my third attempt to win an All-Ireland minor medal. However, Fan and I were to play together on many successful sides in later years.

Fan was now playing with the James Stephens senior team, but following a dispute he left the club to join another city Club, Eire Óg in 1960. Gossip at that time told that his father influenced him to leave The Village, but Fan told me that his father never knew of his decision until after he had signed the transfer form. He played with Eire Óg until 1966, but he had no successes with the club. In 1967, he broke his leg playing football with Kilkenny and by the time he regained fitness, Eire Óg had disbanded. He rejoined James Stephens in 1968.

While he won no honours with Eire Óg, he did have the pleasure of playing with one of his heroes, Jim Langton, who hurled with that club well into his forties. In 1966, Langton played at full forward for Eire Óg against Freshford marking none other than Pa Dillon. Pa was one of the most respected full-backs ever to play for Kilkenny and was generally regarded as a man who did not make life easy for any forward. On this occasion, Fan recalled, Pa was careful not to injure the ageing legend in any of the tussles and Langton was able to demonstrate the skills, which made him famous and scored seven points. I asked Fan how a man could still have played to that age. 'Langton always had a hurl in his hand,' he said. 'He never lost his touch. He was not fast to run, but he had great anticipation and great skill to take up the ball. He was a hardy boyo with strong wrists and he could strike equally well left and right. He was also an accurate free-taker.'

On a Wednesday night in the late autumn of 1962, Fan was notified that he had been selected at right full back to play against Tipperary in Thurles in a League match. The regular man in that position, Tom Walsh from Dunnamaggin had retired, and Fan got his chance. Tom's brother, Jim 'The Link' Walsh and John Maher completed the full back line. Ollie Walsh was in goal. The trio were gods to him, having watched them perform in the 1950s and particularly in the All-Irelands of 1957 and 1959. It was a big day for the 21-year-old, particularly when it appeared that he would be marking Sean McLoughlin who was nearly twice his size, but Sean cried off as he had being playing with his club the day before. Liam Connolly stood in as Fan's first opponent at senior level. Larkin played well enough to retain his place for the remainder of the League, and was delighted when he was selected on the panel for the Championship for the 1963 season. He was named as a substitute for the semi-final of the Leinster Championship against Wexford for a full-back line of Cha Whelan, Link Walsh and Martin Treacy. 'I was like a child that day travelling up to the match with the legendary Ollie Walsh and Paddy Grace,' he recalled. As he sat in the dressing room, Paddy Grace suddenly threw him a jersey and said 'you're playing!' 'What?' said Fan. 'You're playing,' said Paddy authoritively. It appears that Cha didn't want to play at right full-back on Aidan Quirke who was a small speedy forward and he considered that Fan would be better equipped to deal with him.

Kilkenny won the game and went on to play Dublin in the Leinster final. Before the game, Sean Clohosey came to him. 'You'll be on Mick Bermingham,' he said. 'He's a good hurler, but he'll suit you. Keep on top of him.' He must have kept too much on top of him, because when the first ball came down between them, Fan was badly cut across the forehead. He continued to play, although heavily bandaged and more than held his own for the hour. 'Ollie was outstanding in goal as was Seamie Cleere in front of me, and Ted Carroll at centre-back, which made it very easy for me,' he said modestly.

Kilkenny had now qualified for the All-Ireland final to meet a much-fancied Waterford team who had beaten Tipperary in the League final and had an impressive run in the Munster Championship.

'No one in Kilkenny gave us a chance,' Fan suggested. 'The only people who were confident were the team members and coach, Fr Maher. I don't think that even the selectors thought that we'd win. You will recall,' he continued 'that the usual after-match banquet was not even arranged. We just had dinner in the hotel after the game.'

Fan could not believe that he would be at last be filling the shoes of his father in the number two jersey in an All-Ireland final. He was marking the great Philly Grimes and he recalls that Grimes caught the first two balls that came towards them and scored two points. It was a bad start, but he gradually got into the game and matched the Waterford man for the rest of the game. He gave great praise to Seamie Cleere for another outstanding performance in front of him, which earned him the Texaco Award as 'Player of the Year'. 'Ted Carroll had a great game too on Tom Cheasty, and the forwards got some great scores to ensure victory for us, and my first All-Ireland medal. Denis Heaslip was an outstanding forward and would be brilliant in today's game. He was as skilful as DJ Carey, and as fast, and he had a great eye to find the gaps in the defence. But, at that time, the backs could pull and haul the forwards and they mostly got away with it. An alert referee, Jimmy Hatton, from Wicklow, awarded a number of frees for fouls on Heaslip. Fan will never forget the reception the team got on their return to Kilkenny. The crowd, who were expecting defeat, were ecstatic at the result.

The following year was totally different. Kilkenny were fancied to beat Tipperary in the final. Fan thought that Kilkenny were in with a chance at half time, but the loss of Martin Coogan through injury had an unsettling effect on the backs and after the first goal, the rot set in. Tipperary won by 5–13 to 2–8. Fan accepted responsibility for one goal but claimed that he was blamed for three, and after the game the hatchets were out and he was dropped from the panel. 'In those days you were never told, you just read on the paper that you were not on the team, and you had to accept that. That Tipperary team was a super team, but they were not 14 points better than us. We played them two weeks later in Birr and they beat us by four points. That was a fairer margin.' Fan said that the selectors should have taken some of the blame too. 'They picked Seamie Cleere at right half-forward for that game, and Seamie had been the previous year's 'Hurler of the Year' at right half back. It just did not make sense,' he concluded.

Fan was naturally very disappointed to have been dropped, but was very determined to get his place back. However, he was now taking on new responsibilities. He married a city girl, Eileen Hogan, in 1964 at the age of 23 and during the remainder of the 1960s, like any young couple, they had to contend with the financial pressures of making a home and raising a family. Fan qualified as a plasterer and was working long hours in the building industry. Other than a period of ten years, when he was employed with the Kilkenny Corporation, he worked in the private sector with various builders in the trade. They have six children, Ann, John, Padraig, Eileen, Philip and Eamonn.

He rejoined James Stephens in 1968. In that year, they were defeated by Freshford in the semi-final. In 1969, Kilkenny won the All-Ireland final and there was no Village man even on the panel. To some extent, that must have inspired them to greater things for the 1969 county championship which was completed after the All-Ireland. James Stephens had beaten Castlecomer in the first round. They beat Kilmacow then to qualify to play Bennettsbridge in the semi-final. Bennettsbridge was the outstanding club in Kilkenny at the time and it took three marvellous matches to decide a winner. In the first game, the Village were losing by eight points early in the second half and made a great comeback to draw level. In fact they went ahead by one point, but Seamie Cleere soloed up the field to snatch an equalising point on the call of time. For that revival, Fan was moved out to centre-back to mark Jim Treacy who was surprisingly placed at centre-forward and was causing havoc. Fan succeeded in cutting off the supply of ball to the 'Bridge full-forward line and was able to deliver good balls to the forwards where Georgie Leahy and his colleagues got the vital scores.

In the replay, the city club had to come from behind to draw level, but they emerged victorious in the third game and went on to beat Johnstown in the county final by 8–5 to 2–7. The three games with the 'Bridge had stood them in good stead.

This was the start of a glorious and proud chapter for the James Stephens GAA Club. They revitalised the Kilkenny senior championship and people came from all over the country to see the great tussles they had with Bennettsbridge, The Fenians (Johnstown), the Rower-Inistioge and the Shamrocks (Ballyhale). They won four county finals in all, 1969, 1975, 1976, and 1981. On top of that, they were the first Leinster club to win the AIB All-Ireland club championship in 1975–1976 when they defeated Blackrock by 2–10 to 2–4. They won their second All-Ireland in 1981–1982 beating Mount Sion by 3–13 to 3–8, but it was the game against Blackrock that really captured the public imagination.

Placing Fan Larkin at full back to mark the 6'3" Ray Cummins seemed a mis-match to say the least. Ray was at his peak at that time and was consistently beating much bigger opponents with devastating effect. But Fan was an astute player who studied the game deeply and studied his opponents even more so. He had played on Ray in a League match that year when Nicky Orr was injured. He had also played on him in a number of challenge matches that the 'Stephens had with Blackrock over the years. 'Cummins usually took me to the cleaners in those games,' declared Fan. 'Most forwards you played from the front, but Ray Cummins, no. Even when Ray played on big full backs like Pat Hartigan, he stayed behind him and as Pat went out to catch, the Cork man was able to jump higher than him from behind and sweep the ball and he then had a clear run for the goal. I knew that, even though I was conceding almost a foot in height, I had to stay between him and the goal at all times. My strategy was to get my hurl in front of the dropping ball and keep it out of his hand. Once I succeeded in getting the ball to the ground, as a small man I now had the advantage.'

James Stephens played against the wind in the first half and Blackrock's Eamonn O'Donoghue had the ball in the net within a minute. They followed up with a goal from a penalty by Pat Moylan and were 2–1 to 0–0 ahead after 15, but after a few positional changes, the Village clicked into gear and the Cork team only scored two more points by half time to the 'Stephens 0–3. On the resumption, they began to whittle down the lead and in the ninth minute of the second half, Chunky O'Brien scored a goal from a penalty to put them ahead for the first time, but it took a great goal from Mick Leahy to put daylight between the two teams and they held out to the end.

Fan Larkin was the proud captain who received the cup, and most of the newspaper photographs the following day showed the happy picture, but also some of the more imaginative photographers captured some great shots of the 6'3" Cummins standing 'dwarfing' the 5'4" Larkin. Apart from writing their own proud history during that period, the James Stephens Club contributed many outstanding players to the senior county team, Fan Larkin, Chunky O'Brien, Mick Crotty, Eamonn Morrissey, Joe Hennessey, Ned Byrne, Brian Cody and Tom and Dinny McCormack. It is no coincidence that this period coincided with another glorious period for the Kilkenny senior team.

As county champions in 1969, James Stephens had the honour appointing a captain of the Kilkenny team and of picking the selectors for the 1970 season. Fan had earned his place back on the team following his outstanding games for his club, and was nominated to lead Kilkenny in the 1970 Championship to defend their All-Ireland crown. It was not to be, however, as Kilkenny were beaten by Wexford in the Leinster final by five points in the first 80-minute game. Fan was now firmly re-established on the Kilkenny team, but 1971 turned out to be another disappointing year although Kilkenny won the Leinster final.

Larkin received a bad injury in the All-Ireland final against Tipperary and had to leave the field and watch the Premier County score a narrow victory by three points. 'We were unlucky that year. A few incidents in the second half turned the game for the Tipperary men,' he recalled. 1972 was one on the best finals ever when Kilkenny made a great comeback to defeat Cork. It seemed that Fan would never finish an All-Ireland final when he had to retire in that game with an injured knee to be replaced by Martin Coogan. 'I tore ligaments in my knee three weeks before the game and could do no training beforehand,' he said glumly. 'I went over to Nowlan Park one evening the week before the game to try it out and it held up, and I was selected. Dr Cuddihy strapped it up before the game (which is why Fan did not appear in the official team photograph) and I had no problems in the first half. During half time, I sat down and the bandage began to cut above my knee and I attempted to loosen it myself, but I could not get it tight enough to support the knee properly. The ligaments tore again in the second half and I had to come off. However it was great to have played a part in such a great match and to collect my second All-Ireland medal.'

Like Noel Skehan in another chapter in this book, Fan regarded the 1973 display of that Kilkenny team in the Leinster final as the best performance he ever saw. History shows that Kilkenny lost four players through injury and the emigration of Eamonn Morrissey for the All-Ireland final. They were defeated by a great Limerick team. Kilkenny went on to win two-in-a-row by getting revenge on Limerick in 1974 and beating Galway in 1975. Fan Larkin gave outstanding displays in all of those championship matches in the early 1970s. He was the cog in the wheel of the solid full-back lines that had Pa Dillon at full back in 1971–1972 and Nicky Orr for the 1973 to 1975 campaigns. Jim Treacy was in the left corner up to 1974 (other than when injured for the1973 final) and Brian Cody took over in 1975.

In 1975, Galway made their amazing breakthrough by beating a star-studded Cork team in the semi-final. Despite this, Kilkenny were 'hot' favourites to take the title. Kilkenny had appeared in every All-Ireland since 1971, and the exasperated newspaper reporters had all the 'quotes' they could get from that seasoned team. Consequently, they almost camped in the Galway training ground and did story after story on the Galway build-up to the game. This gave a huge imbalance to the pre-match reporting, so the experienced Paddy Downey felt that he should go to Kilkenny to try to get a new angle for *The Irish Times*. At Nowlan Park he could get nothing, but he decided to go down to Langtons after the game to join the players for their meal. He saw Fan Larkin eating his steak and thought that he might approach him for a comment. Paddy realised that Fan was now 34 years of age and slowing down and that he would be marking young Padraig Fahy who had given the Cork defence the 'run around' by turning up all over the field. It was probably the forerunner of the 'third man midfield' tactic that Galway developed later.

'How are you going to cope with Fahy when he goes out to the middle of the field?' Downey quizzed. Without breaking his stride with the steak, Fan retorted, 'he can run wherever the hell he likes, Paddy, as long as he hasn't the ball!' Padraig did run in the match, but it was Fan who was doing the cleaning up and had a star game.

Fan continued on to 1979 during which time he collected four All-Star Awards. Fan Larkin collected his last All-Ireland medal in 1979 against a much better Galway side. I was joint coach with Pat Henderson for that season and it could have been awkward to have to tell a former hurling colleague how you wanted the game played. But Fan was most receptive at all times and I knew that I could rely on him to be a leader on the field when contact from the sideline was impossible. He was the steadying influence on the then relatively inexperienced Paddy Prendergast and John Henderson who made up the full-back line. I remember that, at a crucial stage of the game, John Connolly took a penalty, which was marvellously saved by Noel Skehan. Fan was there like a shot from a gun to 'double' on the ball, as it dropped from Skehan's hurl to clear it out 40 yards to the sideline and out of danger.

When the final whistle went, Fan went immediately to the dressing room and did not join the players on the stand for the presentation of the cup. The television cameras were already set up in the Kilkenny dressing room to capture the match aftermath and celebration of the players. A surprised Mick Dunne saw Fan arrive early and he posed the question to him on camera. 'Why are you in so early, Fan?' 'I have to go to Mass, Mick,' replied Larkin with a wry smile. That quote was good enough to make the six o'clock news, and was repeated many times after. I asked Fan what really happened. 'I never went up to the Hogan Stand after any All-Ireland,' he replied. I went up in 1963 and nearly got killed with lads beating me on the back. I never went up after. I always went to Mass on Sunday evenings anyhow, and on All-Ireland day I certainly was never up in time to get Mass and meet the train as well. So I had a routine of going to Mass on the evening of the All-Ireland.'

Fan was captain of the Kilkenny team again in 1976 and he was there to accept the National League Cup after beating Clare in a replay. 'Although I was delighted to win my one and only National League medal, it probably cost us the All-Ireland,' he suggested. 'We had a replay with Cork in the semi-final and we should have beaten Clare the first day. We had to play them again on our return from an exhausting American trip and then turn immediately into the Championship. Because of all the draws, the local championships were behind and the county board decided to play the first round of the Championship the Sunday before the Leinster final. We played the Fenians that day in a gruelling match and between us we had eleven of the Kilkenny panel in action,' he continued. 'We were all "burned out" by the following Sunday and were heavily defeated by Wexford,' he concluded.

In January 1960, Paddy Grace brought Fan and minor star Joe Ayres to play in a trial for the Leinster team. Kilkenny were due to play the rest of Leinster. The Kilkenny secretary knew that some of his more established players would probably not turn up at that early stage of the year. He always took some reserves and Fan knew that he had no chance of making the team, but was delighted to have the opportunity to meet and mix with some of the Wexford, Dublin and Kilkenny stars of the day. 'I also got a feed and a new hurl, and what more would a young fellow want at 18 years of age,' he said smiling. Twelve years later, in 1972, he was a certainty for the team, and Pa Dillon, Jim Treacy and himself made up the full-back line that defeated Munster to retain the title and continue a marvellous running sequence of five-in-a-row wins over the Munster men. He won six medals in all and had the honour of being captain of the side in 1979. 'We should have won in 1976 too,' he said, 'but we went down by a single point to Munster. I was invited to Thurles some time ago to the Munster celebration of that victory and I was presented with a framed photograph of the Munster team,' he went on, 'but I couldn't bring myself to hang the picture up, but the frame is very good,' he said with a twinkle in his eye!

Fan considers that the All-Star trips to the west coast of America in the 1970s were the best things that happened for GAA players. 'Kilkenny, Kerry and Dublin teams were very lucky that they were prominent in those years to qualify for these trips, either as All-Stars or members of the All-Ireland winning teams,' he stated. 'Those trips were brilliant and we made long lasting friendships with players from other counties as well as our own, but also with American families. We were treated so well over there, by our hosts the Hamiltons, the Oettingers and the Whelans, and they still keep in contact and call to Kilkenny frequently.'

Fan had great praise for Georgie Leahy who put all his time into coaching teams in this county and further afield. He did a great job on the James Stephens team and had a great way for handling players. 'He would "dress you down" but when that was over, he never held a grudge. He regards Fr Maher as undoubtedly the greatest hurling coach of the millennium. 'He revolutionised coaching and won seven All-Ireland titles for Kilkenny in the process,' he said with conviction. 'He was a shrewd hurling man. He never went up and down the line shouting and roaring, but stood in the middle 'eyeing' the game. He told you privately what you were doing right or wrong. His coaching methods are still being used today,' he said with admiration.

From his own era, he named Chunky O'Brien as his favourite player. 'Chunky was a natural. As a young player, he was naturally fit and fast and needed very little training. He was a great hurler with amazing ball control. You could give Chunky the handle of a hatchet and he could hurl with it,' he said with a smile. 'It's a pity, though, that he was not more dedicated to training in his late twenties. He retired at 30, but could have gone on for many more years and collected medals in 1982 and 1983 with a bit more dedication.'

Larkin believes that the hurling played today is as good as was ever played. 'The present players are every bit as good as those of the past, but there is far more pressure on them. They're under far more scrutiny nowadays in their private lives as well as on the field. The television cameras are picking up every move on the field and replaying it. If they were there in our time, we'd all be in jail.' he laughed.

Fan believes that the players should always be well looked after. He feels that the present players give wonderful enjoyment to many people and should get rewarded. But he considers that they are treated very well in most counties and should have no complaints. He is very unhappy with the direction that the GPA is taking. He believes that hurling is a team game and any financial benefits that are gained from sponsors should be mostly for the team and not exclusively for an elite group.

Larkin is very much against the back-door system. He regards it as being very unfair that a provincial winner might have to meet the beaten finalist again in the All-Ireland final, as has happened three times already. He believes that the time has come to run the provincial championships separately and have a complete open draw for the All-Ireland series.

Fan's son Philly won his first All-Ireland medal in 2000 and became the only hurler whose father and grandfather were also All-Ireland medal winners. I asked Fan if he talked to young Philly about his game, as his father did with him. 'I always talk to him and try to help him in any way I can,' he replied, 'but Philly has been very lucky that he has had Brian Cody to coach him in the primary school and up through the under-age grades. He has already won All-Ireland minor and under-21 medals, and is still under the guidance of Brian with the senior team. My main job is to keep the pressure off him.'

I know Fan Larkin since we played together as minors in 1959. He has a sharp tongue and a quick wit, and I have given up (as most people in Kilkenny have!) of trying to get the last word with him. He has a long memory and still accuses me of hitting him in some match in Nowlan Park a quarter of a century ago, which I have long forgotten about. But we are great friends and we have shared many wonderful team trips abroad together. I have played against him in many great games between The Rower-Inistioge and James Stephens, and he was my direct opponent in a few of those games. When I was moved into corner forward on the county team, I generally had to mark him in training. He was a most difficult opponent, small, but as strong as an ox on the ball, but he was also a super ball player and it was difficult to cover the ball to gain possession. If you delayed a split second, he would have stroked it from under your nose up the field. Inch for inch and pound for pound, he was the best corner back that I have seen or encountered.

Fan Larkin's Team of the Century

Noel Skehan
(Kilkenny)

Paddy Larkin   Nick O'Donnell   John Doyle
(Kilkenny)   *(Wexford)*   *(Tipperary)*

Tommy Doyle   Billy Rackard   Ger Henderson
(Tipperary)   *(Wexford)*   *(Kilkenny)*

Timmy Ryan   Ned Wheeler
(Limerick)   *(Wexford)*

Christy Ring   Mick Mackey   Jimmy Doyle
(Cork)   *(Limerick)*   *(Tipperary)*

Jimmy Smith   Billy O'Dwyer   Eddie Keher
(Clare)   *(Kilkenny)*   *(Kilkenny)*

Leinster Team Of The Century

Noel Skehan
(Kilkenny)

Paddy Larkin   Nick O'Donnell   Peter Blanchfield
(Kilkenny)   *(Wexford)*   *(Kilkenny)*

Seamus Cleere   Billy Rackard   Ger Henderson
(Kilkenny)   *(Wexford)*   *(Kilkenny)*

Chunky O'Brien   Ned Wheeler
(Kilkenny)   *(Wexford)*

Mick Crotty   Pat Delaney   Jim Langton
(Kilkenny)   *(Kilkenny)*   *(Kilkenny)*

Tim Flood   Billy O'Dwyer   Eddie Keher
(Wexford)   *(Kilkenny)*   *(Kilkenny)*

10 – Ger Loughnane

Ger Loughnane celebrates victory.

How will Ger Loughnane be remembered? The image that will remain in our minds is that of a tall upright figure in navy tracksuit bottoms and the familiar white polo shirt prowling the sidelines. We will remember his confident assertion, 'We will win!' after the thrilling first half of Clare's first All-Ireland appearance in 81 years when a forlorn RTE microphone was thrust at him as he went to the dressing room at half time. They did win, and that Clare hurling team went on to become recognised as one of the outstanding teams of the 1990s.

As a player, Loughnane was one of the most brilliant half-backs in the country on a Clare team that won back-to-back League titles in 1977 and 1978 – a Clare team that many would contend was better than the All-Ireland-winning team of 1995 and 1997. They were good enough to win at least one All-Ireland title in those years, but with no disrespect to the management at that time, they did not have a Ger Loughnane to manage them. In those years Ger was a thoughtful, resourceful player who was an excellent reader of the game. He was strong and competitive and had an abundance of skills but would be the first to admit that he did not have the management skills then either that would have steered the two times League champions through a Championship campaign. But Ger is a good learner, a good observer, and what is more a good teacher. He has learned a lot from his experiences, but he knows that it takes time to put together a successful formula, and that you must also get the opportunity and the right players to put your plan into action. He knew what was required, and he did it. Yet Loughnane's own outstanding hurling abilities will be overshadowed in GAA history by his marvellous achievement of bringing Clare from the bottom to the very top of the hurling ladder.

I met Ger for the interview for this chapter a month before Clare were to meet the winners of Tipperary and Waterford in their first match of the 2000 Championship. In the space of two hours I got a great insight into what made the Feakle man so successful as a hurling manager.

We met at his office in St Aidan's Primary School in Shannon Town where he has been principal since 1982. I had encountered him briefly on a few occasions when our hurling paths crossed in the 1970s, but I really only knew his image from the media. As another schoolday finished, we moved on to his attractive home a short distance from the school. His wife, Mary (née Minogue) is also a native of Feakle, from a family of seven – none of whom had any interest in hurling until Ger came on the scene! Their two boys, Barry (17) and Conor (14) acted as 'water boys' for the Clare team and were the envy of their pals because they knew all the players and experienced the atmosphere of the big games in the dressing room and on the sideline! Barry made the county minor panel, while Conor is playing under-14 hurling. Ger is not unhappy that they won't let their father see them play, as he does not want to put any pressure on them!

While we talked, the Feakle man dealt with the many phone calls in a business-like manner. Some were personal, others business, and one or two were from members of the team. I gathered that the players had a problem attending training that evening. Ger was very sympathetic to their plight but I had the impression that they were still expected to attend, at some time – and I bet that they did. He would move back and forwards from the interview to the phone calls and other interruptions with ease and it is clear that he has the ability to keep many balls in the air at the same time, a quality that has served him well as a hurling manager.

Ger Loughnane was born in Feakle, a small parish between Tulla and Scarriff in 1953. The late John James Loughnane and his wife, Veronica raised four girls and three boys on their east Clare farm. John James did not play hurling, but was an outstanding athlete and won four All-Ireland cross-country championships with Feakle in the 1940s. Life on a busy farm did not leave much time for hurling, but he had a passionate interest in the game and was very supportive when his sons started to play. He loved to see the three boys practising in the yard against the big wall of an outhouse. The wall was painted each year, but in no time it was full of the marks of a sponge ball as the young Loughnanes vied to strike the ball into an opening over the door. Of Ger's two brothers, Michael lost interest in the game after a while and took to hunting. Sean, also a teacher, played minor hurling for Clare before emigrating to Australia.

One of Loughnane's earliest memories is of going to a neighbour's house to listen to a Munster or All-Ireland final. Neighbours would gather to listen to Micheál Ó Hehir's broadcasts, and the atmosphere was magical. These were the years of the great Tipperary team of the late 1950s and early 1960s. The big names were Donie Nealon, Theo English, Liam Devaney and Jimmy Doyle.

'There was nothing like the radio in those days, it got you to use your imagination more. You visualised the game better. Television hasn't really the same impact. Micheál Ó Hehir must have been responsible for getting so many young lads all over the country to play hurling' Loughnane stated with conviction. 'After every broadcast, we always had a massive battle in our own Croke Park or Thurles living out the match.'

The Feakle National School had only a small pebble yard, but shortly after Ger started there, a new school was built beside the parish hurling field. They hurled there in the morning, at lunch time and in the evening. The principal was Sean Harrington, who was a great Clare and Munster hurler, but was then coming up to retirement and although most supportive, did not have the energy to train them. They were fortunate that local man, James Moloney had just returned from England and he took a huge interest in the team. Like most school teams in those days, transport to matches was a problem, but that was solved by Dan Joe Moroney who had a lorry. The brave Dan Joe would load them all into his lorry to go to the matches. Ger still remembers vividly the thrill of getting into the lorry on a summer's evening to go to play a match, and coming back as night fell with all the lads having great fun. As a parish with a small population, they would have players as young as eight years old to make up a team, and they were invariably well beaten by the teams from the towns. He remembers been beaten by 14–6 to 2–2 by Ennis in his first ever match. Although he was very young at the time, he was playing at centre-field and was marking a huge 14-year-old, twice his size. He still remembers the impact of their first clash on a ball! 'He nearly murdered me,' laughed Ger!

When he entered St Flannan's College in Ennis, he was very lucky that the present Bishop, Willie Walsh and Fr Seamus Gardiner had taken a decision to bring up the standard of hurling in the college by concentrating on the first years. 'That was the biggest break I got in hurling', Ger enthused. 'The two priests gave a huge amount of time to the players, and were very patient with their charges. They complemented one another in styles, and devoted most of the time to skill training. They won the Munster under-15 competition, and succeeded in bringing them up to Harty Cup standards.'

The biggest occasion Ger remembers was when they met Ennis CBS in a Harty Cup semi-final in Tulla. Ennis had beaten Flannan's in a Harty Cup final in the early 1960s, and this was the first time since then that they had met. A legend had built up about that game and huge crowds travelled to Tulla for the showdown. Flannan's won and went on to be well beaten by St Finbarr's, Farranferris in the final. Ger played at centre-back that day, but they were no match for the Cork side who were well-tutored by Fr Michael O'Brien for this

13-a-side competition. Colm Honan and Johnny Callinan were on that St Flannan's team.

Ger did his teacher training in St Patrick's College, Drumcondra. They had a fine hurling team that included Brian Cody of Kilkenny and Pat Kearney who had been captain of a winning Kilkenny All-Ireland minor team. They won the Dublin under-21 championship easily and the Dublin Advanced Colleges competition. Loughnane regretted that they were not allowed to play in the Fitzgibbon Cup, as he felt that they would have had a good chance with the team they had in those years.

His first job was in a school in Chapelizod in Dublin. He spent a year there but had tremendous difficulties travelling up and down to Clare for training. Fr Harry Bohan, who was manager of the Clare team at that time, arranged a job for him in Shannon. The interview consisted of a brief meeting with the local PP after Mass, after which he was told that he would start the following Monday! 'That wouldn't work now', laughed Ger, but he was delighted to get back to his native sod, working under principal, Sean Cleary, who I had played against in those great League clashes with Clare in the 1960s. That was in 1974, and he was appointed to his present position in the same town in 1982.

Because of their small population, Feakle struggled at under-age level, but they had a great win over St Joseph's in the minor 'B' Championship in 1969. In 1974, with that famous Clare goalkeeper, Seamus Durack playing outfield, they won the intermediate title. Newmarket were so strong at senior level that most clubs opted for intermediate status which made that grade very competitive. Feakle had been unable to field a team at all in the late 1960s and early 1970s and it was a great boost for the club to win the final in 1974 when they beat neighbours, Broadford in a game that created a huge interest due to the local rivalry. They were promoted to senior level and have retained that status to this day.

In the 1980s, Ted Harrington, son of Ger's primary school teacher had great success with the under-21s who won four-in-a-row county championships. That team was the backbone of the team that won the Croke Cup (League) twice and contested the senior county championship final twice in-a-row.

In the twilight of his hurling career, Ger was coaxed back to the club in 1988 to have a go at the county title. He had thrown in his lot with Wolfe Tones of Shannon where he lived and worked, but Tony Hayes approached him to come back, and he answered the call. 'Tony was a marvellous trainer and a great manager of people', said Ger. 'He got all the players on side, and his training consisted solely of ball work, and he made it very interesting for the players. 'There was a full turn-out at training every evening, and I gave him a commitment for one year, but that turned into two, and we were successful in the second year'. 1989 was a great year for the parish in that it was their first title for 45 years. Like Clare's breakthrough in 1995, there was great support for the team from outside the parish as well as within. They had a tough battle against Eire Óg, Ennis in the semi-final, only barely scraping through, but the won the final well against Ruane. The celebrations in the parish were amazing, and they had a great reunion of that team in 1999, and the spirit of that famous victory still lives on.

Ger still has the little card he got from the county secretary in 1971 telling him 'a Chara, you have been selected to play for the county minor team against Cork...' He remembers that he was standing at the back gate when the postman arrived with the card. He could hardly believe that he would be wearing the Clare jersey for the first time. A Jimmy-Barry-Murphy-inspired Cork team beat them well that day, but his disappointment faded when he found that the minor team were seated right on the sideline for that famous senior clash between Tipperary and Limerick. That was the day of the Donie Nealon/Babs Keating 'dry ball' incident. It was such a thrill to be so near to the action, and Ger will never forget the display of Mick Roche that day. Mick was Ger's boyhood hero. 'Mick always seemed to be playing at his ease when everyone else was flailing around', he said. 'The Tipperary man would just glide out of the ruck with the ball and send a lovely long clearance down the field.'

He does not have a card informing him of his first selection on the senior team. 'I think that they had graduated to the telephone by then,' he said with a laugh. His first match was against Tipperary in the 1972–1973 League, and he was marking Jack Ryan on the day. When he arrived at the ground, he was apprehensive about going into the dressing room with people like Gus Lohan, Jimmy Cullinane and Vincent Loftus who were his heroes. His first reaction was to get a seat quickly and sit down unnoticed, but when he looked beside him, he was sitting beside Gus Lohan. Gus was very helpful, and gave him great encouragement. 'Some older players feel threatened when younger players arrive,' Ger said, 'but not Gus, the success of the Clare team was his priority.'

Ger remembers the drawn game with Kilkenny in the 1975–1976 League final. Kilkenny went to America, and played the replay on their return. Kilkenny won by 6–14 to 1–14. 'Pat Delaney went to town that day, scoring three great goals', Ger recalled. I have good reason to remember that day too, as it was one of the few occasions that I had to leave the field injured, after an altercation with Martin McKeogh. I remember that Ger was the first man over to me with the consoling words, 'Jesus, Keher, there's nothing wrong with you', as the blood flowed down my neck. Martin was extremely apologetic and wrote to me afterwards.

'I learned one great lesson in that game,' said Ger. 'I was marking Billy Fitzpatrick that day, and at one stage the ball was in the far corner with Mick Brennan. Billy took off down the wing. I remember saying to myself 'I'll let him off, I'll chance it.' Billy caught the ball coming across the square and stuck it in the net! The lesson stays firmly in my mind to this day. You can never take a chance against a good team. One moment of laziness can be the losing of a match.'

The following year, that Clare team began to make progress, and they met Kilkenny again in the League final. This time the tables were turned and the Bannermen emerged victorious on a scoreline of 2–8 to 0–9. Ger recalls that the winning of the League final that year was as big for them as winning a Munster final. There were huge celebrations around the county, but that led to huge expectations from the supporters for that team to win a Championship. They played well in the first two rounds of the Munster Championship and went on to meet All-Ireland champions, Cork in the Munster final. They were doing well in that game until full-back, Jim Power was sent off. Their pattern of play was disrupted from then on, but they were only beaten by five points, 4–15 to 4–10 in the end. Cork went on to win the All-Ireland.

In 1978, they went on to record the double by beating Kilkenny by 3–10 to 1–10 in the League final. 'That year we were more focused for the Championship,' recalled Ger. 'A time comes when you have to win. The time came that year, but we just did not make it. Clare totally underperformed in the Munster final against Cork, and went down 0–13 to 0–11. Four of Cork's points came from the stick of John Horgan who was playing at corner-back. If we had won that day, we could have gone on to great things, but it was not to be.'

Ironically, that was Ger's best performance ever in the Clare jersey. He seemed to be everywhere that day, breaking up every Cork attack and firing ball after ball down to his forwards. Cork tried several players on him, but even the great Gerald McCarthy and Pat Moylan could make no impact. It was not surprising that Cork had to rely on the long-striking John Horgan to save them, though Tom Cashman was also very instrumental in Cork's victory by controlling the game from mid-field. Cork went on to win their third All-Ireland in-a-row, and that was effectively the end of that Clare side.

Ger played his last game for Clare in the 1987 Munster Championship against Tipperary. The Premier County, under the management of Babs Keating was emerging from a lean period and were gaining in confidence with each hour of hurling. Ger was now playing at corner-back and was assigned to mark Pat Fox. He was reasonably satisfied with his performance and held the Annacarty wizard to two points. But he recalls that he was satisfied to stick closely to his man for the hour and content to merely hold his own. 'A sure sign of a man on the way out,' laughed Ger!

Ger Loughnane, in his last game in the Clare jersey, clears under pressure from Tipperary's Donie O'Connell in the replay between the two teams in the Munster Championship, 1987.

Ger played for five years on the Munster team before winning a Railway Cup medal. Leinster had a great run in the early 1970s, and Munster were also beaten by Connacht before Loughnane won his first of three Railway Cup titles. He enjoyed very much playing with players from other counties and felt that playing for his province on St Patrick's Day was of special significance. 'Donie Nealon was a great manager of the Munster team and got the players to gel together', said Ger. He believed in the competition and treated the Munster team with the same interest as he would Tipperary or his own club.'

Ger Loughnane never attended an official coaching course, but sort of 'drifted' into it. As an inter-county hurler, it was natural that he would take his class team and he went on to take various school teams who became very successful. His involvement deepened and he often found himself taking an under-14 team after school, a club team at six o'clock and going on from that to train himself with the Clare team!

He got great pleasure from the team he coached to win the All-Ireland Féile competition. 'But apart from the success, it was the way they played that gave me the greatest pleasure', said Ger proudly. 'They were totally disciplined, no wildness about them and they played the ball intelligently to one another. People came from miles away to see them in action. The strange thing was that none of them made outstanding players afterwards, but when they came together they were something special.'

'I learned two very important lessons from my involvement with that team', he went on. 'First of all, a player does not have to have exceptional ability to play an important role in a successful team if you can get them to gel together. Secondly, it is so important to concentrate on ball work to improve skill and speed of striking left and right. I realised that slowness of thought, and of striking and moving of the ball was where Clare hurling teams fell down when it came to the Championship. They got away with it in the League, but on the fast sod, they were blown away. When I took over the Clare hurling team the most important part of my strategy was to correct those faults with my training methods', he declared.

His first involvement with a Clare team was with the county minor team with Fr Seamus Gardiner. They were hammered by Limerick in the first round and that was the end of that.

He was appointed manager of the under-21 team in 1991, and in 1992 they found themselves in the Munster final against Waterford. Anthony Daly and Brian Lohan were the backbone of the Clare fifteen. 'That was a marvellous Waterford team containing players such as Tony Browne, Fergal Hartley, Johnny Brenner and Paul Flynn', Ger recalled. 'It was a fantastic final with superb hurling from both teams'. Waterford emerged victorious, 0–17 to 1–12, and went on to beat Offaly in a replay in the All-Ireland final.

In the same year Loughnane assisted Len Gaynor who was managing the Clare senior team who were also beaten. For the second time in his coaching career Ger got the sack, but this time from two teams in the same year!

Ger was not involved at all in 1993, but following Clare's big defeat by Tipperary in the Munster final, Len Gaynor asked him to come back to assist with the team. Loughnane considered the offer for some time and eventually told Gaynor that he would accept on condition that he would be appointed manager when Len's term was up. He told Len to put the proposition to the county board believing that they would not accept it. But to his surprise, Chairman, Brendan Vaughan steered it through and he was appointed a selector. Ger also assisted with coaching. Their target was to avenge the previous year's defeat by Tipperary which they achieved in the first round. However Clare then lost impetus and went down to Limerick in the Munster final. Len retired and Ger took over.

When Loughnane took over the team, he felt that he would have to make sweeping changes. He let go many of the players from the previous years and kept only those who he felt had the right mental attitude to win important matches. From his previous experience he felt that was the most important attribute. Skill levels could be improved upon, but attitude can't be taught, he believed. He had seen a lot of players in club games and had coached some of them at under-21 level, so he brought in a group of young players like Colin Lynch and Conor Clancy who he felt could do the job.

He asked physical trainer, Mike McNamara to put them through an intensive winter training programme, stories of which stunned the hurling world. 'Many of those stories were greatly exaggerated', said Ger. 'Those sessions were severe, but no different than gaelic footballers had gone through for years. We had to build them up physically to be ready for the physical confrontation that would be the Munster Championship. We had to increase their speed to enable them to keep up an unrelenting pace for the entire game in every game.'

'We went on fine during the winter games and arrived at the League final but Kilkenny hammered us, which was an awful set back to our plans. They looked unbeatable with DJ Carey, Adrian Ronan and Denis Byrne in devastating form. But Kilkenny were beaten in Leinster which shows how deceiving the League can be'. He remembers the late Ollie Walsh coming to the dressing room and giving the Clare team great encouragement, but in talking to him and to Cyril Farrell later on in the hotel, Loughnane felt that they did not give them much chance in Munster.

In analysing that performance, Ger realised that Clare were still 'off the pace' with the speed of their hurling. They had five weeks to go to the first round of the Championship. In training, Loughnane concentrated on increasing the speed of their striking and of moving the ball. It was a painstaking work, as players who were weak on one side or who had poor ground hurling skills had to get up to standard.

Ger felt that they were lucky to get over Cork in the first round. 'We did get a few lucky breaks, and the game could have gone either way. Nevertheless, beating Cork was a milestone, and it did our confidence the world of good.' Limerick had recovered from the devastating defeat by Offaly in the All-Ireland of 1994, and disposed of Tipperary in the first round. They were firm favourites to beat Clare in the final but the intensive training programme that Clare had undertaken took effect that day and they ran Limerick ragged on a scoreline of 1–17 to 0–11.

'Once the breakthrough was made, all the obstacles fell down', declared Ger. 'We thought that we would have a job to focus their minds on a semi-final with all the hype that surrounded Clare's first Munster final win since 1932. The supporters were ecstatic and they all wanted part of the team. We arranged our next training session for the following Friday, and the team travelled the county visiting every parish. Everywhere they went, celebrations were in full swing. The players were pulled and dragged here there and everywhere, and by the end of the week they were totally fed-up and couldn't wait to get back to training! 'Playing neighbours, Galway, in the semi-final was a good thing, because there was no problem in motivating the players for the game. I was a little concerned that Galway were well used to playing in Croke Park, while it was merely a dream for all of our lads. However, they took to it like ducks to water and turned in their best display of that year.

'This was a game that I could watch again and again,' said Ger proudly. 'The pace was tremendous, and we held it for the entire game. Jamesie O'Connor got some marvellous points that day. Galway did come back at us for a while, but we pulled away again to win comfortably by 3–12 to 1–13. It was a wonderful feeling after the game to realise that we were going to play in an All-Ireland final.'

Loughnane was very much aware of the skill and teamwork that was inherent in that great Offaly team they were to meet in the final. 'We had to devise a strategy to counteract that. Our policy was to close them down all over the field,' he told me. 'We had to keep them under constant pressure. We had to keep squeezing them so that their brilliant teamwork could not be allowed to function. That was our only chance of disabling their machine.'

I asked him how confident he was when he told the RTE reporter at half time that they were going to win.

'I was totally confident', he said, 'although [goalkeeper] Davy [Fitzgerald] had made an uncharacteristic mistake for Offaly's goal, I saw that Offaly were not playing with their usual fluency and were a bit disjointed by our tactics. I knew that if we could hold our heads, we would win. After Taaffe's goal, I knew that we were on our way. And when Daly stood up to take the "65", that was it.'

I asked him about the strange decision of taking Taaffe off after he scored the goal. 'You know the funny thing about that', Ger replied with a laugh, 'from where I stood, I thought that it was Fergal Hegarty that scored it at the time! Eamonn had been suffering from a hamstring injury during the week, but made a good improvement in the final night's training. We decided that if we needed a goal, we would chance him. We did, but very soon we noticed that he was struggling and couldn't chase. In fact he had to pull up when chasing Kevin Martin who went on to score a vital point. We decided to replace him again, but while we were writing down his replacement's name, he flashed in the goal!'

Loughnane's special moments from that day were going out on the field and feeling the atmosphere as the Clare supporters roared their hearts out, the final whistle, and the crowds of supporters running on to the field with a look of amazement, almost disbelief on their faces. Claremen and women standing around the pitch for hours taking away souvenirs of grass from the hallowed sod! Yes indeed, it was an occasion to be savoured!

The defeat of Clare by Limerick in the first round of the 1996 Championship came as a surprise to most people, not least the management team. Many thought that the 1995 celebrations carried on too long and affected the players. People thought that the defeat, particularly in the way it happened, would finish that Clare team. Loughnane, however, felt that, in many ways, it was a good thing. It gave them a much-needed break so that they could come out fresher the following year. It also gave them time to revise their strategy. In a relatively short space of time they had experienced the highest high and a crushing low. They must learn from defeat. They must also learn to deal with the 'favourites' tag. As Clare entered the 1997 Championship, they were reasonably confident that they could be a force again. They knew that they had the winning formula, they just had to continue to speed up the way they played.

As they travelled to Cork to play Tipperary in the Munster final, Ger and his team knew that they would have to win to be finally recognised as a hurling force. Clare supporters came to Leeside in their thousands. Pairc Uí Chaoimh was an ideal venue for such a super-charged occasion. The electric atmosphere was recharged again and again by a super display by both teams. Clare were on top in the first half, but Tipperary came back strongly in the second. If John Leahy had not missed that open goal, anything could have happened, but Clare held on to win 1–18 to 0–18. Loughnane felt a great sense of achievement in beating the Premier County in a Munster final. But it was to get better. Clare easily defeated Kilkenny in the All-Ireland semi-final. Though the black and amber came back at them in the last quarter, Loughnane still felt that Clare were the better team on the day.

Tipperary had all the aces going into that 1997 All-Ireland final, Ger felt. Clare had narrowly beaten them in Munster but they came through the back door by beating Wexford in the semi-final. They had the psychological advantage after the pain of defeat in the Munster final, and were highly motivated. 'We had a big job to do to get that monkey off our backs.'

'The pressure showed in the early stages of the game', Loughnane recalled. 'We were uncharacteristically slow to start, and were very jittery in our play. But just before half time we started to hurl in our usual style. We were only four points down when the whistle blew for the break. I told them at half-time that four points was nothing, considering the way they had played for 25 minutes. I said that if they continued as they left off, they would win well. Clare did dominate the second half and went well ahead. But Tipperary got two goals against the run of play and nearly pipped us. I remember particularly Davy Fitz's save from Leahy, and Jamesie's final point from a brilliant flick on by Colin Lynch.'

Clare had won their second All-Ireland title under Ger Loughnane.

The legend of Anthony Daly's 'whipping boys' speech after receiving the Munster trophy grew with time. Just like Babs' equally famous 'donkeys and derbys' quote some years earlier, it kept on growing. Even the Clare supporters were embarrassed, and one of them called to Daly in his sports shop in Ennis and said, 'You shouldn't have said it!' 'What did I say', said Anthony? 'I don't know' was the reply, 'but you shouldn't have said it anyway!' The media and particularly the *Clare Champion* devoted pages to the story, and the letter page was crammed with comment. The Clare captain approached Loughnane and told him that this had gone too far and could he do anything to stop it. Ger decided to write a letter himself to the *Clare Champion*. Of course, that added fuel to the fire. The whole controversy was compounded when Ger was asked in an interview by Jim O'Sullivan, a most honourable reporter with *The Examiner,* for an opinion on the other semi-final between Wexford and Tipperary. Ger stated that he thought that Tipperary would win. Jim responded by asking if he thought that Wexford would be tough enough for Tipperary. To which Ger replied 'The biggest mistake anyone could make when playing Tipperary was that rough-house tactics would win against them!'

A sub-editor of *The Examiner* got hold of the quote and ran a headline 'Loughnane accuses Tipperary of rough-house tactics!' 'That totally twisted the meaning of my comment', said Ger. *The Examiner* subsequently issued an apology, but the damage was done.

With all that in the background to the 1997 final, tension was almost at breaking point. Whatever rivalry had existed before between Clare and Tipperary was increased a hundredfold. However, the match itself was magnificent with the game in the balance to the final whistle.

Ger got great satisfaction from the win, but it was tempered somewhat when he saw the devastation on Len Gaynor's face when he went to offer his sympathy after the game. 'I have great time for Len', he said. 'He was a brilliant manager. He was totally committed, and drove every evening to Ennis when he was training Clare without any financial reward. We were through the good and the bad together. The fact that he was involved with Tipperary took a lot out of the victory for me'.

Ger has a very high regard for Eamon Cregan. He regards him as a great hurling man with a true passion for the game. On *The Sunday Game* television show that night, he felt that the Limerick man was sent in to pick out the negative points of the game. 'I don't know what was wrong with Eamon that night, he must have been in bad form or something', commented Ger. 'Here we were in the hotel with all the Clare supporters getting more agitated as he continued to criticise the game and had nothing good to say about it. Naturally we all thought that it was a super game, and the fury of the supporters grew as the programme went on. Ger Canning could sense my anger and tried to steer me away from making a statement, but as soon as they switched over to our hotel, I opened my remarks by saying "after that ten-minute whinge from Eamon Cregan..." That started the verbal battle over the airwaves which was further great fodder for the print media.'

The controversy continued into 1998. Clare got to the League semi-final and, after a lethargic display against Cork, were beaten 2–15 to 0–10. A rumour went out that Clare had trained for three hours in Templemore on the morning of the game, and a journalist even contacted the sergeant there to find out. 'That was total rubbish', declared Ger. 'The truth was that we were not totally fired up for that game, knowing that we would be meeting Cork in the Championship when we totally overpowered them, and that was our strategy.'

'We were now in the 1998 Munster final against Waterford, but we were certainly not the darlings of the media by then! We had started the tactic of issuing 'dummy' teams to the press, which they certainly did not like,' Loughnane continued.

I asked him how the players felt about that strategy, and he told me that they got used to it very quickly. 'My priority was to win matches' Ger declared. 'I think that I have the right to do what I think is best to achieve that. I felt that it was better to keep all the players on edge right up to the game. They were told to ignore whatever team appeared in the papers and that the real team would be announced to them on the morning of the match. They accepted that, and it worked for us. The players got used to it but the journalists didn't', he concluded with a laugh. Later, when the Clare team went out on the field for the replay of the Munster final wearing the tops of their tracksuits because it was raining, a reporter in the press box was heard to say in frustration, 'What's the bastard up to now!' Ger felt that paranoia had set in!

Clare went in to that first, drawn game not totally fired up. Waterford were trying to make a breakthrough as they had done three years before, and there was an underlying sympathy for them in the Clare camp. However, Ger contended that the Clare team and management were incensed by the behaviour of the Waterford management team on the sideline, and approached the replay in a different frame of mind. 'The players could not wait to get back to play them again,' he recalled. 'I never experienced such a hostile atmosphere before a game. There was a time-bomb waiting to explode, and it did even before the throw-in.' (there were some scuffles between the four midfield players as they awaited the throw-in). When the game settled, Clare totally overpowered the Decies men and ran out easy winners 2–16 to 0–10.

'During the last ten minutes when the issue was in no doubt, Gerald McCarthy and I made our peace, and Gerald was marvelling at the Clare display', he continued. 'The Chairman of the Waterford County Board described the Clare performance as the best he had ever seen.'

But the next day all hell broke loose in the papers and on radio. Brian Lohan had been sent off during the game, but in a subsequent investigation, Colin Lynch was suspended for three months by the Munster Council. Loughnane was not at all happy with the decision or the way it was made, 'but that's all water under the bridge now!' he commented.

Clare had to take on Offaly in the semi-final without the services of two of their key players, Lohan and Lynch. In addition, Loughnane himself was banned from the sideline. When he went out from his seat in the front of the stand to speak to one of the players before the game, he could not believe the reaction from the Clare crowd.

They barely survived the first day by a 'doubtful' free, Ger admits, but they were back to their best for the replay and gave an exhibition of hurling that left them comfortably ahead when the referee blew the full-time whistle with clearly two minutes of normal time to go. While the Offaly team and officials accepted at the reception after the match that Clare had won the game and wished them the best of luck in the final, GAA officials were not thinking the same way. The first inkling that a replay was on the cards was when Marty Morrissey rang Loughnane in the hotel that night to say that RTE had been put on 'standby' for the following Saturday in Thurles! Next morning it became official.

Everything was in Offaly's favour for that third meeting of these two great sides. The tough series of matches that Clare had put behind them had taken its toll. The team was tired, and six days were not sufficient for them to recharge their batteries. Offaly was a fresher team at that stage and they knew that they were close to a place in the All-Ireland final. Ger described Clare's performance in Thurles as the most courageous from his team. 'Offaly played magnificently, and with their skill and teamwork they are very difficult to beat in that sort of form. But our lads dug deep and came back at them in the second half, and it took three unbelievable saves from Stephen Byrne to enable them to hold out,' said Ger proudly.

Offaly won by 0–16 to 0–13.

'If we had won,' continued Ger, 'I don't think that we would have beaten Kilkenny in the final. We wouldn't have been as sharp as them on the big day.'

The 1999 Championship continued in the same vein. Clare drew with Tipperary in the first-round match in Cork. 'We were very lucky to survive that day', recalled Ger. 'Tipperary played marvellous hurling. They owned the ball, exploited every weakness we had, dragged us all over the field and finished every opportunity. They should have beaten us by ten points. Still, they were only three points ahead with minutes to go and we got the penalty, and we survived! But Tipperary had played all their cards in the first game and we had time to plan for the replay.'

Loughnane described the tactical moves that they made for the replay as the most successful in his career to date. 'We played three men in the middle of the field which totally shut them down and put them off their stride. They had hoped to open up our defence, as in the drawn game, but when our plan counteracted that move, they had no time to devise an alternative strategy.' Clare played superbly and ran out easy winners, but at a cost. Ger remembers Nicky English coming into the dressing room afterwards and praising Clare's display. The Tipperary man prophetically wondered what a performance like that so early in the Championship would do for Clare's prospects later on.

'It actually destroyed us,' said Ger. 'We went in to play Cork in the Munster final a tired team. Even at that, we only lost by four points. Cork were much better than us that day. We gave another tired display against Galway in the quarter-finals and were lucky to snatch another draw. But we managed to rekindle the fire for the replay and won comfortably but six hard championship games had taken its toll, and we were unable to get into our stride for the semi-final against Kilkenny,' he continued. 'Kilkenny controlled the game from the half-back line with Pat O'Neill and Peter Barry breaking up every attack. But it took DJ's magnificent goal to finish us in the end,' he concluded.

Ger had a long hard look at the situation and felt that the only way to get back on the winning trail was to add a whole new freshness to the camp, as he did in 1995. 'So we changed the selectors, physical trainer, our captain, our way of training and our way of eating!' Ger said with enthusiasm. 'We brought in some new players and went back to the very hard winter training from January to March. We needed to toughen up both physically and mentally. 'Cusack Park has been re-sodded and is in magnificent condition and we are now hurling there every session at 90 miles an hour trying to bring the speed of their hurling back up to what it was. We hope to be able to keep up the intensity of our play for all our games as we did when we won our two All-Ireland titles. Only time will tell,' he concluded.

When I asked him what was the most difficult decision he had to make as a manager, he replied that he never had any difficulty in that regard once he knew that it was for the good of Clare hurling. However he conceded that changing the captain this year was perhaps the most difficult. 'If you trawled the country in any sport you would not get anyone better than Anthony Daly. He was a natural leader, and telling him that the time was up was the hardest of all,' he said with a hint of nostalgia.

Of the modern-day players, Ger named Brian Whelahan as his favourite. 'He has a huge level of skill, is outstanding left and right and reads the game very well. He has a great presence on the field, always uses his head and never gets ruffled. He is fiercely competitive, and a very clean player and always performs well on the big day.'

He instances Pat Fox's goal in the 1981 Munster final against Cork as the best he has seen. He remembers Aidan Ryan getting the ball under the old stand in Thurles and sending it towards the goal. It looked like that Ger Cunningham was going to get it, but Fox bravely kept going and stuck the ball in the net with a super flick from 20 yards. 'Fox was an exceptional player, very competitive,' he said admiringly.

Like most hurling people, Loughnane disagreed with the back-door system when it was first mooted but his views have changed and he feels that it has worked so well that it will be hard to change it now. He is very happy about the future of the game. In recent years, a huge interest has developed particularly amongst young people and women. Colour and excitement are now very much part of the games and people are travelling in their thousands to be part of what is almost a 'concert' atmosphere. He feels that the games will continue to progress and he could see further changes in the Championship in years to come.

'I would like to see an open draw at some stage', he said. 'The Leinster and Munster Championships could be played first, and the provincial champions could get a bye into a quarter or semi-finals. The remaining counties could go into a hat and the draw for the All-Ireland series could be made on television. That would bring many unusual pairings, and would create a huge interest throughout the country.'

Loughnane is somewhat concerned, however, about standards in some counties. 'Dublin, Kerry, Westmeath, Antrim and Laois have fallen behind, somewhat', he ventured. 'I am also disappointed in the standard of minor hurling. The finals have been very poor for the last few years.'

Professionalism? 'A total non-starter' he said firmly. 'A county can barely meet the costs of running their teams now. Even with sponsorship, it is only possible to look after the teams well with proper meals, good medical treatment, nice gear, adequate travelling expenses and a good holiday for the players. You can't go outside that. It is a total red herring. Anyway, it would ruin the game, and would create petty jealousies amongst the players.

'The GPA is doomed from the start,' Ger said forcefully. 'I see it as totally ineffectual. The way it is based, the fact that it encompasses the whole country will make it very hard to unite players. When the Championship starts, a player's greatest concern is getting on the team. How could he be expected to fight some player's battle at the other end of the country? I know of some prominent hurling counties who warned their players not to get involved, that it would take their minds off the main objective, which was to win. I didn't say that to our players, but I told them the most effective way would be to have a small organisation themselves and get the best possible deal from their own county board. In any case, I do not agree with the motivations behind the leadership of the GPA. Players will see through that in time, and it won't last.'

Ger Loughnane is one of the great hurling characters – friendly, a wonderful conversationalist, marvellous company with a keen sense of humour. He exudes a passion for the game of hurling, and is totally focused on what is important for the success of his team. Other things related to the game, he regards as trivial and does not take seriously, something that drives his 'friends' in the media berserk. After Clare's defeat by Cork in the 2000 Munster semi-final, Ger Loughnane resigned as manager of the Clare team. I can see that, before long, he will be head-hunted for the world of punditry and television.

Ger Loughnane's Team Of The Century

Ger selected his team from those he had seen playing from 1968 onwards.

Noel Skehan
(Kilkenny)

Fan Larkin   Brian Lohan   Martin Hanamy
(Kilkenny)   *(Clare)*   *(Offaly)*

Brian Whelahan   Mick Roche   Sean Foley
(Offaly)   *(Tipperary)*   *(Limerick)*

Frank Cummins   John Connolly
(Kilkenny)   *(Galway)*

Nicky English   Pat Delaney   Eddie Keher
(Tipperary)   *(Kilkenny)*   *(Kilkenny)*

Pat Fox   Ray Cummins   Eamon Cregan
(Tipperary)   *(Cork)*   *(Limerick)*

Munster Team Of The Century

Ger Cunningham
(Cork)

Brian Murphy   Brian Lohan   Brian Corcoran
(Cork)   *(Clare)*   *(Cork)*

Con Roche   Mick Roche   Sean Foley
(Cork)   *(Tipperary)*   *(Limerick)*

Ollie Baker   Gerald McCarthy
(Clare)   *(Cork)*

Nicky English   Gary Kirby   Eamonn Grimes
(Tipperary)   *(Limerick)*   *(Limerick)*

Pat Fox   Ray Cummins   Eamon Cregan
(Tipperary)   *(Cork)*   *(Limerick)*

11 – Paddy Molloy

Paddy Molloy

If ever there was an example of the weak becoming strong in hurling terms, then surely the Faithful County is the one to look at. For a relatively small county, a football stronghold where hurling is confined to the southern tip, the achievements of the Offaly hurlers since 1980 are truly amazing. At the beginning of every championship since then, Offaly is always mentioned as one of the leading contenders to take the All-Ireland title. They have delivered on four occasions and won nine Leinster Championships playing an intelligent brand of skilful hurling that is beautiful to watch, coupled with a 'never say die' attitude. Surely this is the place that the so called 'weak' hurling counties should look to for inspiration.

If anyone was born into the wrong era, Paddy Molloy from Ballinree in the parish of Drumcullen was such a man. Though he may not have senior inter-county medals to show after his long and distinguished career, his achievement of gaining national recognition for his hurling displays with an unsuccessful team may be all the more admirable. I would love to have seen Paddy perform in a forward line with Padraig Horan, Mark Corrigan and Pat Carroll around him, or on a later team with the Dooley brothers and John Troy, and with Brian Whelahan delivering pin–point passes to him from the half–back line.

That is not to take from his own great team of the late 1960s which contained Pat Joe Whelahan, father of the present Whelahan brothers and Paudge Mulhare who have contributed much to Offaly's success in the last two decades from behind the scenes. They were an unlucky team that almost made the breakthrough. I have very good reasons to remember them because of the very close calls we had with them in 1968 and 1969.

As All-Ireland champions, we travelled to Portlaoise in 1968 in our opening defence of the title. We barely survived by four points in the end, 3–13 to 4–6 and that was with Offaly playing with 14 men for 50 minutes, after full forward, John Kirwan was sidelined for a stroke on goalkeeper, Noel Skehan. Pa Dillon and Ollie Walsh were unable to play due to injuries, and Paddy remembers meeting Pa outside the grounds before the game. 'You're in with a great chance today, Paddy,' predicted the Kilkennyman. How right he was. Paddy was up against the tight-marking Jim Treacy that day and still managed to score three points. He remembers that he got a chance of winning the game for Offaly in the closing stages. Always meticulous about having his own special hurleys for a game, he was horrified when his last one was broken just before Offaly were awarded a 21-yard free with minutes remaining. When he was thrown one in from the sideline that he did not like, Eamonn Fox saw his dilemma and rushed up with his own. 'Is it any good?' enquired Paddy. 'I can hit straight with it anyhow,' said the wing-back. Paddy looked at the Kilkenny players lining the goal and could only see a small gap between Seamus Cleere and the goalpost. He shot for the space only to see the ball shave the post on the wrong side. He nearly beheaded a neighbour who was standing on the bank behind the goal. Kilkenny were lucky to get through that contest, and we knew that, with a little bit more experience, that Offaly team would be a force to be reckoned with.

Our feeling proved correct when we came up against the same team in the Leinster final the following year. Offaly had come through the hard way by beating Westmeath in the first round. They also disposed of their 'bogey' team, Laois at Portlaoise. Paddy Molloy 'went to town' that day, scoring 5–4 of Offaly's 8–10.

They now faced All-Ireland champions, Wexford in a double header at Croke Park. Offaly defeated Kildare in the football championship as a curtain-raiser, and Paddy remembers meeting the football corner back, Paddy McCormack coming off the field. 'Come on Molloy,' he said. 'We'll win the two All-Irelands this year.'

The footballers went down to Kerry in a replay in the final. The hurlers showed great promise by defeating Wexford that day, 5–10 to 3–11. Paddy scored 3–6 of that total while marking no less than Tom Neville.

I had the honour of being captain of the Kilkenny team that year, following my club's one and only county championship success in 1968. I was very conscious of the previous year's game with Offaly, and their performance in the Championship, particularly their defeat of Wexford. We were well prepared for a tough struggle, and that is what it turned out to be. Offaly set the pace with the wind in the first half and kept forging ahead. Kilkenny could only keep in touch with some well-taken goals by Pat Delaney. He scored two in the first half, the second on the call of half time to bring us level at 2–4 to 0–10.

Paddy was 'marked' by his good friend and foe, the late Ted Carroll, on that day. He was high in his praise for the Lisdowney man who he described as 'a true gentleman.' 'He was a hard man to beat' he recalled. 'He never let you away from him, and he was always there to tip the ball away just when you thought you had possession.' He remembered the first ball that came down the left wing towards them that day. Paddy broke first to the ball, but Ted was right with him, and he pulled the hurl from the Offaly man's hand as he took off. Ted naturally got possession and made an easy clearance. Paddy thought that he would get his own back for the next ball and did the same to the Kilkenny man. He was just bending to control the ball when Ted's boot came from behind and drove the ball 40 yards down the field. 'What an embarrassment,' said Paddy.

But Paddy turned the tables on his other great hero, the late Ollie Walsh that day. He had studied Ollie's style for years, how he sidestepped the in-rushing forwards before making one of his spectacular clearances. When Ollie broke out with a ball in the first half, Paddy timed his run to perfection, and grabbed the ball when the goalie threw it up. To his surprise he found himself inside the defence on his own and he hurriedly sent the ball over the bar, when he probably could have scored a goal. It was just as well for Kilkenny that he didn't, because Kilkenny just barely scraped through by two points in the end despite having the wind advantage in the second half.

It is probably stating the obvious that Kilkenny would not have won but for the performance of Pat Delaney that day. He scored three great goals, and I remember the third particularly well. Offaly had gone into a two-point lead, 0–15 to 2–7 with only seven minutes remaining and we were pressing hard for a goal. Delaney got the ball and fired a shot that was stopped by Damien Martin. The Johnstown man had lost his hurl in the tackle as he was striking, but as the ball hopped in the square from the save he continued through the flailing hurleys and met the ball with his hand first time to palm it to the net. We got two more points to Paddy Molloy's one to leave the full time score Kilkenny 3–9, Offaly 0–16. 'We were probably a bit in awe of Ollie Walsh in the Kilkenny goal that day,' he suggested. 'We were told to take our points, and after Ollie made a magnificent save early on, we did just that. But in hindsight, we might have scored a goal or two which could have won the game for us, if we had the confidence to try.' That great challenge by Offaly probably won the All-Ireland for us, and we went on to beat a much-fancied Cork team in the final that year.

You could say that Paddy Molloy was born with a hurley in his hand. His father, Larry Molloy was involved in the GAA, and particularly hurling all his life. In the early days Larry played for Fortal which was a club that drew its players from Drumcullen and part of Birr. Drumcullen then formed their own team and they won their first senior championship in 1908. With his two brothers, Paddy and Mikey, he played for Offaly senior team for years. He was chairman of the county board from 1920 to 1925, and Paddy remembers reading recently that he was credited with bringing in a rule that each senior club would have a selector on the county team. Before that, the county champions picked the senior team.

Larry married Kathleen Troy from Kilcormack and they had three sons and two daughters. Paddy was born on 4 June 1934 and was only five years old when his father passed away. As soon as he could walk, Paddy was out hurling with his brothers using what he called a 'crookie' stick. This was an ash stick with a crook cut from a ditch and pared to a flat surface. His earliest memory of his father was one day when his brother Mikey had a 'real' hurl and his father came out to the field where they were playing. He took the hurl and hit the ball out of sight. The young Paddy Molloy could not believe that a human being could puck a ball the length of their field. The local pitch was only two fields away, and he remembers his father taking them to matches there. Every chance they got, they were out hurling at home, and as they got older, as soon as they heard a ball being pucked in the parish field, they raced there to join in. 'There could be a hundred lads playing there on a Sunday,' he recalled.

'We had great matches in our own field too,' he said. 'We were inspired by Micheál Ó Hehir's commentaries, and I remember, for the 1943 All-Ireland final between Cork and Antrim, we went to a house in Killyon to listen to the broadcast. As usual, as soon as the match was over, we rushed back to our field with our neighbouring friends to replay the game. Cork had won by 5–16 to 0–4, and we had a row about who was going to be Antrim. My mother had to come out to make the peace.

'Micheál Ó Hehir did more than any other person I know to promote Gaelic Games,' Paddy stated. 'He inspired all young people to play the games. He was my idol. It was unreal the way he used bring the games to every corner of rural Ireland. After listening to a match, I used go around for days 'broadcasting' the game into a bucket, to get the effect. I knew every player on every team. When I listened to him saying, "Christy Ring, Mick Mackey or Jim Langton has the ball," I wondered if the time would ever come when Micheál Ó Hehir would say "Paddy Molloy has the ball."'

When the Molloys were tired hurling or when it was raining they liked nothing better than calling into Mick White who lived in a house down the lane. 'Mick was a living encyclopaedia on all the old hurlers. He read every paper about hurling, and used have the hair standing on our heads with stories of games. He had a special 'grá' for Kilkenny hurling, and I knew as much as anyone about the great Kilkenny hurlers of the past. Names like Peter Blanchfield, Mattie Power and even going back to Eddie Doyle were familiar to me.' Paddy remembers that he used make rag balls for them to play with, and he used to seal it by following it around the edges with wax end. '"That's as good as a Kilkenny ball" he used say!'

Paddy eventually got to see his hurling hero, Mick Mackey play. The good curate, Fr Clarke took a load of youngsters to a Munster final, probably the 1944 or 1946 clashes between Cork and Limerick. He still can remember the wonder of such a crowd of people. Mackey was at the end of his career, but he can still see him going through on a solo run and the Cork backs pulling across his big chest, and the Ahane man laughing at them as he returned to his position.

The Molloys lived on the same boreen as the national school. They had a lady teacher who was not interested in hurling, so they organised games themselves in a neighbour's field adjacent to the school. The major games of the year were contested between the 'Ups' and the 'Downs.' The 'Ups' were those who came up the lane and across the fields to school, while the 'Downs' came to school in the opposite direction! These games meant a lot to the young hurlers, and they were keenly contested.

His mother, a young farming widow, had to rely on the children to do many of the farming duties. Paddy remembers how his mother sent a note to the teacher one day to say that he was sick, and kept him at home to sort potatoes. Unfortunately it was also the day when the 'Ups' were playing the 'Downs' in an important game. He worked hard all the morning, but could not stick it any longer when lunch time came and he heard the lads getting ready for the match. He grabbed his hurl and raced down to the field to join in. It is unknown how he explained himself to two furious women. His mother must have wondered what happened to the potatoes, and the lady teacher must have been mystified how a sick boy could star for the 'Downs.'

Paddy was a small boy and he played for six years at under-14 grade. He was ten years old when he started at that grade, and finished as a small 16-year-old! He remembers in his first year he went to block John Pilkington (father of the present Pilkington brothers) only to mis-time his effort and get John's hurl down on top of the head. In his last year, he was playing at full back on a short juvenile pitch and early on he scored two points from puck-outs. The trainer rushed down to him and whispered, 'for God's sake puck the ball to one side or the other, or they will be asking your age.'

Paddy could not get enough hurling in those days. The rules were somewhat 'elastic' at that time and he recalls that he played on different occasions with Seir Kieran and Kinnity as well as his own club. He was on holidays in Clareen one summer and he turned out with the local team, Seir Kieran against Coolderry. They won the game, and Coolderry objected and were awarded the match because Paddy was an illegal player.

On another occasion he was on the street in Birr, when the Kinnity under-16 team was passing by on their way to play Birr. They stopped and asked him to play which he was delighted to do. They lost the match, but he never forgot how the Kinnity mentors brought them all down to Paddy Conroy's shop and treated them all to fruit ices. He had never seen a fruit ice before.

In 1949, he won his first medal when his own parish team, Drumcullen won the county minor title, beating Tullamore in the final. He played in goal or corner forward in different games. His two brothers played with him that day. 'Willie Mitchell was the star of that team. He carried us on his own,' Paddy recalled. The local curate, Fr Clarke was their coach, ably assisted by Tom Dooley.

Tom Dooley was Paddy's hero from childhood. He was about 14 years his senior, but Paddy had the honour of playing beside him on the senior team before he retired from the game. Paddy had seen Dooley play with the parish team in the 1940s. They had a poor team in those days, and Tom seemed to be trying to hurl the opposition on his own. 'He was the greatest striker of a ball that I ever saw,' said Paddy proudly. 'He could hit left or right and I remember him frequently cutting side-line balls over the bar.' The highlights of the Paddy Molloy's young life were when he would cycle with Tom to Birr to a match. When Paddy started playing with the senior team, he lined out at wing-back. Tom was at centre-back and gave him great advice before and during each game.

Paddy won four senior championship medals with Drumcullen. They beat Coolderry in 1954 and 1958, and St Rynaghs (then known as Shannon Rovers) in 1957. His greatest honour with his club was when he was captain of the team that beat Shinrone in the 1960 championship. He was the first man to be presented with the 'Sean Robbins Cup,' which was named after a great Offaly Gael who was chairman of the county board immediately after his own father. Sean made a huge contribution to the success of the GAA in Offaly. Paddy was no mean footballer either. There was no football team in his parish, and he was asked by Andy Gallagher to play for Tullamore. He got special permission from the county board to do so, and they won the county final in 1963.

The long hurling tradition in their area was probably influenced by their proximity to Tipperary. One time during his career, he got a shoulder injury and went for treatment to a bone-setter in Toomevara called O'Meara. During the treatment, the 85 year-old asked him was he related to Larry Molloy from Drumcullen. 'I'm his son' replied Paddy. 'Well I can tell you,' said the old man 'He was a right hurler. We brought himself and Jim Toohill and Mick Spain over to play with us against Nenagh-De Witts one time, and they made all the difference for us.' So the Toomevara Greyhounds were poaching from Offaly in those days! Times have changed.

At the age of 19, Paddy got his first taste of inter-county hurling when he was included in the substitutes on the Offaly junior team in 1953. It was a great thrill for him to even get a spin in a motor car, and he really felt he had 'made it' when the car arrived to collect him. Pat Bracken and Mick Spain junior were on the team from the club. They won the Leinster junior title that year, beating Kilkenny in the final by 3–7 to 2–2.

He played in goal in his first match with the seniors to be beaten well by Westmeath. Two goals were scored against him, but Westmeath ran up a big score of points, most of them by the legendary 'Jobber' McGrath with his unorthodox one-handed style. Paddy said that he was fed up pucking out the ball that day.

Apart from the great days of 1968 and 1969, Paddy remembers with pleasure beating Tipperary, then All-Ireland champions in a League match in 1966. The victory gave Offaly great confidence when playing the top hurling teams in later years. He was marking John Gleeson and succeeded in scoring a few goals early on in the game.

In 1962, Paddy was selected for the Rest of Leinster to play Leinster champions Dublin in the trial for the Railway Cup team. Although the final selection was made from the stronger hurling counties at the time, Dublin, Kilkenny and Wexford, Paddy impressed sufficiently to make the panel. Leinster beat Munster that year by 1–11 to 1–9. He won his second medal as a substitute in the final of 1964 when Leinster came out on top again by 3–7 to 2–9. Paddy played his first full game with the province in 1965 in the semi-final against Connacht at Pierce Stadium Galway. Leinster won by 4–9 to 2–3 on a freezing cold February day. Paddy retained his place for the final against Munster playing at left half-back with Ted Carroll at centre half and Seamie Cleere at right half-back.

Paddy was always grateful to Ted Carroll and to Seamie Cleere for the encouragement they gave him before and during the game. Every time he made a clearance or an interception, Ted was over to him shouting him on. He had the task of marking the great Jimmy Doyle that day, and he was apprehensive going into the dressing room. He was immediately welcomed by Martin O'Neill, the genial secretary of the Leinster Council, and the players from Kilkenny, Wexford and Dublin went out of their way to make him feel relaxed. He played well that day, and Leinster won again by 2–8 to 2–7 in a nail-biting finish. Paddy partnered Brian Cooney from Dublin at centre-field the following year, but was injured in the final and had to leave the field. Leinster was beaten by Munster by 3–13 to 3–11 that day.

Paddy got his last Railway Cup medal in 1967 playing at right full-forward. We had a big win over Connacht in the semi-final at Croke Park for another showdown with the Munster men on St Patrick's Day. I was playing outside Paddy that day at right half-forward, and we combined well for a number of scores. We got on top of the Southerners in the second half and were leading by six points just on full time. As we were waiting for the full-time whistle to blow, I remember a long ball dropping in to the corner between Paddy and Denis Murphy, his marker. I moved in front of them hoping that Paddy would win the ball and pass it out to me. At the last minute, they both decided to pull on the dropping ball and it caught me straight in the nose as the full-time whistle sounded.

The X-ray showed that it was not broken but as they were preparing me for examination, I winced as the nurse removed my sock, and she noticed a swelling from a knock I received early in the game. They decided to X-ray that too, and they found a crack in the bone. They put a plaster on my ankle and sent me home on crutches. My wife was amused that I should go in with a broken nose and come home on crutches. When the swelling went down on my nose, I was convinced that it was broken, and I returned to the hospital for examination again. I was right, it was broken and they took me in for the operation. I remember thinking as I lay in hospital, 'Paddy Molloy, why did you not catch that ball instead of trying to pull on it.'

I played with Paddy on the Leinster team for the following three years, and we were beaten each year by Munster, twice and Connacht once. Molloy remembers meeting Pat Henderson during in 1970, and telling him that he was 'calling it a day.' Pat encouraged him to give it one more year and that we would beat Munster the following year. Paddy was now 36 and said that he had no more to give. Unfortunately for the Drumcullen man, he lost out again, because Leinster went on the next year to start a run of five-in-a-row Railway Cup final wins.

Paddy went to that great rivalling parish of Coolderry to find a wife, and in 1968 he and Bernie Carey walked up the aisle. They set up house in the town of Birr. I was made to feel very welcome by Bernie and Paddy and their family when I called to their lovely home on the edge of town. They have five sons, Enda, John, Paul, Padraig and the youngest Darragh, who is 12.

All of the boys played hurling at various levels. Enda won an All-Ireland minor medal with Offaly in 1986, and won three intermediate county medals with Birr. Paul and Padraig played at all grades and made the county minor team. John was very promising but gave up the game after under-14 level. Darragh was on the Birr under-12 team at the age of eight, and is very proud of his All-Ireland Community Games medal that he won last year to emulate the success of Paul and Padraig in the same competition.

Paddy enjoyed these games very much, and remembers in particular Dessie Haines going up to receive the cup. It wasn't so much that Birr had won against the odds, but that their captain was the first boy with black skin to be presented with an All-Ireland cup.

When Paddy retired from the game, he tried to give back what he had learned to his own children and to the other youngsters in Birr. He loves coaching the young teams as they are so receptive to advice. He gets a great thrill from watching the young lads put his coaching tips into practice, and seeing how it improves their game.

Molloy follows closely the fortunes of the county senior team and was thrilled when they made the breakthrough in 1980. He gives great credit to Dermot Healy for bringing that team to a new level of skill and know-how so that they were able to defeat Kilkenny in 1980. He remembers going to see a Leinster trial in the spring of 1981 between Offaly and the Rest. He was highly impressed with what he saw and remembers coming home to Bernie that evening and saying, 'You know Bernie, Offaly will win the All-Ireland. Healy has them playing a different brand of hurling, a brand that I like.' Offaly won their first All-Ireland hurling title that year. Paddy was also full of praise for the work done at under age level, and the three minor All-Ireland wins in 1986, 1987 and 1989 built a great foundation for the later successes.

Peter Nolan, who played at centre-back for Offaly in the late 1950s was the best footballer Paddy ever saw in that position. 'He was a fine specimen of a man, and a great fielder of a ball,' said Paddy. 'Unfortunately he had to emigrate to America, and he was lost to the great team of 1960–1961. Had he been available to that team, they might have won two All-Ireland titles rather than being pipped by Down in the semi-final and the All-Ireland in those years.'

On the current scene, he was full of praise for Trevor Giles and John McDermott of Meath, and Michael Donnellan of Galway.

Of the present-day hurlers, Paddy is a great admirer of Brian Whelahan. 'I have watched him since he was seven years old, and I never saw him pull a foul stroke on anyone,' he said. 'He has tremendous skill and a great temperament for the game. He and DJ Carey are geniuses, and have given us all so much enjoyment over the last decade.'

While he is happy that Offaly was able to take advantage of the 'back-door' system in 1998, he is uncomfortable with the system. He feels that a Championship should always be on a 'knock-out' basis. He admits however that we have had a number of great hurling games as a result of the experiment.

Molloy is more vociferous on some of the more recent 'innovations.' 'Please leave our great game of hurling alone,' he appealed to the authorities. 'Various committees are obsessed with making rule changes every year that are not adding to the game.' As a retired farmer, he used a farming term to describe the red/yellow cards. 'Get rid of those 'Blue' cards' he fumed. 'They have no place in our games. They are an insult to amateur players.' Paddy was equally angry at the decision to forbid the supporters from going on to the pitch after a final. 'The captain and the team should be allowed to go to the stand to be amongst their own to receive the cup,' he said. The supporters of both teams should be allowed on the field to congratulate and console their heroes.' He was very angry last year to see professional security men act like thugs with peaceful, life-long supporters of our games.

Paddy cannot understand the mindset of players looking for a Players' Association. 'They should feel privileged to play our games for their county for the few short years that they are honoured to do so,' he said. He would much rather see the thousands of unsung heroes of the GAA, who work hard for the Association and give much of their time to young players, getting any perks that were going. 'They are the ones who are responsible for creating the present senior players. They should at least get access to All-Ireland tickets,' he continued. 'The players are sufficiently rewarded and are well looked after. If I have any worry for the future of the GAA it is that these great club stalwarts may not always be there. They should be looked after well,' he concluded.

Before I left Paddy Molloy's home, he showed me a Christmas card from the late Christy Ring. He met Christy when they were guests on a trip to the USA for the Cardinal Cushing Games. Tom Neville and Jimmy Duggan were also invitees. Christy and Paddy remained firm friends, and he was shocked when he heard of his untimely death. The last time he saw the maestro was in Birr when Cork played Offaly in a League match in November. Offaly won the match, and Paddy went into the dressing room to see his friend who was involved with the team. After exchanging the usual pleasantries, Christy looked at him from under the peak of his cap and said, 'ye're going well boy, but we'll be back with the cuckoo!' In other words, Cork would be back for the start of the Championship.

Paddy Molloy finished his career without any All-Ireland medals, but he left his mark firmly on the game of hurling. Apart from his achievements with the Leinster team, he was selected on the Ireland team in 1966, which was the forerunner to the 'All-Stars.' He was also honoured in his own county by being awarded the 'Offaly Sportstar' of the same year. He got a 'Hall of Fame Award' in 1997. His selection on the 'Offaly team of the Millennium' ensures that he will go down in history as one of the best 15 hurlers ever from the Faithful County, and that says it all.

Paddy Molloy's Team Of The Century

Tony Reddin
(Tipperary)

Bobby Rackard	Nick O'Donnell	Mark Marnell
(Wexford)	*(Wexford)*	*(Kilkenny)*
Brian Whelahan	Pat Stakelum	Seamus Cleere
(Offaly)	*(Tipperary)*	*(Kilkenny)*

Mick Roche
(Tipperary)

John Connolly
(Galway)

Eddie Keher	Mick Mackey	DJ Carey
(Kilkenny)	*(Limerick)*	*(Kilkenny)*
Christy Ring	Nick Rackard	Josie Gallagher
(Cork)	*(Wexford)*	*(Galway)*

Leinster Team Of The Century

Ollie Walsh
(Kilkenny)

Bobby Rackard	Nick O'Donnell	Mark Marnell
(Wexford)	*(Wexford)*	*(Kilkenny)*
Brian Whelahan	Billy Rackard	Seamus Cleere
(Offaly)	*(Wexford)*	*(Kilkenny)*

Harry Grey
(Laois)

Frank Cummins
(Kilkenny)

Jim Langton	Terry Leahy	DJ Carey
(Kilkenny)	*(Kilkenny)*	*(Kilkenny)*
Eddie Keher	Nick Rackard	Johnny Dooley
(Kilkenny)	*(Wexford)*	*(Offaly)*

12 – Michael O'Grady

Most of the people featured in this book have achieved the dream of every young hurler. They have had the experience of pulling on their county jersey and running out on the pitch before thousands of their cheering supporters. They have played in provincial or All-Ireland finals and have medals to prove it. A few have experienced the ultimate honour of walking up the steps of the Hogan Stand to accept the McCarthy Cup. Their young formative years were spent hitting thousands of balls with a hurl, learning and developing the skills of the game and trying to copy the heroes of the day. They were inspired or got a helping hand from a willing schoolteacher or club man along the way and, with blood, sweat and tears and a sprinkling of luck they achieved their ambitions.

For Michael O'Grady, the early years were like this, but his pathway in life dictated that he would never achieve his boyhood dreams. Very early in his young life, he listened to a call from his God and he answered it. It is hard for those born into the Celtic Tiger culture to visualise a time in this country when an education was only available to the few who could afford it, that the State could not afford to educate all its young people and that this task was undertaken by a group of unselfish people who had to sacrifice much in order to do so. In the case of the young men of Ireland, the Christian Brothers fulfilled that role.

Michael O'Grady as Dublin hurling manager, Leinster Championship 1997.

When Michael O'Grady answered the call to become a Christian Brother, he knew the sacrifices he would have to make to do so. Apart from the obvious ones of having to leave family, friends and townland, he knew too that he would never be able to fulfill the dreams of his childhood. His hurling career would be finished.

Patrickswell, Co. Limerick is, in fact, half of the parish of Lurriga, the other half being Ballybrown. But they are very definitely separate hurling clubs! It is an amazing achievement however that both teams contested the AIB All–Ireland club finals in consecutive years only to be beaten by Kilkenny teams on each occasion. In 1990, Ballybrown were beaten by Ballyhale Shamrocks by 1–16 to 0–16, and in 1991 Patrickswell lost out to Glenmore 1–13 to 0–12.

Michael O'Grady was born in Patrickswell on 22 April 1948 into a strong hurling family. His father was heavily involved in the local GAA club, Patrickswell, holding different administrative positions including that of a selector on various teams. But it was his mother who had mostly the hurling blood. Her brother, Ger O'Brien, had the honour of wearing the Limerick jersey with distinction on the senior team.

Michael remembers having a hurl of his own from the time he was able to walk. It was not surprising that the three O'Grady brothers, PJ, Michael and Jim spent all of their free time hurling in a field at the back of the house. But Michael was not content with that. When the others got tired, he spent hours developing his skills in the back yard by hitting a ball on his left and right side alternately, on either side of a small window. His mother loved hurling, but she wasn't so keen on having her windows broken and close calls were greeted with screams of 'mind the window!' Sometimes she was too late as glass flew from a misdirected shot. When he returns home now and sees the spot where those thousands of balls were struck, Michael wonders how that window escaped so often for so long.

As the O'Grady boys grew bigger, bigger areas to hurl were required, and a field belonging to neighbours, the Griffins, became their own Croke Park. With another family, the Higgins, they played five-a-side games. The games were preceded by a spectacular parade around the field, and were so intense at times that they ended with a row and were never finished. When hurls were broken, they went down to Griffin's farmyard to pick up a board or lathe to fashion their own sticks.

There were no under-age competitions in the club before under-15, so the long summer days were spent hurling matches all over the parish in various farmers' fields. In those days, with limited transport available, hurling was played in many different fields in the parish, now it is played in one, the club grounds.

Adare CBS was the local school, although a separate parish, and there was intense rivalry between Adare and Patrickswell. Most of the Patrickswell children attended school there, and although outnumbered by the Adare boys, they were the better hurlers. At the age of six, Michael took his first tentative steps into the school where Brother Dwan, a Tipperary man looked after the hurling. They hurled every day, at lunchtime and in the evenings. Michael was naturally left-handed, and he remembers Brother Dwan instructing him to learn to hit the ball on his left side which would give him a more 'wristy' stroke. This was his first experience of coaching, though it was not called that at the time.

Although they played a great deal of hurling in the school, they never had much success in the Limerick schools competitions. The school, however, boasted of producing the likes of Richie Bennis and Frankie Nolan who later gave sterling service to the county team.

They had little success at under-age level with Patrickswell either. The club was formed in 1949 drawing on a small population of about 400 to provide an adult team. In the 1950s, they won three-in-a-row county junior championships, and the young Michael O'Grady got his first experience of what the true spirit of supporting your club team was. He was there shouting for his uncle Ger O'Brien, Willie O'Brien, former Fine Gael TD and Tom Boland who was later to become county secretary. The club went on to win their first county senior title in 1965 with the services of Phil Bennis, Eamonn and Pa Carey, Gerry Casey who played in goal for Limerick and the late Tony O'Brien. Richie Bennis was making his presence felt, though still a minor.

But in 1961, at the age of 14, Michael left it all to join the Christian Brothers. It used to break his heart when Patrickswell or the Limerick county team was playing that he could not hear the matches on radio, or read the reports in the newspapers. He merely heard the results on the day after the game.

However, things began to look up in 1968 when he was sent teaching to Drimnagh Castle. Christian Brothers were still forbidden to play hurling, but it was the worst kept secret that many did play under assumed names! And so a new star from Patrickswell under the name of 'Mick Ryan' was born. He was approached by Bill Walsh, the Kilkenny star of the 1940s and 1950s to play for Young Irelands Club in Dublin, and he remembers playing his first match against Crumlin in 1969 with whom the Boothman brothers were still playing. He scored three points from wing forward.

The Second Vatican Council (Vatican II) was now beginning to impact on religious orders, and the new 'boss' in Drimnagh Castle was a keen hurling man and turned a blind eye to the fact that many of his young men were playing for clubs in town. In fact, they formed their own team called 'An Caislean,' and the 'reborn' Michael O'Grady joined up with them together with a number of other Brothers who could now use their real names! They had limited success, winning a few secondary club competitions.

It was at Drimnagh Castle that Michael O'Grady got his first taste of coaching. When he started teaching there, he was given the under-12 team to look after. For a young man with such a passion for the game and no great opportunity to express it, this was manna from heaven. It meant that, instead of sitting in the monastery after school reading books, or dare I say it, praying, he could take his under-12 team for two hours each evening for hurling. He immersed himself in the job and found that there were no books available on how to coach hurling teams. He found himself reading books on basketball, soccer and other field games to get ideas that he could adapt to hurling. He devised his own hurling skill drills and put the boys through their paces. The coaching bug had caught him.

Michael was transferred to the CBS in Cashel in 1973, a great hurling town. He was now based nearer to his home club, Patrickswell, and he signed up for them initially. While he did go there for a few training sessions, he quickly realised that travelling was not easy or attractive, so he started going down to local field to train with the Cashel King Cormacs team.

Cashel were drawn against Lattin-Cullen in the first round of the Championship, and on the day of the match he was having his dinner when the doorbell rang. Aongus Ryan, club secretary and team captain was at the door. 'Are you coming?' he said. 'What do you mean?' said the surprised Christian Brother. 'You're picked,' was the reply. He was signed up for Patrickswell but had not played a game with them. He had not transferred legally to Cashel, but the thought of playing with the club was so attractive he went along. He had a good day scoring 2–1 from wing forward. He was playing outside inter-county star, John Grogan and both were wearing similar helmets. The local reporter, Bill O'Donnell mixed them up and credited John with the scores in the paper. Maybe he was cleverer than the good Brother thought – no point in splashing the exploits of an illegal player all over the paper! He did make an escape in that Mick Maguire, who was chairman of the West Tipperary Board was playing at full back for Lattin-Cullen and would have known of his status, but there was no objection lodged. While the team boasted inter-county star goalkeeper Peter O'Sullivan, Pa Fitzelle and a youthful Cormac Bonner, they could only go as far as winning the west division final. The finalists from the other divisions like Moycarkey, Nenagh and Silvermines were too strong for them.

By now, however, coaching was beginning to take over from Michael's playing career. He was having great success with the school team and he coached the Cashel minor team to win the county final in 1974.

To his surprise as a Limerick man, the club nominated him as a county minor selector for the following year. He regarded it as a great honour to be so closely involved with a county team.

However, he was very quickly disillusioned when he found that the team had no manager and that the training and preparation of the team was totally haphazard. They were given a few hurls and sliotars but there was no planning or preparation. It was no surprise to him that they were beaten well by Cork in the Munster final. Michael was so annoyed that he wrote a letter to the county board asking them never to appoint him again. He told them in his letter that it was a disgrace that a county team should be sent out to represent their county so ill-prepared. He said that under-12 teams were better managed.

Like any good county chairman, the late Tom O'Hara took his comments on board and the following year he arrived up to the local ball alley where Michael was playing and put to him a straight question: 'will you manage the county minor team this year?' The onus was now back on him to implement all his great ideas.

He asked for a day to think about it as he did have some reservations about having to face Limerick in the Championship. He telephoned a friend in Limerick who told him, 'you're working and living in Tipperary, it is a great honour, go for it.'

This was his first big test, but he had great selectors in Mick Minogue from Roscrea and Billy Carroll from Clonmel. They were older and more experienced at this level, but they were most supportive of Michael from the start and built up his reputation with the team, which in turn gave the team confidence in his methods. 'That was crucial,' said Michael 'as we had to take some very hard decisions early on. We dropped two players who had been on the team the previous year because they did not train adequately.' The strategy worked because they now had a good solid team, with no stars, who worked well together.

They were unimpressive in their first match against Kerry and Michael was not surprised when he heard a Kerryman say 'they'll go no further anyhow!' The first big test was against a Pat-Horgan-led Cork and O'Grady could see in that game that the players were doing as he had asked them to do in training. They came away with a two-point victory and he could now face the Munster final with confidence that his coaching strategy was working.

However, there was a different test to overcome in the Munster final, a loyalty test. They were facing his home county, Limerick in the final, but he realised early on that he was so close to the Tipperary team that loyalty did not become an issue. There were one or two good-natured jibes from Limerick supporters, but Michael went about his business and Tipperary won by 5–10 to 5–6. They went on to destroy Kilkenny in the final with a score of 2–20 to 1–7. Michael Doyle, son of the legendary John Doyle and Eamonn O'Shea from that team went on later to perform on the bigger stage. Brother O'Grady was now a national figure in coaching circles.

In 1978, he was asked to take charge of the Tipperary under-21 team, which was made up mostly of players from the successful minor team of 1976. This team showed the same promise when they drew with Cork in Thurles, Tipperary 3–13, Cork 4–10. It was on the during that match that Michael came in close contact with the great Christy Ring, who was a selector on the Cork team. The encounter was not too pleasant however, as the maestro reprimanded him because one of the Tipperary players made a heavy tackle on Tom Cashman.

This match created a huge interest in Tipperary, and a massive crowd travelled to Cork for the replay causing a traffic jam in Cahir on that Sunday evening. Tipperary won the replay by 3–8 to 2–9 in another exciting game. Tipperary were going through a lean patch at senior level and their supporters started to gain confidence that this group of players might bring senior honours to the county within a few years.

This put a certain amount of pressure on the players, and it was just as well that few supporters travelled to Belfast for the semi-final against Antrim. The team stayed in a hotel in Belfast the night before the game, and were unable to sleep due to the noise outside. Antrim were totally disorganised for the game. They played an important under-21 club championship before the inter-county match in which eight of their team took part. Those players merely changed their jerseys to take part in the game against Tipperary. Whether it was due to complaisance or lack of sleep the night before, the Tipperary team were a disaster on the day. Michael said that it was the first and only time he broke a hurley in a dressing room in frustration. They had forgotten everything he had told them. Despite his efforts to motivate them, they were still two points down with three minutes to go on a wet day. He remembers thinking that they could never go back to Tipperary after such a defeat. But a last-minute free was sent to the net, and they got out of jail.

They faced Galway in the All-Ireland final and drew, 3–5 to 2–8. They missed an easy chance from 25 yards in the last minute which would have brought them victory. Michael remembers reprimanding the culprit for doing the same thing on the last night of training.

The extra game was of greater benefit to Galway who had their usual easy passage to the final. Michael also got an unsettling report from Galway on the week of the match saying that one of his players had played illegally in England. While the player denied it, he did not have enough time to investigate the allegation fully. It was sufficient, however to disrupt and knock their focus off the game. Galway won the replay well on a score of 3–15 to 2–8.

By this time, Michael had been transferred to Dublin and, with some reservations, he agreed to manage the Tipperary senior team for a year. They had a very successful 1978–1979 League campaign beating Clare by two points in the semi-final. They had a big win over Galway in the final 3–15 to 0–8 which set them in a confident mood for the Championship. However, they went down to Cork by a point who comprehensively defeated Limerick in the Munster final later that summer.

O'Grady had been a regular attender at the national GAA coaching courses in Gormanstown College since 1974. These courses had been devised and set up by Fr Tommy Maher (Kilkenny), Donie Nealon (Tipperary), Des Ferguson (Dublin) and Ned Power (Waterford). He could not believe that, by attending these courses he could get so close to these famous men who had a great track record, and also famous inter-county stars who attended as guests. He learned much at these events, not only from the excellent lectures and notes they received, but also during the night-time discussions at meals. The social aspect was tremendous too which was tirelessly orchestrated in his own inimitable way by Ballyboden's Tommy O'Riordan. Another man who enjoyed the social aspect was Kilkenny man, Liam Hinphy who attended the course every year. He came from his teaching post in Dungiven, Co. Derry, and it is assumed that he eventually got his qualification.

The matches were serious too. Michael remembers Buffer's Alley coming to play a team selected from those taking part in the course. Jimmy 'Puddin' Cullinane from Clare and Colm Doran can still show the marks from their encounter that day.

My first time working with Brother O'Grady was at the time we were both appointed to the National Coaching Council by President Paddy Buggy. Our term of office was from 1982 to 1984. Michael was appointed chairman, and the other members included Jim McKeever (Derry), Mickey Whelan (Dublin) and Padraig O'Gorman (Sligo). Muiris Prendeville acted as secretary. We were given the task of devising and putting together a coaching manual and a coaching video. Michael and I took on the hurling one, leaving the football to the others. We worked hard on the manual only to be frustrated at every turn by the

Management Committee who seemed to think that we were going in the wrong direction. Large parts had to be written and rewritten. Eventually the final document was ready, and we were running up against a printing deadline. The document had to be finally proof-read, but I had arranged a family holiday to France. The chairman coolly suggested that I would have plenty of time to read it on the boat to France. Not a man to take 'no' for an answer, I had little option. I found a quiet corner on the ferry and started the task on the way out and finished it on the return journey. The coaching manual never saw the light of day and the manuscript is probably still lying in a corner of an office in Croke Park, if not buried in the rubble under the new stand! We were told that there was a lack of money for the project, but we think that we know the real reason.

The second project was more successful. We set out to make a hurling skills video, and having agreed on the particular skills to be demonstrated and a rough script, we arranged for the filming to take place. We selected Marley Park in Rathfarnham as a location that would give us some lovely, scenic background scenery and we were lucky to have two of the nicest days in the summer of 1984 to do the outside work. We used a group of young, skilful players from Dublin schools and four inter-county stars of the day, Joe Hennessey, John Fenton, Conor Hayes and Paddy Kelly. I took two days off from work for that part, but the editing was a horrific experience.

I had to keep the day job going, but Michael was on school holidays and the only one available with some help from Muiris and less from myself. The proposed 30-minute film was now running up against a deadline, as the GAA and the sponsors were anxious to launch the video on the weekend of the All-Ireland hurling final. Michael got his first taste of the Editing Room in Anner Communications on the first night when they started at 7 p.m. At 2 a.m., they had only half a minute of this half-hour film 'in the can.' They continued until 5 a.m. and went through the same hardship for the following five nights after which 15 minutes was completed. However, the project was completed in time, and the launch by Paddy Buggy took place during the Centenary celebrations as scheduled on the weekend of the All-Ireland hurling final in Thurles. I was very pleased with the end result.

That was not the first time that Michael O'Grady had been involved in producing hurling skills on film. While he was in Cashel, he and John Darby, a teacher who was also an excellent photographer, launched a film strip of still photographs of various skills accompanied by a small booklet with matching text. These were packaged and sold very successfully to clubs and schools. With Matt Kelly, he also produced and sold a hurling skills video when he was teaching in Limerick CBS in 1983. He was already a budding Steven Spielberg, but I think it was the editing room in Anner Communications that killed off his ambitions in that regard.

Back to the real world: while in Limerick CBS in 1982, he was asked to take charge of the Limerick under-21 team. They were defeated by Cork in the Munster final by 1–14 to 1–4. He took over the Limerick senior team the following year when they got to the League final only to be beaten by Kilkenny by two points, 2–14 to 2–12. They drew with Cork in the Munster Championship, having withstood a number of extraordinary setbacks. Their regular free-taker, Paddy Kelly was unable to play due to a broken finger, and they tried four different forwards who between them sent ten scoreable frees wide.

Eamon Cregan was a selector, and he resigned so that he could make himself available as a player for the replay. A bye-law existed in Limerick which stated that 'a player may not be a selector.' They lost by two points to Cork who were rescued by a last-minute point-blank save by Ger Cunningham. Cork went on to contest the All-Ireland final and were beaten by Kilkenny.

In 1986, Michael was transferred to Wexford CBS. He was principal of the school which carried its own heavy demands, and he had no wish to get involved in coaching. However, he was persuaded by John Doyle to take the job as manager of the Wexford team. Before accepting, he set out three conditions that would have to be accepted by the county board: that he could pick his own selectors, that he could pick the captain of the team and that all home League games be played in Wexford Park. Up to then, League games were rotated between other venues. Michael felt that improvement could only be achieved by playing all their games on the best pitch available. His selectors were Tom Neville and Tom Mooney and the captain was John Conran.

His demands had a rough passage through the county board, and he knew that if he was not able to deliver, his sojourn would be short. They won the Oireachtas Competition and beat Kilkenny in the Walsh Cup, which gave them confidence when they were drawn against them in the Championship. For that game, O'Grady took the unprecedented step of breaking with tradition and re-designing the purple and gold Wexford jersey. The wives and girlfriends of the team did the new design. Kilkenny defeated them heavily and the good Brother got the sack! The re-designed jersey never again saw the light of day!

In 1989, Martin Quigley was appointed manager of the team and he asked Michael to help him with the coaching. Martin had always heard that the Wexford teams never trained hard or properly, but he was pleasantly surprised on both occasions that he was involved. There was a marvellous commitment from the players. He felt that they should add another dimension to their game by playing more ground hurling, and he tried to do that with them. He enjoyed his short stint with the teams, but was glad of the rest from team coaching when the year was up.

Brother O'Grady's life was going to change dramatically over the coming years. In 1991, he was sent to Chicago to do a two-year management course. While in the States he met his future wife, Irene, and they became close friends. When he returned home, he had to think seriously about his future and he decided to leave the Brothers in 1994. He had served with the Christian Brothers for 33 years. In 1996, he and Irene were married and set up home in Dublin. Michael became deputy principal post in the community school in Celbridge while Irene took a job teaching Biology and Religion.

But the GAA world was not going to let him settle down to tend to his garden and play golf. In 1997, he was approached by the Dublin county board to become manager of the Dublin senior hurling team. He felt that he was burned out from team management at that stage and was going to refuse, but the GAA had just restructured the National Hurling League calendar by eliminating the pre-Christmas games and playing the entire League in the spring. This was more attractive to him, and he also felt that Dublin would have good spring-time games against the top teams, which would serve to prepare his team for the Championship.

He knew that it would be a mighty challenge, but he was prepared to take it on for the term 1997 to 2000. He found that the hurlers were the poor relation of the footballers and were badly looked after. He got great co-operation from the county board and now the hurlers get the same perks and treatment as those playing the other code. The commitment of the players has been superb. They arranged and financed a trip to the Canaries that helped to bond the players from the various clubs together. He gets full attendance at training sessions, many having to take time off work for the Saturday get-togethers.

He found that their skill level was very high, but they needed to be able to perform at greater speed to compete with the top teams. Playing in Division One has been a great help in that regard. They were made to realise that at that level, a player only gets one chance to gain possession. O'Grady also found that their support play was poor, in that they were inclined to leave their colleagues isolated when fighting for a ball. They were being beaten by teams who were not better hurlers but were more clever at team play. With the help of fellow selector Tommy Naughton and trainer John Thomson, Michael has devised drills and routines to try to improve these deficiencies. The strength of football in the county continues to be a problem, particularly with dual players. but they have taken a decision that they will have to get players to commit themselves to hurling. This year, they will not include any dual players in their panel. The better players still practise on their own in ball alleys, but it is becoming harder for hurlers everywhere to give that sort of time to the game with so many outside attractions.

Michael believes that the basic skills have to be practised thousands of times before games for a player to have any chance of doing the right thing under pressure in a match. He enjoys the fact that hurlers love the game so much that they rarely make demands, but he feels that they should. He said that they are entitled to be clothed, fed and taken on a holiday each year. The holiday does not have to be exotic to be beneficial.

Michael O'Grady's views on the structure of the Championship are well known, and he is likely to continue expressing them until a change is made. He says that it is nonsense that teams can be beaten in the first round of the Championship in May and spend the best hurling months of the year idle. O'Grady contends that every major sports organisation runs its major competition on a league basis, and he sees no reason why a 'Super League' for all inter-county teams could not be played during the summer months. This could culminate in the top teams of each division playing off in a semi-final and final to replace the existing All-Ireland final series. He believes that the provincial championships could still be run with the winners coming in at quarter-final stage.

His points are thought-provoking and well made, but there are obviously a number of serious hurdles to be overcome before they would receive unanimous approval. Consideration would have to be given to running the club competitions in both hurling and football as well as the inter-county football championship. I put it to him that he would need to draw up a calendar of events for the year before people would be persuaded – and this could well be his next project!

Michael had some interesting views on the game itself. He is happy with the current playing rules, but he feels that suspensions should only apply to the grade of competition. In other words, a suspension incurred in an inter-county match would not carry in to a club competition. This would eliminate postponements of club games while inter-county players are under suspension. He also favours the idea of the 'sin-bin.'

He thinks the Players Association is a good idea and that they should be listened to. However he also believes that professionalism should be resisted because it would destroy the clubs and would not lead to higher standards.

Michael O'Grady has made an enormous contribution to the GAA and the game of hurling in particular over more than 30 years. He still has much to contribute. He told me that his most rewarding period in coaching was with the Tipperary minors in 1976. They did things that time that were not done before, and they worked.

He has another interesting project 'on hold' which he may well finish now that his term with the Dublin hurlers is completed. He has started to write a book of GAA stories and anecdotes, and I thought that I might finish with a sample from his collection:

Tipperary senior hurlers struck a very bad period during the late 1970s and early 1980s. After a poor display in a League game in Thurles against what many people would regard as a second-rate team, one disgruntled Tipperary supporter caught up with former great defender, Mickie Byrne, holder of four All-Ireland medals. The frustrated supporter asked Mickey what he thought of the team's display. Fast as lightning came the retort: 'I've seen better men go to Lourdes!'

Michael O'Grady's Team of the Century

Michael restricted his choice to the years 1968–2000

Noel Skehan
(Kilkenny)

Fan Larkin   Brian Lohan   John Horgan
(Kilkenny)   *(Clare)*   *(Cork)*

Brian Whelahan   Mick Roche   Sean Foley
(Offaly)   *(Tipperary)*   *(Limerick)*

Frank Cummins   John Connolly
(Kilkenny)   *(Galway)*

Francis Loughnane   Joe Cooney   Eddie Keher
(Tipperary)   *(Galway)*   *(Kilkenny)*

Nicky English   Ray Cummins   Eamon Cregan
(Tipperary)   *(Cork)*   *(Limerick)*

Leinster Team 1968 to 2000

Noel Skehan
(Kilkenny)

Fan Larkin   Eugene Coughlan   John Horgan
(Kilkenny)   *(Offaly)*   *(Cork)*

Brian Whelahan   Mick Jacob   Joe Hennessey
(Offaly)   *(Wexford)*   *(Kilkenny)*

Frank Cummins   George O'Connor
(Kilkenny)   *(Wexford)*

DJ Carey   Martin Quigley   Eddie Keher
(Kilkenny)   (Wexford)   *(Kilkenny)*

Liam Fennelly   Tony Doran   Joe Dooley
(Kilkenny)   *(Wexford)*   *(Offaly)*

13 – Noel Skehan

Noel Skehan pucks out.

Bennettsbridge is a small picturesque village situated on the Nore about five miles from Kilkenny city. At one time Mosses Mills were the main sources of employment, but nowadays, local people go to work in nearby Kilkenny City. In recent years, it has become a centre for the craft industry and there are numerous nationally and internationally known arts and crafts people located in the area, which they find ideal to work in, and close to the Kilkenny Design workshops and the city trade.

From the 1950s to the 1980s, the name of Bennettsbridge was nationally renowned for its exponents of that other art, the art of hurling. They won five senior county titles in the 1950s, another five in the 1960s and their final one in

1971. During that period, players from the club had very influential roles in winning ten All-Ireland titles for Kilkenny. There was no All-Ireland club competition in those years, but the famed club took part in many of the top club tournaments of the time including the famous Dunhill Tournament and were able to beat the best clubs from Cork, Tipperary, Wexford and Waterford.

It may be an exaggeration to say that they play 'pitch and toss' with All-Ireland medals in this village, but when I drove into the small and beautifully kept estate of Woodlawn, I was conscious that in those 24 houses alone there were 24 All-Ireland medals. Seamus and Liam Cleere, Paddy Moran, Pat Lawlor and John Kinsella hold 15 between them, and as I walked into Noel Skehan's house, I knew that I was entering the only home in the country with nine All-Ireland medals. It was said about all those players that they lived on the hurling pitch as youngsters. They still do, as Woodlawn was built on the old hurling pitch in 1971.

Noel Skehan was born in December 1944 in the village. His father, Dick and his uncles on that side of the family all played hurling, with Johnny Skehan winning an All-Ireland junior medal with Kilkenny in 1928. But an even more famous hurling pedigree came from his mother's side. May Kennedy was a sister of Dan Kennedy who was captain of the Kilkenny team in 1947 when they had a marvellous one-point victory over Cork in what is regarded as one of the best finals ever. May was also a first cousin of Ollie Walsh, which made the two greatest net-minders Kilkenny ever had, and possibly the hurling world has ever seen, second cousins.

Noel married Mary Scott from Lisdowney in 1968, and they have three children, Brian, Niall and Noelle all of whom are now living in Dublin.

Noel lived with his parents, his brother PJ and sister Patti in 'The Ring' in Bennettsbridge, which in those days was where all the hurling was done. As a very young boy, he watched the lads playing in the green area in the middle of the estate and it wasn't long before he was hurling himself with pieces of broken hurleys that had been discarded by the older boys. Skehan remembers well the Saturday evening that his mother came home from Kilkenny with a brand new hurl, which she had purchased for him in Liam Moore's shop in Parliament Street. It was such a thrill to have a new hurl which had the name of the shop stamped on it. For weeks afterwards, he continued to wash the hurl any time it got dirty, and he was particularly careful to wash around the shop's brand, of which he was very proud. The next big thrill was when his uncle, Paddy Kennedy sent him home a pair of hurling boots from England. He was about six years old at that time and he wore the boots all day every day for about three weeks.

His uncle, Dan Kennedy was a passionate hurling man and lived, ate and slept hurling. Dan lived next door to the Skehans and instilled his own love for the game into the hearts of the young boys of the village and especially his nephew. 'When coaching wasn't structured as it is today, Dan was all the time coaching us,' recalled Noel. 'As well as watching us playing the seven-a-side matches in The Ring, he encouraged us to practise on our own. If he saw any faults in our game, he pointed them out, and got us to change.'

Noel remembers that he was mainly a left-handed striker of the ball in those days, and Dan took him aside and told him that he was 'at nothing' if he did not develop his right-hand stroke. He brought him to the wall at the back of the house and told him to puck the ball for ten minutes every day with his right hand. This wall became the training ground where most of the Skehan skills were developed. He spent hours there, belting the ball against the wall. On the other side of the house from Kennedys lived Paddy Kelly who threw back the stray balls that went into his house. Windows were constantly broken, but luckily Paddy was a hurling man too and as long as it was a hurling ball that broke his windows, he didn't mind!

As they grew a little older, the young boys ventured up to the hurling field in the evenings to watch the club seniors training. They usually positioned themselves behind the goal to puck the ball back, but as a young teenager, Noel was thrilled one evening when he was asked to go out on the field to puck the ball in for 'backs and forwards.' 'The Bridge,' as they are known locally, were now county champions and were winning all before them. It was a huge honour for a young boy from the village to be allowed to take part in their training sessions. The next big break for Noel came one evening when they were short one player to play a match amongst themselves and he was told to 'go up on the far goal.' Little did the exasperated trainer know, when he was hurriedly trying to sort out two teams for a match, that he had unwittingly assigned a youngster to a position where he would be part of a Kilkenny senior panel for over 20 years, win seven All-Star Awards as a goalkeeper and amass a record total of nine All-Ireland medals! Noel became a regular for the goal for those training sessions, and particularly when regular goalkeeper, Liam Cleere went to Dublin to work and was not available during the week. Noel became the number one keeper for the weekday sessions.

Ollie Walsh was by now making a name for himself as a goalkeeper for Thomastown and for the Kilkenny minor team, and was a regular caller to Skehans with his parents for family visits. Noel was small in stature, and he liked playing in goal, but when he saw that his cousin was over six feet and well built, he began to have doubts about his ability to 'make it' in that position. He accepted later that he was not going to be a big man, but if he was going to make a success of the position, he would have to learn to deal with high balls differently to his illustrious cousin.

Bennettsbridge did not take part in the primary schools championship, but following his showing in the training field with the club senior team, Noel was selected as goalkeeper with the minor team at the age of 12. He continued to do practice routines to improve his reflexes and he worked harder at the back wall of the house. He would start about 20 yards out, hitting the ball against the wall and controlling the return. Then he would move closer and closer to the wall hitting harder and harder until he was confident that he could react and stop a ball from as close as ten yards. Out on The Ring, he would set up two goals 25 yards apart, and with another boy, they would belt balls as hard as they could at each other. Despite all that practice, he still worried that he would not be big enough to be accepted as a goalkeeper, and he played as often as he could out the field. As he got older, he played in the forwards for the club under-16 and minor teams.

When Noel he went to the Vocational School in Kilkenny, he was on the team as a half- forward, and they won the Leinster senior final in 1960 and 1961 only to be beaten by Tipperary and Cork in the All-Ireland finals. Tom Walsh from Thomastown and Claus Dunne from Mooncoin were in the half forward line with Noel. Both were outstanding in those days and made it to the top with the Kilkenny seniors later in that decade. In that illustrious company, Noel did manage to make his own contribution to the scoreboard.

At the age of 15, Noel went with his father to Thomastown to see the Bennettsbridge play St Aidan's of Wexford in a tournament game. He was standing at the railing at the sideline before the game when Dan Kennedy came to him and said, 'Noel, I want you to hurl.' He could not believe his ears. It appears that the regular goalkeeper, Liam Cleere had not turned up. 'But I have no gear,' Noel responded. 'We'll get you gear,' was the reply. So they got him a hurley and a jersey and the young Noel Skehan made his debut with the seniors wearing his runners and short pants.

The 'Bridge won well. Skehan had little to do, fronted as he was by the famous Galway brothers who were a formidable full-back unit. From then on, he played in many tournament games either in goal or in the forwards. He was sub-goalie for the county finals of 1960 and 1962, and collected his first county medal at the age of 16. He played at wing-forward in the county final against Glenmore in 1964 and scored 1–2. He won six medals in all playing in goal for the 1966, 1967 and 1971 finals. My own team, The Rower-Inistioge beat them in the 1968 final and stopped them winning three-in-a-row. Noel regrets that there was no All-Ireland club championship in those years, particularly for those players who were outstanding for their club but never got their place on the county team.

Fr Nugent, a former St Kieran's College man, was hugely influential in developing that Bennettsbridge team in the 1950s to be one of the best club teams in the country. He had a passion for hurling. He was a good disciplinarian and in the early days 'hounded' the lads up to the field for training. He accepted no excuses for anyone missing a session, and questioned them the next night as to why they were not there. He even checked up at their place of work if he was told that they were working. Nugent was also good at skill and team play and organised routines to improve these aspects of their game each night.

While Fr Nugent was not involved with the minor team, he made sure that they were being coached and organised a match between an 'A' and a 'B' team each year so that he could spot any new talent emerging.

Following his performances with the Vocational School team, Noel was in contention for a place on the 1961 Kilkenny minor team as a forward and was thrilled to get the card asking him to attend a trial. Kilkenny had won the Leinster minor final at that stage and were trying to finalise a panel for the All-Ireland semi-final against Galway. The printed card stated 'a car will collect you at 7 p.m.' Noel had his gear and hurl ready in good time and waited outside the door for the car to come. He waited and waited but the car failed to arrive. Eventually as darkness fell, the disappointed young Skehan had to go back into his house knowing that he had lost his chance. Kilkenny went on to win the All-Ireland minor title that year.

The following year, Skehan was impressive as a goalkeeper playing with the Bennettsbridge senior team, and was short-listed for a trial for that position for the Kilkenny minor team. 'A car will collect you at 7 p.m.,' read the card. Noel took no chances this time and cycled to the venue. He impressed sufficiently to be called to a second trial in Kilkenny. The car did arrive this time and he sat in beside Tom Walsh and Johnny Delaney from Thomastown, who were stars from the All-Ireland win the previous year and Mike Twomey from Stoneyford. They were all selected and travelled together to training and to matches for the rest of the season.

For a man who had achieved so much subsequently in his career, I was amazed how passionate he was in describing the thrill of being selected for a Kilkenny team for the first time. 'Unbelievable, just unbelievable, all my dreams were coming true,' he enthused when he described how he felt when he knew that he would be wearing the black and amber jersey and playing for his county. Noel retained this passion for the game right through his playing career, which was what made him so great over a long number of years.

His first match was against Dublin in Nowlan Park and they qualified to meet Wexford in the Leinster final in Croke Park: another milestone for the enthusiastic young Bennettsbridge man. Noel recalled vividly how he felt 40 years ago when he knew that he would be togging out in Croke Park where so many great men had done so before. He would be standing between the posts where Tony Reddin, Art Foley and Ollie Walsh starred for their counties.

Kilkenny had a tough struggle against a great Wexford team that day and barely survived to win 5–7 to 5–4. 'The forwards, particularly Tom Walsh won it for us that day,' recalled Noel.

Kilkenny qualified to play Tipperary in the All-Ireland final. Tipperary had the young prodigy, Babs Keating, who was making his third attempt to win a minor All-Ireland medal against Kilkenny. Pat Drennan was detailed to mark the Tipperary star, and there was considerable talk in Kilkenny before the game as to whether the Gowran man would be able to hold young Keating or not. Noel recalled that he got a few tricky shots to save early on in the game which settled him down and he grew in confidence as the game went on. Pat Drennan succeeded in marking the Tipperary star very effectively, and when Babs was moved to full forward to try to salvage the game, Pat moved with him to full-back. Noel remembers that when he was taking a puck-out late in the game, he asked the umpire how much time was left. 'Only two minutes, ye have it won anyhow,' was the reply. But before the final whistle, Babs Keating made one final effort and caught a high ball. His way was barred by Drennan, but he laid it off to the incoming Francis Loughnane who sent a pile-driver towards the net. I remember seeing Skehan making a tremendous reflex save in that final minute of the game, and I knew that Kilkenny had another star goalkeeper to follow in the footsteps of the great Ollie Walsh. Skehan cleared the ball up the field and the final whistle blew leaving Kilkenny winners by 3–6 to 0–9. Noel had kept a clean sheet in his first All-Ireland.

Noel continued to impress as a goalkeeper with his club and was selected on the Kilkenny intermediate team in 1962 only to be beaten by Carlow who went on to win the All-Ireland that year. In 1963, the Kilkenny intermediate team was defeated by Wexford in the Leinster final by 3–8 to 3–6, and Noel thought that his days with Kilkenny were finished for that year.

However, after the Leinster senior final, a card arrived telling him to go to Nowlan Park for training. He thought there was some mistake, as they were out of the Championship. The mystery was solved shortly afterwards when Paddy O'Neill from the local club, and a selector on the Kilkenny senior team, told him that he had been selected as sub-goalie for the All-Ireland final. 'I could hardly contain my excitement,' said Noel. 'It was unreal that I would be now training in Nowlan Park with players who were my heroes.' He travelled to the first session with clubmate Seamus Cleere, and he remembers seeing Sean Clohosey and Billy Dwyer for the first time at close quarters. 'I looked forward to every training night and I enjoyed playing in goal and trying to stop shots fired at me by all those greats. When the big day came, I was overwhelmed by the occasion and I remember sitting on the bench hoping that Ollie would not be injured and praying that I would not be called in.'

Kilkenny won that All-Ireland, defeating Waterford by 4–17 to 6–8. Noel really savoured the celebrations and the homecoming to Kilkenny City and hoped that he would keep his place on the panel and some day take over the number one jersey when his cousin retired.

His hurling career was nearly brought to an abrupt end in 1964 when he broke a bone in his neck in a car accident on his way to work. He spent three months in hospital and had to wear a collar for a further six months. However, in 1965 he began hurling again for his club and was recalled to the Kilkenny senior panel following their defeat in the 1966 final. Noel remembers going with the team to Croke Park to play in an Oireachtas or Walsh Cup game. He got his first chance to stand between the posts when Ollie Walsh had to retire injured.

From then until late in 1971 he sat on the subs' bench watching and cheering on his team. He saw Kilkenny defeat Tipperary and Cork in the 1967 and 1969 All-Ireland finals and he saw them being beaten by Tipperary in 1971. He studied the play of the legendary Ollie between the posts and the way the backs defended. He saw what it took for a team to win matches and he also saw where mistakes were made which led to defeat for his county.

In September 1971, Ollie stepped down and Noel took over the number one shirt at the start of the League, a shirt he was to wear with distinction for another 14 years.

Bennettsbridge beat The Fenians in the 1971 county final by 3–10 to 1–7, and the club nominated Noel as captain of the Kilkenny team for 1972. Kilkenny and Wexford drew in the Leinster final in a pulsating, high-scoring 80-minute game. Wexford led by ten points at one stage and it looked as if the writing was on the wall for Kilkenny when they were reduced to 14 men after Mick Brennan was sent off. There were still 23 minutes left in the game and they were seven points in arrears. But Kilkenny clawed their way back and Mick Crotty sent over the equaliser on the call of time. The score was 6–13 each.

The Wexford backs had pulverised the Kilkenny goal and there was talk in Kilkenny about changing the goalkeeper for the replay. The selectors kept faith in the captain, and Noel justified their confidence by having the game of his life, conceding only one goal and making a series of miraculous saves which kept Kilkenny in the game. The sides were level with ten minutes remaining, but Kilkenny scored two goals and a few points during the final minutes and won by 3–16 to 1–14. Noel had the honour of lifting the Bob O'Keeffe trophy on the steps of the Hogan Stand.

Kilkenny had an easy win over Galway in the semi-final and Noel led his team out in Croke Park in September of that year to take on the much-fancied Cork in the final. Cork justified their rating in the first half and, with Ray Cummins in devastating form, they bombarded the Kilkenny goal and had scored an amazing 5–11 with 20 minutes still remaining. Con Roche's point from over 80 yards out was Cork's last score and Kilkenny went on to score 2–9 without reply and won by 3–24 to 5–11 in one of the most amazing finals ever played. Noel had the honour of lifting the McCarthy Cup before thousands of delirious Kilkenny fans.

When the Kilkenny team of the 1970s is being discussed in the county, there is a general consensus that the display given by the team in the 1973 Leinster final against Wexford was the peak performance of that team. Noel and I had, in some ways similar views of the game from different sides of the field. I was playing at left corner forward and, of all the games I ever played in, I never had so little to do. The ball was worked down the field. Players ran into position perfectly and most of the scores were created and finished before the ball reached the full-forward line.

Noel recalls too that he never saw a team working so well together for a full game. 'Every member of the team did everything to perfection, passing, supporting, running into position and striking. It was like clockwork.' For the record, the final score was Kilkenny 4–22, Wexford 3–15.

Things, of course, changed dramatically for the All-Ireland final with four players missing through injury for the game against Limerick. The cohesion and combination of the team was naturally disrupted for that final, but that great Limerick side had a comprehensive and well-deserved win by 1–21 to 1–14.

Noel still has nightmares about that controversial goal in the second half when the sides were level. He described how the ball ended up in the square on that very wet day. Backs and forwards were on top of each other with the ball underneath. He saw three or four hands trying to grab the ball off the ground. Then someone picked it up, was pushed over the line and dropped it. 'To this day,' sighed Noel, 'I can't believe how the flag went up. It was like a push-over try!' But Kilkenny went on to win two-in-a-row in 1974 and 1975, which Noel felt made up for that defeat.

*Noel Skehan concentrates on stopping the ball in the 1974 All-Ireland final.
From left to right, Ned Rea (Limerick), Fan Larkin (No. 2, Kilkenny),
Jim Treacy (Kilkenny), Matt Ruth (Limerick), Noel Skehan (Kilkenny).*

By the time Kilkenny reached their next All-Ireland final, I had retired from the game and I was appointed joint manager of the team with Pat Henderson for the 1979 campaign. The team was in a transition period and we introduced some new players who fitted in very well. We came through Leinster beating Wexford in the final by 2–21 to 2–17. Galway had surprised Cork in the semi-final and were an exceptionally good team, and I really thought that we would not have the experience and overall strength to overcome them in the All-Ireland. On a very wet day, we did have the luck and got two rather fortuitous goals, which kept us in touch. With 12 minutes to go, we were ahead by 1–10 to 1–8 when Galway were awarded a penalty. Skehan, Larkin and Ger Henderson had been detailed to defend the goal. Noel remembers saying to his colleagues, 'Lads, it can't go in, if we stop it, we'll win.' John Connolly, who had scored two goals against Kilkenny in the previous year's semi-final stood up to take the shot. Noel saved brilliantly with the ball falling dead in front of him. The ever-alert Larkin 'doubled' on it as it fell and drove the ball out to the sideline before the speedy Galway forwards arrived. Liam O'Brien scored a good point shortly afterwards to put us three points ahead before we got the second of our 'lucky' goals to clinch the game.

I saw Noel Skehan play as a minor with Kilkenny. He was a colleague on the senior panel for eight years before he took over from the great Ollie Walsh. I played with him for a further six years and watched him play for almost ten years after I retired myself. He had many great games in the black and amber jersey, but I don't think I have seen him better than in the All-Ireland final of 1982.

Cork were red-hot favourites again to take the title, but the game was fairly evenly balanced after 20 minutes. Then Cork made their bid to establish their authority on the game when Jimmy Barry Murphy and Ray Cummins combined well and opened up the Kilkenny defence before passing to the unmarked Seanie O'Leary. Skehan read the move well and was out on O'Leary in a flash to throw himself in front of his shot and block down the ball. O'Leary met the rebound, but it hit the crossbar and Paddy Prendergast cleared.

Kilkenny then took the initiative and made no mistake with their first serious challenge on the Cork goal when Christy Heffernan deflected a centre by Frank Cummins to the net. He followed up almost immediately with another goal and from then on Kilkenny were in the driving seat. If that first attempt had gone in for Cork, it could have been an entirely different game. In the second half I recall Noel making a series of marvellous saves as the Cork forwards made an almighty effort to get back into the game, but they could not get the ball past the Bennettsbridge man. Apart from stopping the balls, Noel controlled them perfectly and gave the in-rushing forwards no chance of latching on to a rebound. In a last desperate effort, Eamonn O'Donoghue walked the ball from the 21-yard line into the net with half the Kilkenny defence on his back. Even the lanky Eamonn could not have covered the distance in regulation four steps but Kilkenny had no complaints as the match was well and truly wrapped up by then.

Towards the end of the game, Cork had scored a point and the ball was driven into the crowd at the back of the goal. Noel went back with his hand up waiting for them to throw back the ball. No ball was forthcoming and an irritated Noel O'Donoghue who was the referee rushed in as he thought that the Kilkennyman was time-wasting. As he came in, a spectator threw in an apple, which Skehan caught thinking that it was the ball, as did the referee. Noel dropped the apple and the referee charged up to him and said, 'puck it out or I'll abandon the match!'

'What will I puck out?' replied Noel, 'that?' showing him the apple. The referee could only laugh, and Noel put the apple beside the goalpost. After two more puck-outs, the long whistle sounded and Noel went back to the goal to take a bite out of the apple. As the players came in to celebrate, they all got a bite as they danced around the square. It made good television, and Noel told me that he has since met fellows from Mooncoin, Conahy, Carlow, Wexford and even Antrim who claimed that they were the generous benefactors of the fruit. Talk about the GPO in 1916. The final score was Kilkenny 3–18, Cork 1–13.

Noel won the Man of the Match award on 'The Sunday Game' on RTE for his performance and later the Texaco Award as Hurler of the Year. He went on to win his ninth and last All-Ireland medal in the following year when Kilkenny confirmed their 1982 win by beating the Rebels by 2–14 to 2–12. That was effectively the end of the famous 'double double' team who won both the League and the Championship in 1982 and 1983, a feat that will probably never be equalled.

Noel was hugely dedicated to the game of hurling and spent hours practising on his own and was always in Nowlan Park well before the appointed time for training. When I moved to Kilkenny in 1973, I usually tried to get into Nowlan park early to practise frees and my own routines. However, I don't think I ever got there before Skehan and he liked nothing better than having someone there to blast shots at him.

The day before an All-Ireland can often be very difficult for players. Noel used say to himself, 'don't worry, don't get excited. The match is not until 3.30 tomorrow. There are no goals gone in yet.' He established a regular routine for himself. On the Saturday evening before the game, he always went to the hurling field on his own pucking the ball, and practising the puck-outs. Then at 5.30, he went to Kilkenny and played squash for 30 minutes. Then he had a shower and went home to relax. He always made sure that he stuck to his routine and that everything was right for the game and always went into a game feeling confident that his preparations were perfect.

Noel found that squash was very good for sharpening his reflexes, and although he took up the game initially for that purpose, he became the number one squash player in Kilkenny and held the rank for ten years. He also got three caps playing for Munster at senior level (Kilkenny played in the Munster division).

Noel felt really honoured to have been selected on the Leinster Railway Cup team in 1973 after one year as first-choice goalkeeper with Kilkenny. 'It was something I always dreamed about,' he said. 'It was a great chance to meet and play with players from the other Leinster counties.' He mentioned particularly Tony and Colm Doran from Wexford, but he was loud in his praise for Pat Dunny from Kildare who played at corner-back and gave an outstanding display against Connacht in Ballinasloe in 1974. Padraig Horan played for four years at full-back in front of him and was outstanding.

I saw Noel make one of the outstanding saves of his career in the Railway Cup final of 1975. We were going for a record five-in-a-row wins over Munster and they were throwing everything at us in the second half to snatch victory. Noel made a brilliant interception that saved us. I asked him to describe the save. 'The play was over at the Hogan Stand and I saw that all the backs and opposing forwards were being dragged over to that side of the field. I then saw Jimmy Barry Murphy moving in on the other side totally unmarked. I knew that if the ball came across quickly he would have a goal for the taking. Ray Cummins won the ball out on the sideline and I saw him looking up and knew that he had spotted his colleague who was now on his own on the 21-yard line. I left my line as Ray sent it across and just arrived as Jimmy was about to catch the ball. I tapped the ball away before sending a clearance down the field. I knew that if the Cork sharpshooter had got a shot at me from there, I would have no hope of saving it.' Kilkenny held on to win by 2–9 to 1–11.

Noel holds a record seven All-Star Awards and he considers it a great honour to have been selected. He thinks that it is a shame that the trips to America for the All-Stars were discontinued. 'It was another great opportunity to meet hurlers and footballers from other counties and to play and socialise with them abroad,' he said. His first trip across the Atlantic was in 1967 with the Kilkenny team. Tom Walsh and myself were injured in the All-Ireland final of that year and were unable to play against New York in the Gaelic Grounds. Also, there were a number of the Kilkenny team unable to play in the first match due to reactions to the compulsory injections that were required to enter the USA at that time. As a result of the defections, the selectors were forced to play Noel as a forward in the first leg but he had to go back in goal after Ollie Walsh was knocked out by the uncompromising New York forwards midway through the game.

Noel played most of his inter-county hurling under the 'new' 1970s rules which gave protection to the goalkeeper, and I have heard commentators from time to time wonder how the Bennettsbridge man would have fared under the old rules. I saw him play that day, and he gave a display of fearless goal-keeping under the most difficult conditions, and with the New Yorkers trying everything to drive him into the back of the net. I can assure those who did not see him play under the 'old' rules, he could hold the net intact in any situation.

Apart from his uncle, Dan Kennedy, Fr Nugent and the tips he got from watching Ollie Walsh while he sat on the bench as his understudy for eight years, Noel credits Fr Tommy Maher as the man who had the biggest influence on his career.

'Fr Maher was a huge influence,' Noel enthused. 'Taking over from the outstanding and popular Ollie Walsh wasn't easy, but Fr Maher made it easy for me. He would talk to me during every training session and tell me what he wanted me to do. I always felt happy going out for the game knowing what was expected of me. He was dead honest and genuine in the way he advised, and he would tell you nicely if you didn't do as he said! He didn't complicate matters with too much detail or instructions.'

Noel remembers Fr Maher taking him into the small dressing room in Croke Park before the Leinster final in 1973. 'You'll have no bother today stopping or clearing ball,' he told him.

'But Wexford have Murphy, Jacob and Doran – the best half-back line in the country. I don't want you hitting any puck-outs down on top of our half-forwards. I want you to puck them to centre-field.' Noel followed those instructions, and as he told us earlier in this chapter, he considered the Kilkenny performance that day as the best he had seen.

Noel Skehan's achievements are extraordinary. He holds nine All-Ireland and eleven Leinster medals. He won three National Leagues, four Oireachtas and four Railway Cups. He has five Walsh Cup medals, and three AIB Wembley tournament medals. He was awarded seven All-Stars, one Texaco, four B & I monthly trophies and won RTE's 'Man of the Match' for the 1972 and 1982 All-Irelands. He also won the RTE 'Save of the Year' competition in 1980 following a brilliant save from Padraig Horan in the Leinster final. He regards the 1976 Leinster final as his best game in the black and amber jersey and the 1973 Leinster final as his most enjoyable. He played for the last time for Kilkenny in a game in Callan in March 1985.

When I asked Noel for his special memories with his county, he replied, 'every day I put on a black and amber jersey was special for me, but to select one I would have to say the 1972 All-Ireland when I was captain.'

From that statement alone it is easy to see how Noel Skehan was so dedicated to training, so focused on striving for perfection in the very onerous position of goalkeeper. But the fact that he still spends his time coaching teams shows that his love for hurling and the GAA continues to motivate him. He became involved through Leinster Hurling Officer, Brendan O'Sullivan and went around Leinster with him to many coaching sessions. He then went to the GAA coaching courses and obtained his qualification. He has been the Kilkenny junior, intermediate, under-21 and minor coach for various terms winning nine Leinster titles and one All-Ireland. He is the current intermediate team coach and an advisor to the senior team.

Noel is somewhat worried that more counties are not coming through to be real contenders for the top honours. He is not convinced that the back-door system is helping in that regard. It has provided some great matches, he concedes, but maybe the re-entry of the first round losers would be of more benefit to the so called weaker counties.

He is concerned that too much time is taken up with physical training and not enough with the skills. 'Soccer players train five days and play a match every week, and we are told that there are about 20 skills in the game to be perfected. There are 125 skills in hurling and hurlers expect to perfect them with two nights training. I would like to see players spending more time practising on their own,' he concluded.

He believes that the present hurling ball is far too lively and light and that the puck-outs from the goal are travelling too far and taking centre-field play out of the game. Noel is totally against professionalism in the GAA and feels that the players are very well looked after. He questions the motivation behind the newly formed Players' Association and wonders if there is a need at all there. He is horrified that an outside body should be trying to undermine the Association. He is very loyal to the GAA, but he feels that they have erred by keeping the supporters off the pitch in Croke Park at the end of the finals. He said that there was nothing like receiving the cup with the fans milling around the old presentation area in the Hogan stand. 'Players should be able to experience that,' he said.

Kilkenny have been very lucky that they had two goalkeepers of the sheer genius of Noel Skehan and Ollie Walsh to mind the net for a total span of 30 years. It is remarkable that both goalkeepers were second cousins and it is no coincidence that Kilkenny won a total of ten All-Ireland senior titles during that period. They could justifiably wear the mantle of 'The Princes of Goalkeepers.'

Noel Skehan's Team of the Century

*(selected from players he played against in the
Championship and League from 1972 to 1984.*

Seamus Durack
(Clare)

Tadgh O'Connor
(Tipperary)

Pat Hartigan
(Limerick)

John Horgan
(Cork)

Tom Cashman
(Cork)

Mick Jacob
(Wexford)

Iggy Clarke
(Galway)

John Connolly
(Galway)

Gerald McCarthy
(Cork)

Jimmy
Barry Murphy
(Cork)

Ray Cummins
(Cork)

Martin Quigley
(Wexford)

Charlie McCarthy
(Cork)

Tony Doran
(Wexford)

Eamon Cregan
(Limerick)

14 – Tom Walsh

Tom Walsh

'How is Tom Walsh?' In my travels around the country and my meetings with people from all counties and with varying sporting interests, that is the question most frequently asked of me. Tom Walsh from Thomastown thrilled hurling followers from all counties from the day he blasted on to the national scene in the All-Ireland minor final of 1961. His unique hurling style continued to excite the followers during his second year as a minor in 1962 after which he was immediately promoted to the senior team.

'Tom is great form. He has done exceptionally well in his business life. He is a good friend of mine and we play golf frequently together,' is my usual reply to the question.

In the 1963 Championship, he made his mark as a 19-year-old 'boy wonder.' After a series of spectacular goals throughout the season, the late Micheál Ó Hehir colourfully described him as 'the blond bombshell from Thomastown!' He was adding a new dimension to corner forward play, which was unique for the style of game that was played in the 1960s. Sports reporters searched for metaphors, and Mick Dunne, Paddy Downey and John D. Hickey were coming up with 'whirlwind' and 'will o' the wisp'. Like his good friend, mentor and fellow clubman, the late Ollie Walsh who had opened a whole new chapter in spectacular goalkeeping skills in the previous decade, Tom Walsh was now doing the same for the right corner-forward position.

He was the darling of Kilkenny fans and the bane of every corner back's life for a further four years until his hurling career was brought to a sudden and premature end following an injury received in the 1967 All-Ireland final which resulted in the loss of an eye. Although only 23 years of age at the time, he had made such an impact on the game during his all-too-short career, he had established himself as a legend in hurling terms before that fateful day in Croke Park. Thirty-three years later, his extraordinary hurling feats are still remembered by his contemporaries.

'How good was Tom Walsh?' is another question asked by the younger generation of fans, and indeed by some hurling 'greats' of the present day. You have to start by trying to describe what the 'old' game of hurling was like before the 1970s rule changes came into force. 'Hell's Kitchen' is how the late John D. Hickey described the area in front of goal, particularly when his beloved Tipperary team was in full flight. 'Pulling' and 'dragging' was acceptable behaviour, and forwards were 'fair game' from tough, uncompromising backs.

What, you might be asked, was a slightly built, five feet, nine inch tall youngster doing in there then? Well, that 19-year-old knew no fear. He had an amazing turn of speed, a marvellous vision for creating and getting scores. No ball that entered the forward area was a lost cause, and he chased it until it was converted to a score by himself or by one of his colleagues. His hurling action was almost always the first-time pull which never gave his opponent a chance to get close to him. He was always darting into the square to connect on any ball dropping in that area, and most of the spectacular goals he scored were from balls hit first time off the ground in front of goal.

'Who was he like in today's game?' Tom would have been superb in any era. One of my big regrets during my own career was that Tom was not around when the 1970s rule changes came in and when the Kilkenny team of the early 1970s developed. He would have been unstoppable with the newly-found freedom that forwards were given in front of goal, and I would have enjoyed linking with him in the attack during the many great games of that period.

Tom's running with and off the ball was like that of Jamesie O'Connor during Clare's great run in the late 1990s. His bravery in diving to block down clearances, or in chasing the lost ball which invariably ended up in the net was reminiscent of DJ Carey at his persistent best. His clinical finishing of the half chance in front of goal was like that of Joe Deane or Seanie McGrath feeding off crumbs.

Tom was born in 1944, the son of Patrick F. Walsh, a third generation Thomastown man. His mother, Kathleen Cassin was from neighbouring Inistioge parish. His older brothers Larry (known locally as LJ) and Paddy were outstanding under-age and college hurlers before emigrating to America in the 1950s. Brother, Martin was a contemporary of mine and we won two All-Ireland medals together with St Kieran's College. We also played together on the Kilkenny minor team of 1958. Martin played club hurling in Dublin for a few years, but became engrossed in a business venture and his interest in playing hurling waned. The Walsh sisters, Philomena and Breda also emigrated to New York.

Patrick F. Walsh was a publican, auctioneer and undertaker and was a keen sportsman in his day. He was a good boxer, a keen tennis player and a low handicap golfer. But hurling was the sport played by the young people of Thomastown and, with his older brothers making their mark with the local school team, it was natural that Tom would have a hurl in his hand at an early age. In those days, most of the possessions of younger members of big families were acquired through the 'hand-me-down' system, and Tom's first hurls came from his big brothers. His father occasionally employed a local carpenter, Eddie Hogan, to make coffins, and Eddie was prevailed upon regularly to re-model the hurls discarded by the older Walsh brothers to suit the diminutive future hurling star.

Tom remembers spending hours with Martin hurling in their yard across the road. A short distance away was the local ball alley and the two boys got great enjoyment playing handball there. They soon realised that they could use the alley to sharpen their hurling skills, and every day the noise of a sponge or tennis ball could be heard resounding around the walls with the occasional clash of hurls as they tried to beat one another at this 'new' game. Tom regarded that period as a marvellous learning experience in his hurling life. All the skills could be worked on there by meeting the ball coming from all directions, picking out spots on the wall to aim for and doubling on the ball coming off the back wall.

Peadar Laffan was the local schoolmaster and had built up a proud tradition of hurling success in the primary schools championship. Thomastown were almost unbeatable and in that period they won 11 out of 13 Roinn A county finals. When Tom came to the school, there was an absolute confidence amongst the young hurlers that they would win every year. This was an under-14 competition, and he made his debut on the team as a very small nine-year-old. His first match was against Mooncoin, and he remembers getting clear instructions from Mr Laffan that day. 'Tom,' he said, 'you'll be playing right half-forward today. You have one duty only and that's to hit every ball you get straight in to the full-forward. If you do that you'll have done the job I want you to do.' Tom did as instructed and Danny Lannon, who was big and strong at full-forward got a bag full of goals. They beat Castlecomer in the final that year, and Tom went on to win four county medals at that grade only to be beaten in his last year in the school.

The success of Thomastown School did not come without hard work and dedication. Peadar Laffan was well ahead of his time in coaching methods, discipline and in the general preparation of his teams. He never missed a training session in Grennan field and every player knew that every session would be interesting, with some new skill to be worked on. He told each player how he wanted him to play in his position on the field. He also studied other teams and he coached his team on how to counteract the play of the good players on the opposition.

In the backs and forwards routines he pointed out the mistakes as the session progressed and praised a player who carried out his directions well. Laffan appointed free-takers and players to take sideline cuts, and he had them working on these skills at every session. He created a terrific interest in the team amongst the people of the town, and Tom remembers the train to Kilkenny being packed with Thomastown people going to the games. When they won, Mr Laffan would have a lorry organised to parade the team with the cup through the town.

The day after a county final win was a great day in school. They were all given orange and biscuits, and the cup was displayed for all to see. The routine was not so much for the members of the successful team, but to inspire and create an interest for the next generation of hurlers. The following day, the far-seeing schoolmaster would be seen out in the playground observing the very young hurlers and spotting those with exceptional talent to cultivate for the following year's team.

Peadar Laffan's sole interest was with the school teams, and he handed over a pool of players to the club every year for the club coaches to bring to the next stage. Thomastown had some success at under-16 and minor grades, but not nearly to the same degree that the teams had achieved in the schools championship. At adult level they were even less successful. The club had won its one and only senior championship in 1946. Tom Walsh was selected on the team at the age of 18, and they were then a junior club. They had difficulty in winning the Championship, but eventually beat Coon in the 1962 final and were promoted to senior grade.

They made little impact at that level and played in just one county final in 1967 when they were beaten by neighbours, Bennettsbridge.

I put it to Tom that it was extraordinary that a parish with such a pool of excellent under-14 players coming year after year from the school team could not dominate the junior or senior championships to the same degree. He found it hard to come up with an answer, but expressed the view that it could have been that the players might have burned out their enthusiasm in trying to 'win for Mr Laffan,' and that they lost interest when they left that environment.

One player that certainly did not lose interest when he left primary school was the late Ollie Walsh. There is a book in itself to be written about the legendary goalkeeper and his contribution to Thomastown Hurling Club, Kilkenny and to the GAA in general. He was the dominant player in Kilkenny at under-age level as a goalkeeper and a forward. As a young player, Tom Walsh got his inspiration from the great man. 'He was a great example,' Tom enthused. 'His dedication to the game, his club and his county was without equal. His sportsmanship was beyond reproach, and I never saw him hit another player even though he was always the subject of severe provocation in the position he played and under the rules that applied at the time. He was a major architect in the purchase and development of Thomastown's beloved Grennan field, and when his playing days were over, he continued to make his contribution by managing successful county teams at junior, intermediate and senior level.'

Tom made no secret of the fact that Ollie was his idol, and although ten years his senior, they became very good friends. Ollie started working as a driver for the local creamery and Tom regularly went on the milk run with him in the lorry and they talked hurling all day. In the evening, Ollie took him down to Grennan and they spent hours practising. Tom must have hit thousands of balls at him in the goal trying to beat him. 'If you beat Ollie Walsh for a score, you knew you had achieved something. You knew that you wouldn't be meeting any better goalkeeper no matter what team you played against.'

When Tom joined the county minor and senior teams, Ollie took him under his wing and they travelled together to matches. 'It was great to have someone like Ollie Walsh there with you to encourage and support you,' concluded Tom.

Tom's older brothers had gone away to work and it was expected that he would be the one to carry on the family business. However, having seen his parents working long hours in the bar and devoting additional unsociable hours to the auctioneering and undertaking side of the business, he decided that it was not for him. He too left the nest and started his first job in Dunnes Stores in South Great George's Street in Dublin. After a year or so he came back to Thomastown to work in a local retail store. In 1966 he moved to a company, Runtalrad Ltd, which in that year had started operations in the town, manufacturing central heating radiators. This company was owned by the Jones Group, and in the mid-1970s they joined forces with a French company to establish Tube Rollers Ltd in Callan, who manufactured steel tubing. The group then embarked on an expansion programme. During all this time, Tom's career had progressed rapidly and in 1991 he was appointed joint chief executive of the five companies that comprised the manufacturing division of Jones Group plc. After 30 years with the company, he retired in 1996.

Thomastown won the county minor championship in 1959 and Billy Grace was captain of the county minor team the following year when Kilkenny won the All-Ireland against Tipperary. Paddy Dempsey was the goalkeeper and Mickey Kelly was on the panel. Tom was only 16 that year and was not considered for a trial, but in 1961 he made the team along with John Murphy and Johnny Delaney from Thomastown.

He remembers the excitement of learning that he was selected to play a trial match early in the 1961 season. When he went into the dressing room, he was greeted by John O'Brien from Goresbridge. John was a star of the previous year's team, and he greeted Tom with the words 'what are you doing here, sure you must be on the team already.' Tom actually played on John in the trial and to his horror was taken off after 20 minutes, but John O'Brien was obviously right. The young man from Thomastown had done enough already to justify his selection. They became firm friends, even when John emigrated to Chicago and until a few short years ago when the Goresbridge man died prematurely.

It was a great thrill to be collected in a V8 car to go to Croke Park for the first time to play in a Leinster final and he remembers the taxi going to Johnstown to collect Pat Henderson on the way. A great bond developed amongst that team and they had a rather easy victory over Dublin by 4–12 to 0–7.

They had to face a star-studded Tipperary team in the All-Ireland final, which included Babs Keating, Mick Roche, Peter O'Sullivan and Noel Lane. The Kilkenny backs had to withstand ferocious pressure throughout that game with Pat Henderson, John O'Brien and Phil Cullen having outstanding performances. John Murphy and the late Tom Barry, who was playing in his third year at centre-field for the minors were winning the battle in the middle of the field, but scores were hard to come by. With ten minutes to go, I saw Tom Walsh scoring an amazing goal that had the effect of breaking the deadlock and turning the game in Kilkenny's favour. It was not a spectacular score in the terms that we expect nowadays, but the manner in which it was won had to call into play such qualities as speed off the mark, anticipation, judgement and a great deal of courage. These qualities were to become the hallmark of Tom Walsh's play during his all too short hurling career. Peter O'Sullivan fielded a high ball to his right upright and Tom took off from the 21-yard line to dive and block down the ball into the net as the goalkeeper was attempting to clear it down the field. Tom told me that he knew that Peter was so near the post when he caught the ball, he would have to step away from it to strike, so he anticipated his move and just arrived in time. Kilkenny were now in the driving seat and won their second-in-a-row minor final against Tipperary by 3–13 to 0–15.

I had a special interest in those two finals with my own clubmen, PJ Brett and Ollie Ryan starring in 1960 and Pierce Freaney, an outstanding scoring forward giving devastating performances in both years. Pierce linked well with Tom Walsh in the half-forward line.

I knew Tom's brother Martin very well from our days in St Kieran's College, but although we were both in Dublin I had lost contact with him. I was surprised one evening when he arrived in Terenure College as we were training for the Leinster final. Sean Clohosey, Billy Dwyer, Martin Coogan, Sean Buckley and myself were all based in Dublin, and the facilities of the college were made available to us to do our training by two Kilkenny priests Fr Grace and Fr Heaslip.

Martin told us that his brother Tom was now working in Dublin and he wondered if we would mind if Tom joined us for training for the minor team. We were of course delighted to have an extra hurler for our sessions and both of them joined in for the Dublin sessions. We were defeated by Wexford in the senior game, but the minors, inspired by Tom Walsh pulled back an eight-point lead to beat the Slaneysiders by 5–7 to 5–4. Tom regards this as his best game in the black and amber colours. Wexford had a very strong defence led by Dan Quigley and they did very well to score 5–7 against them.

For the third year in a row, they faced Tipperary in the All-Ireland final. Babs Keating was also contesting his third minor final and had with him on that occasion two other future senior stars, Len Gaynor and Francis Loughnane. Tom was playing at centre-forward for that game and his marker was Len Gaynor.

Kilkenny got off to a great start with the Thomastown man scoring 1–2 in the early stages of the game. They kept the pressure on Tipperary all through and kept ahead. A further goal by Tom Walsh in the second half killed off Tipperary's chances and Joe Dunphy became the only Kilkennyman to receive the Irish Press Cup twice. The final score was 3–6 to 0–9.

In the late autumn of 1962 Ollie Walsh brought Tom the news that he had been selected to play on the Kilkenny senior team to play Limerick in a tournament game in the Gaelic Grounds. The only problem was that the Thomastown minor team was playing a game on the same day. Although he has regrets to this day about letting down his club, he decided at the time that he should take his chance and play with the seniors. Ollie took him to the match and he remembers finding the pace of the game very hot and much more physical that he had been used to. However, he impressed the selectors and retained his place on the team and had matured sufficiently to be selected at right full forward for the opening 1963 Championship game against Dublin in Carlow. He was in direct opposition to the inimitable Lar Foley, and he realised after a short time that Lar not too pleased at having a young whippersnapper trying to run around him.

Dublin had a very strong team powered by Des and Lar Foley and the Boothman brothers, but Kilkenny got through to meet rivals, Wexford, in the Leinster final. Kilkenny were beginning to add some youth to their team to complement the experienced players who were still there from the 1950s team. Tom spoke very highly of Billy Dwyer who played a strong play-making role at full forward as well as having an abundance of skill. He was strong and fearless and the 19-year-old regarded Billy as his protector if things got tough. Tom Murphy, from my own club was in the other corner.

'My play was probably unconventional at that time,' Tom said thoughtfully, 'but our coach Fr Maher always gave me my head and I never felt restricted and I moved around the forward line at will.'

Tom played on Tom Neville in the Leinster final and he regarded the Wexfordman as a 'class' player and a great sportsman. Young Walsh got in for a goal early on in the game, which settled him, and he found that his style of play fitted in well with the rest of the forwards and he was very pleased with his overall performance. Kilkenny won by 2–10 to 0–9 in the end.

I remember that Tom was the subject of a lot of media attention before the All-Ireland final of 1963 because of his age and quick progression to senior ranks. I asked him if he felt the pressure or if he was nervous before the game. 'Not really,' he replied, 'I had built up great confidence after two minor wins and did not think of defeat. I had played before huge crowds in those games, so I was well used to that aspect. I was also the junior of the team and I felt that if anything went wrong I would hardly be blamed. We were also extremely well prepared by Fr Maher to face that vastly experienced Waterford side and every player on the opposing team was thoroughly analysed and I knew how I was to play on my marker, Jimmy Byrne.'

Tom was off the mark early in the game with a super goal, which he clipped first time to the net in typical fashion. He knew Billy Dwyer's play well at this stage and when he saw him gaining possession on the 14-yard line he came off his marker and Billy hand-passed it to him and he met the dropping ball on the volley. He got two goals in his first final and his colleague, Tom Murphy in the other corner also got two all snapped up from broken play in front of goal. The game ended as one of the highest scoring 60-minute finals of all time with Kilkenny winning by 4–17 to 6–8.

He still recalls with affection the celebrations after that All-Ireland. The Kilkenny Association had arranged a dinner in the Hollybrook Hotel in Clontarf, which was swamped with fans trying to gain access. It was great to experience the joy on the faces of the otherwise calm selectors who must have been relieved that their gamble to play a number of young players worked so well. There was a reception the following day for both teams in the Players-Wills factory and then the homecoming by train to Kilkenny that night. Tom remembers the experience of being greeted by 20,000 cheering fans as the team was paraded to the centre of the city in a black and amber bedecked lorry. He remembers Fr Maher's rousing speech from the platform as the throng pushed to get closer to the team. Every week there was a celebration in each parish and it was great to go around and join in those celebrations to honour the local heroes.

Kilkenny were invited to play in Wembley for the annual festival at Whit weekend and Tom felt honoured to play in the world-renowned stadium. It was also great to get away with the team to a different environment.

Even better was to come when the Kilkenny team was invited to New York to play Tipperary, who were League Champions in what was billed as a 'World Cup' in June of 1964. The Irish community in Chicago extended the trip by inviting Kilkenny to their city to play a Chicago team that included Tom's old pal from minor days, John O'Brien. The Kilkenny team was accommodated in a motel in the Windy City and it was the first time that they got away together and lived together for any period of time. Tom felt that the trip served to help players to get to know each other better, and great friendships were established which helped them to perform well as a team in subsequent years. The many great stories of that trip are better told verbally or left for another book. The team was given a civic reception by Mayor Daley in the civic offices. On another night, we were introduced from the stage at a major concert where the Clancy Brothers were top of the bill. We then were flown to New York and crowned a magnificent trip by beating Tipperary by 4–16 to 3–13, Tom scoring one of the goals.

Tipperary however got their revenge in an emphatic manner on the day that counted on the first Sunday in September when we went down by an embarrassing 5–13 to 2–8. The great Tipperary team of the 1960s hit its peak in that final and we had no answer. 'The game never flowed for us to put them under any pressure that day,' said Tom. 'We were very disappointing and we could only put it down to experience for the next encounter.'

Tom Walsh strikes in the 1964 All-Ireland. From left to right, Kieran Carey (Tipperary),
Tom Murphy (Kilkenny), Tom Walsh (Kilkenny), Michael Maher (Tipperary),
Seamus Cleere (Kilkenny), John Doyle (Tipperary), Tony Wall (Tipperary),
Tom Forristal (Kilkenny).

Tipperary again confirmed their superiority in the Oireachtas final of 1964 played in October. Kilkenny were well ahead at half time, and Tom remembers the selectors telling them that if they could get one more goal early in the second half, that we would finish them off. Tom got an early goal, but Tipperary clawed their way back and eventually beat us by 5–7 to 4–8.

Tom remembers shaking hands with John Doyle after the final whistle and the Holycross man saying to him 'F★★★ it Walsh, ye'll never beat us!' Those two defeats aside, it had been a good year for Tom Walsh and Kilkenny with the winning of the first of his three Railway Cup medals on St Patrick's day of that year, the Leinster final and of course the trips abroad.

Kilkenny and Wexford had great battles in the 1960s, but there was only one occasion in Tom's career when the Slaneysiders came out on top. Tom recalls two incidents in the 1965 Leinster final which worked against Kilkenny and gave Wexford a narrow win. The match was a draw coming into the closing stages when Andy Comerford got a ball in the left corner and rounded his man and soloed into the centre. He hand-passed the ball, which hit the far upright and dropped down on top of the net and over the bar. Tom's recollection of the incident is the same as my own, as I was standing on the 21 expecting a pass from Andy if he got into trouble. However, the 'point' was signalled a 'wide' by the umpire. Just on full time, Oliver 'Hopper' McGrath came in on the right wing for Wexford and sent in a shot and the umpire at the other end waved the white flag for a point. I had no idea from our side of the field if it was over the bar or not, but I remember the Kilkenny corner back, Jim Treacy being adamant in the dressing room afterwards that the ball was wide of the post. Tom said that he travelled back from the match with Ollie Walsh who he said was the fairest sportsman he had ever encountered. He never heard him criticise a fellow player or an opponent. Ollie said to him coming home in the car 'the ball was a foot wide, but leave it at that.' In all the great games with Wexford for the last 30 years, there were many close finishes where we came out on top. Wexford played better that day and deserved their victory. The final score was Wexford 2–11, Kilkenny 3–7.

1966, in many ways, was a memorable year for Kilkenny in that they defeated Tipperary in the Home League final by 0–9 to 0–7. While Kilkenny had beaten Tipperary in League semi-finals, the team of the 1960s had not beaten them in a final until then. The game was played in Croke Park in a gale force wind, which made scoring very difficult. Kilkenny had the wind in the first half but did not seem to have enough scores on the board at half time to hold out in the second half. I remember handing over the free-taking duties to Tom during that match. My style was to roll-lift the ball and as I rose it for the first two frees, the wind took the ball away before I struck it. Tom used the jab-lift style, which was more suitable for the conditions. We did not get too many frees, but Tom scored any close-in frees we got.

Our backs, led by Pa Dillon at full-back were tremendous, and they kept the Tipperary machine to a minimum of scores and we held out for a narrow victory. Kilkenny avenged the previous year's defeat by Wexford in the Leinster final by 1–15 to 2–6 and went on to meet a youthful Cork side in the All-Ireland final.

Kilkenny were hot favourites to win, but were blown out of Croke Park by a fired-up young Cork side who needed to re-establish Cork's supremacy after 12 years in the wilderness.

'Incidents win matches,' said Tom. 'I remember getting a goal in the first half which was disallowed and a free-in awarded. We got the point, but from the puck-out a Cork forward hit a high ball from the right which looked to be going over the bar. However, it hit the top of the upright and bounced down into the square and was tapped home by an alert Colm Sheehan. That was a turnabout of five points in about two minutes. As underdogs, they were keener and chased everything and made things happen on the day.' It was an expensive lesson but it served Kilkenny well in subsequent meetings with the Rebel County.

Afterwards a story circulated in the newspapers that the Kilkenny team had taken sleeping tablets the night before the game in their Dublin hotel. It was claimed that their lethargic performance was due to the medication. I was living in Dublin at the time so I slept at home, but none of the players I spoke to knew anything about that claim. Tom confirmed to me that he shared a room with Tom Forristal and they talked hurling and about the game until they fell asleep. It must have been a slow news day.

Tom regarded himself as being very lucky by avoiding injury for many years. 'Although I was playing competitive hurling from the age of nine, it was 1964 before I got my first stitch. he said.

However his luck ran out in the 1966 Leinster final when he received a blow to the head by a Wexford defender, following which he had to spend ten days in hospital. In fact he was a doubtful starter for the All-Ireland final that year. The swelling to his face was so bad that his father did not know him when he called to the hospital to see him. There was severe swelling around the eye and it took a week for it to reduce sufficiently for the eye specialist to examine his eye for possible damage. Fortunately there was no eye damage on that occasion and Tom was able to take his place for the All-Ireland final, but he was not so lucky the following year in the Championship final.

The Kilkenny team of the 1960s had matured to its full potential and had a comprehensive win over Wexford in the 1967 Leinster final by 4–10 to 1–12. The stage was now set for an All-Ireland confrontation with arch-rivals, Tipperary. Memories of 1964 were firmly embedded in the minds of the Kilkenny team, and they had been given a confidence boost in 1966 by beating them in the League final. Tom remembers a huge build-up to this game with the print media trying to match the relatively new television phenomenon. Fr Maher and the selectors pulled out all the stops in the preparations for the game. Fr Maher coached each member of the team individually and set goals for them to achieve. The team went into this All-Ireland better prepared than ever before, and was determined to win it. The players felt too that they had thrown away the 1966 final and they were not going to accept defeat on this occasion.

The team management decided that the team should sleep at home the night before the game and travel by train on the morning of the game. Spirits were high and someone had the idea of playing 'pitch and toss' in the corridor of the train. After winning the game with a great pitch, Ollie Walsh went to hit the doorway of the compartment with his fist in the excitement, but the sliding door moved and he drove his fist through the glass. Tom remembers blood squirting everywhere and Dr Cuddihy being called to try to stop the bleeding. They wrapped his hands with towels and took him straight from Kingsbridge Station in a taxi to the Mater Hospital. It was difficult to avoid the Kilkenny fans at the station as people came up to Ollie to try shake his hand and wish him luck. It was vital that the media did not get hold of the story at that stage, so they slipped him out the back way. He had to have seven stitches inserted in the wrist and was told by the doctor in the hospital that there was no way that he could play a game. In fact they wanted to retain him for observation. But Ollie took the field, played the game of his life and won the 'Man of the Match' award, and the Texaco Award as Player of the Year as a result of his great display.

Despite the personal tragedy he suffered in that game, Tom Walsh regards that win over Tipperary as the most enjoyable game of his career. He got great satisfaction that Kilkenny at last beat their great rivals after 23 years. Tom felt that the match was never in doubt from early in the second half when the Tipperary defence untypically started to wilt. I remember Tom scoring a super goal after the break when he hit the ball as it dropped and it shook the roof of the net. That goal marked the beginning of the end for Tipperary, but Kilkenny suffered a number of injuries in the forwards, which disrupted the pattern of play and they found it difficult to clinch the issue until the final whistle. I had my first experience of leaving the field injured in a match when I suffered a fractured wrist. Shortly afterwards, Tom received the blow to his eye. He does not recall specifically how it happened. The severity of the injury almost caused panic on the sideline and it was difficult for the selectors to focus on the play for a number of minutes and to re-arrange the team with two forwards off the field. Full-forward, Jim Lynch had his hand broken later and they had to prevail on him to remain on because three substitutions had already been made. However, Kilkenny held on to win by 3–8 to 2–7.

Strangely, he suffered little or no pain from the injury, and he has some clear recollections of the events afterwards. His brother Martin accompanied him in the ambulance to the hospital and he remembers some priests coming in to see him that night, and also John O'Donoghue and Larry Kiely from the Tipperary team. He also recalls that a young child was crying in the ward during the night. There was no mention of him losing the eye at that stage, but later on the surgeon told him that it was not a question of trying to save it, but that it had to be removed to save the other one. He remembers his mother holding his hand as he went down to the theatre in the Eye and Ear Hospital for the operation, and waking up later heavily bandaged. At that stage no one had explained to him the seriousness of the injury, but when his two brothers, Larry and Paddy arrived home from America to see him, he realised that he was in trouble.

He had great family support during that period in hospital and his brothers spent all day there and they went through a routine of opening and reading the hundreds of cards that came from well-wishers from all over the country. When he left hospital he remembers coming home by taxi and finding it very difficult to measure distance. He thought the buses were almost on top of the car. When he arrived home he was greeted by his father. Patrick Walsh was not normally a very emotional man, but on that occasion he wept. But Tom is a very positive person, and he immediately decided to get on with his life. He drove the car the next day and attended the All-Ireland football final the following Sunday. He decided to immerse himself in his work and family, but he did find it very hard to go to see Kilkenny play for a number of years afterwards. He was only 23 years of age and felt he should really be out there with us, a feeling that lasted until the mid-1970s when his career would have ended anyway. He is now a fanatical supporter, and he travels to every match with his wife, Angela and their friends, Jimmy and Bridie Farrell.

At the time of his injury, Tom was engaged to Angela Grace, the lovely daughter of the well-known secretary of the Kilkenny county board, Paddy Grace. Angela was extremely supportive, and played a big part in helping him to adopt a positive attitude. They decided to get married the following year, and in 1968 they exchanged vows in St Canice's Church in Kilkenny. Brendan Bowyer, who was the singing sensation with the Royal Showband at that time, and a good friend of Paddy Grace sang at their wedding. Their two children, Ronan and Paul, were born in 1970 and 1973. The Walsh family live in a beautiful house in Thomastown in a picturesque setting overlooking the historic Jerpoint Abbey.

Tom spoke very highly of his parents in law, Paddy and Maureen Grace. 'Paddy epitomised everything that was right about the GAA,' said Tom proudly.

'He was a key administrator in Kilkenny from 1947 to 1984, having won two All-Ireland medals in 1939 and 1947. Paddy was the original players' man and treated every hurler with the utmost respect and looked after their every need, even when money was scarce. His heart was always in the right place where hurling was concerned and he loved to see the young hurlers encroach on his beloved Nowlan Park to play hurling during half time of an inter-county game. He looked on those young boys as future Kilkenny stars and treated them accordingly. He always took special care of the Kilkenny minor team too even when the more glamorous senior team was stealing the limelight. He also left as a legacy the tremendous development work he did in Nowlan Park in the 1960s to bring the stadium up to the standard that he felt the players and spectators deserved. He stuck rigidly to his principles as far as the GAA was concerned and sometimes took on the authorities when he felt that there was a need to do so. He had a great relationship with the press and they enjoyed the lengths he went to in playing down the Kilkenny team's chances before an All-Ireland final,' he concluded.

Paddy died in July 1984 and a local supporter penned the following poem, which captured exactly Paddy's dealings with the reporters before an All-Ireland. The poem appeared in the Leinster final Programme that year and is worth recording here.

'GRACE BEFORE AND AFTER'

It would be after the Leinster final and they'd won, but not too well
And you'd meet with Grace in McTernans and ask 'Have they a hope in Hell?'
And he'd fix you with a wounded look, and he wouldn't shout but roar
'They'll beat the pick of Munster, they won't give them a friggin' score!'

And yet in the papers on Monday you'd see a quote from Grace
'Our boys were bad, 'tis very sad, they couldn't last the pace.
They'll never win the All-Ireland, still we won't despair,
We'll feed them up, we'll train 'em well and maybe they'll be fair'

Some worries other than hurling would be the order of the day,
It could be crows amongst the barley or remnants of the hay.
Then you'd meet with Grace in Langtons and say 'Paddy what do you think?'
'They'll beat the pick of Ireland, don't be worrying, have a drink!'

And yet in the papers on Monday morning you'd see a quote from Grace
'Our pick is small, will we have fifteen at all, this we'll have to face.
Still the lads are up there training and they'll try their living best.
And come the day, you can never say, maybe they'll pass the test'

Then on the day, they'd hold the sway and play like men inspired,
And their fame would grow by the firesides glow, passed from man to child.
And you'd meet with Grace in Barry's and say 'Paddy they were good'
'They'd beat the pick of Europe, sure I told you that they would'.

And in the papers on Monday morning you'd see a quote from Grace,
'Our boys were fast, I knew they'd last, they were first in every race.
I knew they'd win the All-Ireland, ah our pick is very strong,
Sure I was saying it in the papers, that they'd win it all along!'

Paddy Grace, ní bheidh a leithéid againn arís.

Tom believes that we are looking at much fitter hurlers today than in the past, but he is not sure if the skill levels have progressed at the same rate, considering the improvements to equipment, pitches and a much livelier ball. The game has changed substantially with players moving all over the field rather than holding the team format.

He recognises that there have been huge changes with media influence, commercialism and sponsorship and that will continue to grow. 'Soccer players have already experienced that development and are earning huge sums of money, but they are not necessarily better sports athletes than our top hurlers,' he suggested.

He believes that professionalism is inevitable, but he hopes that there will first be a thorough debate within the GAA to take all aspects of that move on board. 'The GAA has been successful because of the huge voluntary effort put in by dedicated people at all levels of the association. Those people would have to be taken into account if there are any moves in that direction. If players or officials are to be paid, it should be done up front and be tax compliant,' he believes.

With regard to the Players' Association, Tom would have preferred if the GAA had taken a more pro-active approach earlier to channel players' grievances and to avoid any confrontation.

He is strongly against the back-door system and believes that a Championship must be on a 'knock-out' basis to have any meaning. 'When you no longer see the despondency on the faces of the defeated provincial finalists' faces, then there is something wrong with the system,' he said. He suggested that a good secondary competition, which could be run for all defeated teams should suffice. He criticised the people in the media who whinge every year after the first round of the Championship, and who say that they will not see 'so and so' playing for another twelve months. 'If they put as much effort into promoting that secondary competition, they would ensure that it would gain public interest and be a success,' he suggested.

Finally, Tom was very angry with those politicians and media people who tried to get on a band-wagon by criticising the Government for granting £20m towards the development of Croke Park. 'They know well the contribution the GAA has made to the Irish nation for over a hundred years by challenging the youth of Ireland to become physically fit when no one else had any interest in doing so,' he fumed. 'and still they choose to ignore all that for a cheap headline,' he concluded.

Christy Ring was Tom's childhood hero. He admired the Cork maestro for his ability to score from any angle and his endurance on the field of play for over 20 years where he performed at the highest level and under the most severe pressure from opposing defenders. Mick O'Connell was his football hero for his grace and style and his wonderful fielding ability and speedy distribution skills. Jimmy Doyle was a player from his own era that Tom held in the highest esteem for his scoring ability, style and sportsmanship. Of the present-day players, he singled out Brian Whelahan as an outstanding sporting defender with superb defensive and attacking skills, and is most exciting to watch. He also admires DJ Carey who has scored some magnificent goals and points during the past ten years and whose positional sense and balance is a joy to watch.

Tom, you were up there yourself with the best.

Tom Walsh's Team of the Century

Ollie Walsh
(Kilkenny)

John Doyle	Nick O'Donnell	Bobby Rackard
(Tipperary)	*(Wexford)*	*(Wexford)*
Brian Whelahan	Pat Stakelum	Paddy Phelan
(Offaly)	(Tipperary)	(Kilkenny)

Lory Meagher   Frank Cummins
(Kilkenny)   *(Kilkenny)*

Eddie Keher	Mick Mackey	Jimmy Doyle
(Kilkenny)	*(Limerick)*	*(Tipperary)*
Christy Ring	Nicky Rackard	Jackie Power
(Cork)	*(Wexford)*	*(Limerick)*

Leinster Team of the Century

Noel Skehan
(Kilkenny)

Tom Neville	Nick O'Donnell	Paddy Phelan
(Wexford)	*(Wexford)*	*(Kilkenny)*
Brian Whelahan	Pat Henderson	Martin Coogan
(Offaly)	*(Kilkenny)*	*(Kilkenny)*

Ger Fennelly   Frank Cummins
(Kilkenny)   *(Kilkenny)*

Eddie Keher	Pat Delaney	Jim Langton
(Kilkenny)	*(Kilkenny)*	*(Kilkenny)*
DJ Carey	Nicky Rackard	Tim Flood
(Kilkenny)	*(Wexford)*	*(Wexford)*

Index of Names

A

Alley, John 89
Ayres, Joe 95

B

Barr, Ciaran 38
Barrett, Jimmy 25
Barry Murphy, Jimmy 30, 102, 143, 144
Barry, Paddy 28
Barry, Peter 111
Barry, Tom 153
Bennis, Phil 78, 82, 126
Bennis, Richie 78, 82, 125
Bermingham, Brendan 11
Bermingham, Mick 90
Berry, Jack 37, 39
Blanchfield, Peter 87, 117
Boland, Tom 83, 126
Bonner, Cormac 61, 127
Bracken, Pat 119
Brendan 146
Brennan, Dixie 88
Brennan, Martin 27
Brennan, Mick 84, 102, 141
Brenner, Johnny 104
Brett, PJ 153
Brohan, Jimmy 31
Brophy, Mick 5, 88
Browne, Tony 9, 104
Buckley, Sean 153
Buggy, Paddy 1, 45, 129, 130
Burns, Mick 70
Butler, Henry 15, 40
Byrne, Denis 105
Byrne, Jimmy 154
Byrne, Mickie 133
Byrne, Ned 92

Byrne, Stephen 110
Byrne, Vincent 79

C

Callinan, Johnny 101
Carey, DJ 20, 32, 52, 91, 105, 111, 121, 149
Carey, Eamonn 126
Carey, Kieran 50
Carey, Pa 126
Carr, Declan 61
Carroll, Billy 127
Carroll, Pat 114
Carroll, Ted 8, 90, 115, 120
Casey, Gerry 126
Cashman, Jim 19, 21
Cashman, Mick 31
Cashman, Tom 26, 128
Cheasty, Tom 1–10, 90
Cleary, Michael 60, 61
Cleary, Sean 101
Cleere, Liam 136, 137
Cleere, Seamus 90, 91, 120, 136, 140
Clifford, Donal 27
Clohosey, Sean 88, 140, 153
Cody, Brian 31, 92, 93, 96, 101
Cogan, Frank 25, 29
Coleman, Martin 30, 40
Comerford, Andy 156
Commins, John 17
Conneely, Michael 16
Connolly, John 94, 142
Connolly, Liam 90
Connolly, Mick 4
Conran, John 131
Conway, Phil 59

Coogan, Martin 49, 51, 91, 153
Cooney, Brendan 13, 15
Cooney, Brian 120
Cooney, Jimmy 18
Cooney, Joe 11–21
Cooney, Michael 13, 15
Cooney, Pakie 13, 15
Cooney, Peter 13, 15
Corcoran, Brian 32
Corcoran, Frank 13
Corrigan, Mark 114
Coughlan, Eugene 41
Cregan, Eamon 37, 108, 131
Cremin, Derry 24
Crotty, Mick 82, 92
Crowley, Johnny 12
Cullinane, Jimmy 'Puddin' 102, 129
Cullinane, Sean 9
Cummins, Brendan 23, 26
Cummins, Frank 26, 27, 28, 83
Cummins, Kevin 23, 27
Cummins, Ray 22–32, 80, 92, 143, 144
Cummins, Willie 23
Cunningham, Anthony 16, 19
Cunningham, Ger 19, 58, 61, 111, 131

D

Daly, Anthony 104, 106, 111
Daly, Willie John 5
Deane, Joe 149
Delaney, Ben 5
Delaney, Johnny 139

Delaney, Pat 27, 84, 102, 116
Dempsey, Paddy 152
Dempsey, Tom 17
Devaney, Liam 70, 100
Dillon, Pa 41, 89, 93, 95, 115, 157
Donnellan, Michael 121
Dooley, Tom 118
Doran, Bill 37
Doran, Colm 37, 129, 144
Doran, Joe 37
Doran, Tony 30, **33–42**, 76, 82, 84, 144
Dowdall, Con 37
Dowling, Paddy 45
Downey, Paddy 93, 149
Downey, Shem 34
Doyle, Eddie 117
Doyle, Gerry 46
Doyle, Jimmy 9, 31, **43–53**, 55, 68, 70, 81, 100, 120
Doyle, John 71, 80, 128, 131
Doyle, Michael 56, 128
Doyle, Mike 3
Doyle, Neddy 87
Doyle, Tommy 46
Drennan, Pat 139
Duggan, Jimmy 122
Dunne, Claus 138
Dunne, Coley 88
Dunne, Mick 94, 149
Dunne, Mickey 'Socks' 88
Dunphy, Joe 154
Dwyer, Billy 6, 153, 154, 155

E

Eddery, Pat 21
English, Nicky 34, 57, 60, 61, 110
English, Theo 57, 88, 100

F

Fahy, Padraig 94
Fahy, Pat 13
Farnan, John 24
Farrell, Cyril 12, 105
Feeney, Tom 9
Fennelly, Kevin 12
Fennelly, Liam 17
Fenton, John 20, 57, 59, 130
Ferguson, Des 129
Finnerty, Pete 11, 16, 18
Fitzelle, Pa 127
Fitzgerald, Davy 106, 107
Flannery, Mick 2
Flynn, Austin 9
Flynn, Paul 9, 104
Foley, Art 5, 139
Foley, Des 50, 154
Foley, Lar 154
Foley, Pat 36
Fox, Eamonn 115
Fox, Kevin 55
Fox, Pat 54–63, 111
Freaney, Pierce 153
Fribbs, John 5

G

Galvan, John 4
Gaynor, Len 37, **64–74**, 81, 105, 153
Giles, Trevor 32, 121
Gleeson, John 119
Grace, Paddy 1, 6, 34, 88, 90, 95
Gregson, John 6
Griffin, Liam 41
Grimes, Eamonn 37, 77, 81, 82, 83
Grimes, Phil 6, 9
Guinan, Larry 2

H

Haines, Dessie 121
Harney, Joe 7

Harte, Josie 14
Hartigan, Bernie 2, 78
Hartigan, Pat 2, 31, 41, 62, **75–86**, 92
Hartigan, Seamus 80
Hartley, Fergal 9
Hayden, 'Diamond' 34
Hayes, Conor 58, 130
Hayes, Mick 9
Hayes, Tony 101
Hayes, Tony 'Tuts' 88
Healy, Dermot 121
Heaslip, Denis 90
Heffernan, Christy 61, 143
Hegarty, Fergal 106
Henderson, Ger 17, 142
Henderson, John 94
Henderson, Pat 94
Henebry, Paddy 5
Hennessey, Joe 12, 92, 130
Hickey, John D. 149
Hickey, Martin 5
Hickey, Mick 9
Higgins, Alex 21
Hinphy, Liam 129
Hogan, Eddie 150
Hogan, Jim 81
Honan, Colm 101
Horan, Padraig 114, 144
Horgan, John 26, 103
Horgan, Seamus 82
Hough, John 88

J

Jacob, Christy 39

K

Keady, Tony 11, 18, 59
Keane, John 5, 6, 7, 9
Keating, Michael 'Babs' 37, 59, 60, 67, 81, 84, 102, 103, 108, 139, 153

Kehoe, Padge 38
Kelly, Eddie 38
Kelly, Jimmy 34
Kelly, John 34, 82
Kelly, Matt 130
Kelly, Mickey 6
Kelly, Paddy 15, 130, 131
Kelly, Paul 5
Kennedy, Dan 136, 138, 145
Kennedy, Paddy 136
Kenny, Michael 16
Kenny, Mick 6
Keogh, Christy 30
Kiely, John 3
Kiely, Larry 159
Kilcoyne, Tony 56
Kilkenny, Ollie 59
Kinsella, John 136
Kinsella, Mick 37
Kirwan, John 4, 5, 115
Kirwan, Sammy 88

L

Laffan, Peadar 150
Lane, Noel 12, 19, 20, 153
Langton, Jim 34, 88, 89, 117
Lannon, Danny 150
Larkin, Fan 40
Larkin, Noel 4
Larkin, Philip 'Fan' 26, 40, 87–97
Larkin, Philly 96
Lawlor, Pat 136
Leahy, Bill 89
Leahy, Georgie 91
Leahy, Paddy 48, 51, 70
Leahy, Terry 34
Linnane, Sylvie 14, 18, 58
Loftus, Vincent 102
Lohan, Brian 83, 104, 109
Lohan, Frank 83
Lohan, Gus 83, 102

Loughnane, Francis 37, 139, 153
Loughnane, Ger 98–113
Lynch, Colin 107
Lynch, Jim 159
Lynch, Paul 39
Lynskey, Brendan 17

M

Mackey, Mick 24, 72, 117
Maguire, Mick 127
Maher, Fr Tommy 129
Maher, Hugh 5
Maher, John 90
Maher, Paddy 88
Maher, Phil 77
Martin, Damien 116
Martin, Kevin 106
McCarthy, Charlie 30, 37
McCarthy, Gerald 37, 103, 109
McCarthy, Gerry 68
McCarthy, Justin 27, 37
McCarthy, Lou 88
McCarthy, Mick 5
McCormack, Dinny 92
McCormack, Tom 92
McCurtain, Dermot 26
McDermott, John 121
McDonagh, Joe 13, 20
McDonnell, Pat 30
McGarry, Tom 44
McGovern, Johnny 7, 89
McGrath, Joe 26, 81
McGrath, John 55
McGrath, Michael 'Hopper' 14, 18
McGrath, Oliver 'Hopper' 4, 156
McGrath, Seanie 149
McGuinness, Jack 88
McInerney, Gerry 11, 16, 18
McKeever, Jim 129
McKenna, Joe 78

McKeogh, Martin 102
McLoughlin, Sean 68, 90
McNamara, Mike 105
Meagher, Lory 24, 88
Minogue, Mick 127
Molloy, Larry 116
Molloy, Mikey 116
Molloy, Paddy 114–123
Molloy, PJ 14
Moloughney, Tom 68, 73
Mooney, Tom 131
Moore, Willie 82
Moran, Paddy 136
Morgan, Billy 25, 29
Morrissey, Danny 56
Morrissey, Eamonn 92, 93
Morrissey, Martin Óg 2
Morrissey, Nick 88
Moylan, Pat 26, 30, 92, 103
Mulhare, Paudge 114
Mulkerins, Michael 16
Murphy, Denis 120
Murphy, Joe 37
Murphy, John 153
Murphy, Liam 37
Murphy, Martin 3
Murphy, Michael 71
Murphy, Micheál 27
Murphy, Mike 3
Murphy, Pat 'Blondie' 5
Murphy, Tadgh 51
Murphy, Tom 8, 89
Murphy, Willie 30, 38
Murray, Michael 16

N

Naughton, Martin 14, 19
Naughton, Tommy 132
Nealon, Donie 51, 81, 82, 100, 102, 104, 129
Neary, Mick 88
Neville, Tom 122, 131, 154
Nolan, Frankie 82, 125
Nolan, Peter 121

O

Ó Hehir, Micheál 34, 46, 100, 117, 148
O'Brien, Chunky 92, 95
O'Brien, Fr Michael 60, 61
O'Brien, Ger 125, 126
O'Brien, Jim 82
O'Brien, Jimmy 71
O'Brien, John 152, 155
O'Brien, Liam 142
O'Brien, Tony 78, 126
O'Brien, Willie 126
O'Connell, Mick 80, 162
O'Connell, Tommy 7
O'Connor, Enda 83
O'Connor, Jamesie 2, 106, 149
O'Doherty, Martin 25
O'Donnell, Bill 54
O'Donnell, Nick 36
O'Donoghue, Eamonn 26, 92, 143
O'Donoghue, John 39, 49, 159
O'Donoghue, Liam 82
O'Donoghue, Noel 143
O'Donoghue, Paudie 29
O'Dwyer, Noel 55
O'Gorman, Larry 17
O'Gorman, Noel 37
O'Grady, Jim 125
O'Grady, Michael 124–134
O'Grady, PJ 125
O'Halloran, John 25
O'Hara, Dick 40
O'Hara, Tom 127
O'Keeffe, Bob 141
O'Leary, Seanie 143
O'Muircheartaigh, Micheál 43
O'Neill, Fr Pat 55
O'Neill, Martin 120
O'Neill, Paddy 140

O'Neill, Pat 111
O'Riordan, Tommy 129
O'Shea, Brian 56
O'Shea, Eamonn 128
O'Sullivan, Peter 127, 153
Orr, Nickey 41
Orr, Nicky 92, 93

P

Phelan, Paddy 88
Piggot, Pierce 12
Pilkington, John 118
Power, Jackie 81
Power, Mattie 87, 117
Power, Mick 4, 6
Power, Ned 38, 129
Power, Richie 61
Power, Seamus 3, 80
Prendergast, Paddy 94
Purcell, Kieran 84
Purcell, Padraig 8

Q

Quigley, Dan 37, 38, 153
Quigley, Martin 30, 131
Quigley, Pat 37
Quinn, Billy 17
Quinn, Niall 17
Quirke, Aidan 90

R

Rackard, Billy 24, 34, 36
Rackard, Bobby 5, 34, 36
Rackard, Nicky 24, 34, 35, 36
Reddin, Jack 68
Reddin, Tony 47, 139
Reilly, Peter 87
Ring, Christy 9, 23, 31, 47, 51, 117, 122, 162
Robbins, Sean 119
Roche, Con 28
Roche, Mick 39, 41, 81, 102, 153

Ronan, Adrian 105
Russell, Eamonn 80
Ryan, Aidan 111
Ryan, Bobby 55, 56, 61
Ryan, Declan 73
Ryan, Eanna 19
Ryan, Frankie 67
Ryan, John 56
Ryan, Michael 58
Ryan, Mick 126
Ryan, Mikey 54
Ryan, Ollie 153
Ryan, Pat (Flowery) 56
Ryan, Philly 54
Ryan, Roger 84
Ryan, Timmy 81

S

Sheehan, Colm 157
Simpson, Liam 61
Skehan, Johnny 136
Skehan, Noel 28, 40, 93, 94, 115, **135–147**
Skehan, PJ 136
Somers, Dick 44
Spain, Mick 119
Stakelum, Pat 49
Staples, Vinnie 37
Stapleton, Gerry 55, 56
Stapleton, Timmy 55
Stokes, Dick 81
Sutton, John 88

T

Thomson, John 132
Tobin, Dick 25
Toohill, Jim 119
Treacy, Jim 93, 95, 156
Treacy, Sean 17
Troy, Jim 11
Troy, John 114
Twomey, Mike 139
Twomey, Vince 5

W

Wall, Tony 8, 47, 50, 72
Walsh, Bill 88, 126
Walsh, Denis 61
Walsh, Frankie 2
Walsh, Jim 'The Link' 90
Walsh, Jimmy 88

Walsh, Ollie 2, 6, 7, 45, 80, 90, 105, 115, 116, 136, 137, 139, 140, 142, 145, 146, 149, 151
Walsh, Patrick F. 150
Walsh, Tom 8, 90, 138, 139, **148–162**

Wheeler, Ned 88
Whelahan, Brian 52, 62, 111, 114, 121, 162
Whelahan, Pat Joe 114
Whelan, Cha 90
Whelan, Mickey 129
White, Mattie 87